How to Use

Adobe®

Premiere® 6.5

Douglas Dixon

201 W. 103rd Street
Indianapolis, Indiana 46290

How To Use Adobe® Premiere® 6.5

International Standard Book Number: 0-7897-2826-5

Library of Congress Catalog Card Number: 2002111094

Printed in the United States of America

First Printing: December 2002

05   04   03   02   4   3   2   1

Trademarks

Warning and Disclaimer

Executive Editor
Candace Hall

Acquisitions Editor
Candace Hall

Development Editor
Laura Norman

Managing Editor
Thomas Hayes

Project Editor
Sheila Schroeder

Copy Editor
Geneil Breeze

Indexer
Ken Johnson

Proofreader
Juli Cook

Technical Editor
Alan Hamill

Team Coordinator
Cindy Teeters

Interior Designer
Anne Jones

Cover Designer
Dan Armstrong

Contents at a Glance

Contents

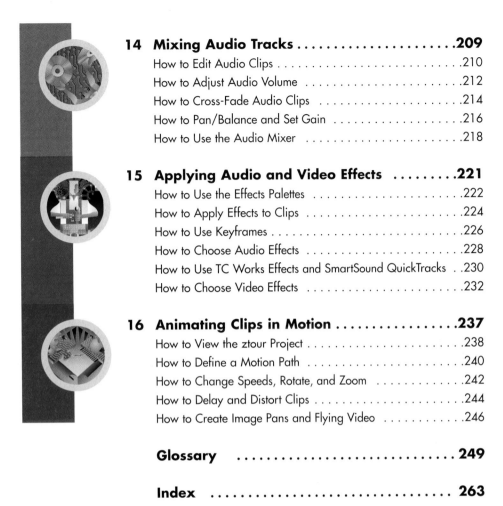

About the Author

Douglas Dixon is a technologist and author who has worked in the "Video Valley" of Princeton, N.J., for more than 20 years, at the bleeding edge where advanced consumer video applications meet personal computers. He also recently authored *Desktop DVD Authoring* (New Riders, October 2002).

As a technology leader at Sarnoff Corp., and previously as a software product manager at Intel Corp., Doug has extensive experience developing multimedia and Web technology into consumer products. A graduate of Brown University, he has published technical articles related to his work in publications ranging from ACM and IEEE journals to *Computer Graphics World*. He holds five issued U.S. patents.

As a technology writer, Doug is a contributing editor for *Camcorder and Computer Video* and *Digital Photographer* magazines, covering video editing and streaming media technology and tools, from DV to DVD, desktop to handhelds, consumer to professional. He has published more than 80 articles since 1999.

Doug also is active in professional activities. He has spoken and presented seminars at local, regional, and national meetings, from user groups to PC Expo, Government Video Expo, COMDEX, and the ACM SIGGRAPH Conference. Doug is a member of the ACM and a Senior Member of the IEEE.

Although he writes about new and cutting-edge technology, Doug's focus is on making technology understandable and useful for real people. For more on Premiere and multimedia technology, see his Manifest Technology Web site at www.manifest-tech.com.

Dedication

To my mother and father, who helped start me on the journey, and to my family, Connie, Karin, and Brian, who make the trip so special.

Acknowledgments

First, I need to acknowledge Brian Dixon for his help in grabbing screen shots, finding inconsistencies, and other helpful stuff.

Not surprisingly, I would like to thank Bruce Bowman and the team at Adobe who brought us version 6.5 of Premiere. It has been a real pleasure working with such a robust application, especially because it makes it so fun and easy to mess around with video on DV, and so painless to help out friends with quick productions.

Thanks also to the great team at Que Publishing, especially Candy Hall, who made this new edition happen, and Laura Norman, who beat it all into shape. And thanks to Neil Salkind and Studio B for their continued help with my career.

This continues to be an exciting time to be in the technology business, especially as digital video becomes accessible and affordable on consumer PCs. I would like to thank Bob Wolenik, Tony Gomez, and Mark Shapiro for the opportunity to cover these developments for Miller Magazines, and Rich Rein and Barbara Fox for the great learning experience of writing for the *U.S. 1* newspaper in Princeton.

Douglas Dixon

We Want to Hear from You!

As the reader of this book, *you* are our most important critic and commentator. We value your opinion and want to know what we're doing right, what we could do better, what areas you'd like to see us publish in, and any other words of wisdom you're willing to pass our way.

As an executive editor for Que, I welcome your comments. You can email or write me directly to let me know what you did or didn't like about this book—as well as what we can do to make our books better.

Please note that I cannot help you with technical problems related to the *topic* of this book. We do have a User Services group, however, where I will forward specific technical questions related to the book.

When you write, please be sure to include this book's title and author as well as your name, email address, and phone number. I will carefully review your comments and share them with the author and editors who worked on the book.

Email: feedback@quepublishing.com

Mail: Candace Hall
Executive Editor
Que Publishing
201 West 103rd Street
Indianapolis, IN 46290 USA

For more information about this book or another Que title, visit our Web site at www.quepublishing.com. Type the ISBN (excluding hyphens) or the title of a book in the Search field to find the page you're looking for.

The Complete Visual Reference

Each chapter of this book is made up of a series of short, instructional tasks, designed to help you understand all the information that you need to get the most out of your computer hardware and software.

 Click: Click the left mouse button once.

 Double-click: Click the left mouse button twice in rapid succession.

 Right-click: Click the right mouse button once.

 Drag: Click and hold the left mouse button, position the mouse pointer, and release.

 Pointer Arrow: Highlights an item on the screen you need to point to or focus on in the step or task.

Selection: Highlights the area onscreen discussed in the step or task.

 **Type:** Click once where indicated and begin typing to enter your text or data.

 **Drag and Drop:** Point to the starting place or object. Hold down the mouse button (right or left per instructions), move the mouse to the new location, and then release the button.

Each task includes a series of easy-to-understand steps designed to guide you through the procedure.

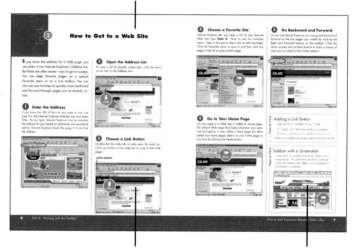

Each step is fully illustrated to show you how it looks onscreen.

Extra hints that tell you how to accomplish a goal are provided in most tasks.

 Key icons: Clearly indicate which key combinations to use.

Menus and items you click are shown in **bold**. Words in *italic* are defined in more detail in the glossary. Information you type is in a `special font`.

Introduction

With this book, you can use Premiere to quickly and easily create your own video productions with professional touches. It takes you through all the major features of Premiere, basic and advanced, so that you can quickly learn how to

- Capture high-quality video from your DV camcorder
- Organize your audio and video clips and edit them into a complete production
- Work faster, and experiment more, with Real-Time Preview
- Enhance your work with transitions and effects, titles and animations
- Add broadcast-quality titles with the new Adobe Title Designer
- Save and share your productions as digital video files
- Export your movies in MPEG format, ready to author to DVD
- Output streaming media formats to share on the Web

As you become more familiar with Premiere, you can return to this book to explore the wealth of additional capabilities and options you can use to create more sophisticated and professional results. You can get started quickly and then still have plenty of room to grow in the future.

Who Should Use This Book?

If you are just starting out with digital video on the desktop, this book can get you started quickly with Premiere 6.5, capturing video; performing simple edits; and exporting your productions for the desktop, DVD, or the Web. Premiere provides convenient tools such as the Storyboard window and Motion Settings dialog to help get you going, and then provides more room for growth as you take advantage of its more sophisticated features.

If you are stepping up from an entry-level video editing application, this book shows you how Premiere frees you from the limitations of more basic tools. For example, now you can have more than one or two video and audio tracks, choose from a much wider range of transitions and effects, customize the screen layout for your working style, and generally have much more control over editing your production.

Finally, if you are upgrading from Premiere version 6.0, this book demonstrates the important new features, including Real-Time Preview, MPEG export for DVD, the Adobe Type Designer, and audio enhancement. If you are upgrading from version 5, this book demonstrates the significant improvements offered in Premiere 6.x, especially with built-in DV capture, Web export, and the dedicated Audio Mixer.

Book Organization

This book is organized into 16 parts, or chapters, each focusing on a major feature in Premiere. Each part contains approximately five to nine tasks, which take you step-by-step through performing a particular operation. Each task presents the operation in a series of steps, each illustrated with a Premiere screenshot annotated to highlight the action being performed.

The examples in this book apply to both the Windows and Macintosh versions of Premiere (although most of the screenshots are from the Windows version). When there are differences between the two versions, the book describes and illustrates operations for both systems. Keyboard shortcuts are provided using a (Mac) [Windows] convention.

Learn More About Using Premiere

To learn more about using Premiere, check the Adobe support Web site for information and updates:

> www.adobe.com/products/premiere

For more information on Premiere and other desktop video topics also visit my Manifest Technology Web site:

> www.manifest-tech.com

Getting Started with Adobe Premiere

Welcome to Adobe Premiere! The best way to learn a new program is to dive right in and get started. Although Premiere's power and flexibility can make it intimidating at first, it really is easy to use for basic editing operations.

This part gets you started by taking a tour of the steps involved in using Premiere: setting up your workspace, importing audio and video clips into a Project window, organizing the clips into bins, assembling them into a project in the Timeline window, and previewing the resulting program in the Monitor window.

Along the way, I will introduce the Premiere user interface and organizational elements, including menus, windows, buttons, and other controls. Premiere provides many options for how you work, so you can go ahead and experiment, and even customize the work area the way that you prefer.

To make sure that you can follow along with what is happening in the book, these first parts use only the sample video clip files included with Premiere and installed with it on your hard disk. So, if you have not done so already, install Premiere (using the instructions that came with your software), and let's get started.

A Quick Tour of Premiere

Adobe Premiere is a powerful video editing tool, but with that power comes many options and controls, and different kinds of windows filling the screen. In this task, you take a quick tour of how to use Premiere, to get a sense of the basic windows and controls and how to work through a video production.

➊ Select the Initial Workspace

The first time you start Premiere, it displays the Initial Workspace dialog. Just click **Select A/B Editing** to configure your default *Workspace*—the layout of windows and tools for using Premiere. If you have already run Premiere, skip to the next step.

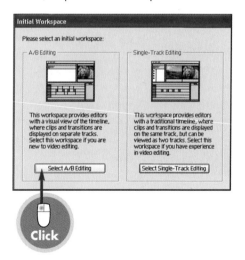

➋ Select the Project Settings

Specify your Project settings to match the type of material that you will be working with by selecting a basic file format from the **Load Project Settings** dialog. For the moment, select **Multimedia** (Macintosh) or **Multimedia Video for Windows** (Windows). Then click **OK** to set up your *Project*.

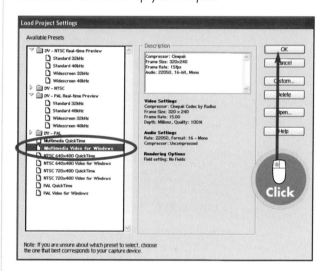

➌ Select A/B Editing

After you have worked in Premiere for a while and have moved around the different windows, the screen layout can become cluttered and disorganized. To restore the workspace layout to the default arrangement, choose **Window, Workspace, A/B Editing**.

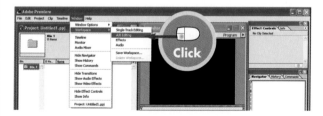

④ Import a Clip

The Project window at the top left of the Premiere work area contains a collection of bins (folders of clips) to be used in the project. To import a clip file into the bin area, choose **File**, **Import**, **File**. In the Import dialog, navigate to the Sample Folder installed with Premiere. Then click to select the **Cyclers** file (.mov on Macintosh) or (.avi on Windows) and click **Open**.

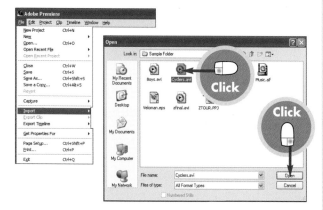

⑤ Add to the Timeline

The Timeline window along the bottom right of the Premiere work area is where you assemble your production by arranging and editing your clips, and adding transitions, effects, and titles. To add the Cyclers clip to the **Timeline**, drag it from the **Bin** area in the **Project** window to the shaded Video 1A track in the **Timeline**.

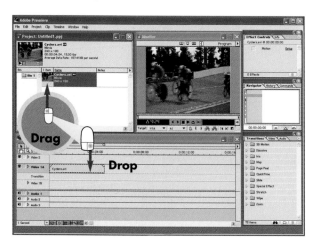

⑥ Play in the Monitor Window

The Monitor window to the right of the Project window is where you can preview the production that you are editing on the Timeline. Click the **VCR playback controls** along the bottom of the window to play through the Timeline.

Windows Keyboard Navigation

You can navigate menus quickly in Windows by pressing the **Alt** key and then the underlined letter in the current menu. To show the underlined letters, open the **Display** control panel, select the **Appearance** tab, click the **Effects** button, and then uncheck **Hide underlined letters for keyboard navigation until I press the Alt key**.

Floating Palette Windows

The three smaller windows down the right side of the Premiere window are tool *palettes*. Although the Project, Timeline, and Monitor windows are contained in the main Premiere window, the palette windows actually float above it. This makes it easy to move them off to the side of the screen, but can also be disconcerting when you move the Premiere window and the palettes stay floating in their original positions.

How to Manage Projects

Premiere organizes your editing activities into projects, which include the collection of material that you are using, the edits that you have performed on them, and even the layout of windows in the workspace. You can save an editing project in process and reload it later to continue working.

1 Play the Thumbnail

For a quick preview of the contents of a clip in the Project window, simply click the clip to select it, and a thumbnail viewer appears in the top-left corner of the window. Click the Cyclers clip (from Task 1) to select it, and then click the **Play** button under the thumbnail window to preview the clip.

2 Save Your Project

To save your open project, choose **File, Save**. Navigate to the **Sample Folder** in the Save File dialog, type **Sample Project** as the name for the project file, and click **Save**.

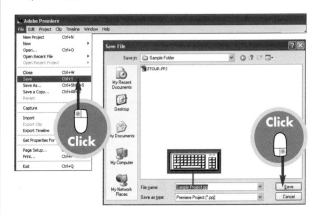

3 Start a New Project

To start a new project, choose **File, New Project**. If you have not saved your current project, Premiere displays a dialog asking whether you want to do so now. Premiere then displays the Load Project Settings dialog. Again, select (**Multimedia**) or [**Multimedia Video for Windows**] and click **OK**.

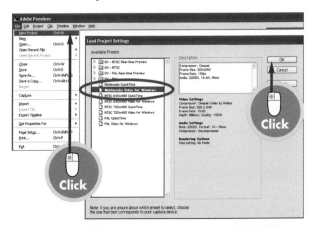

④ Open an Existing Project

To open a project that you saved previously, choose **File**, **Open Recent Project**, and then the **Sample Project** name that you saved previously (or choose **File**, **Open**).

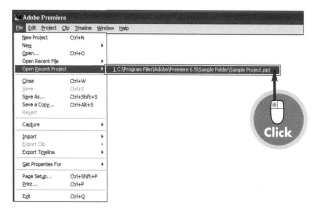

⑤ Save Your Workspace

With Premiere, you can rearrange the windows to fit your own working style. To save your workspace layout to reuse later, choose **Window**, **Workspace, Save Workspace**. Type a name for your workspace in the Save Workspace dialog and click **Save**.

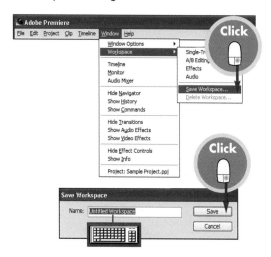

⑥ Resuming an Existing Project

The next time that you start Premiere, it displays the Load Project Settings dialog again. If you want to resume working on an existing project, click **Open** and then use the **Open** dialog to navigate to your saved project file. Premiere then reopens your project back to the bin contents and workspace layout that were last saved.

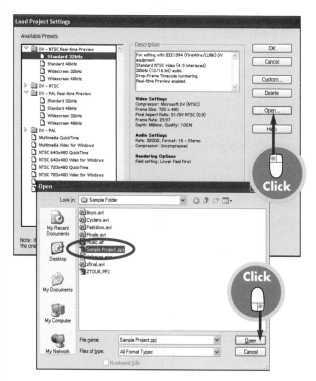

How-to Hint

Save Your Projects

It's a good idea to periodically save your work as you edit. The Premiere project file is not very large because it contains only references to the media that you are editing, and not actual video files. Experiment with Premiere—just save your project first.

Auto Save

You also can have Premiere automatically save your project at specified intervals. You can save to the same file, or even better, save a series of files to archive each state of your project over a period of time. To set the Auto Save options, choose **Edit**, **Preferences**, **Auto Save and Undo**.

How to Organize Clips in Project Bins

Use the Project window in Premiere to organize your collection of clips for editing, and to see information about your clips. You can import both individual clip files and entire bins of clips, and organize them into one or more bins.

1 Import a Folder of Clips

To import an entire folder of clip files into the project, choose **File**, **Import**, **Folder**. Navigate to the **Sample Folder** in the **Browse for Folder** dialog, click the folder name to select it, and then click **OK**.

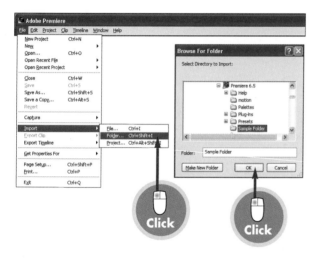

2 Organize Your Bins

When you import clips, they are added to the contents of the current bin. You can organize your bins separately, or by nesting them hierarchically inside one another. Drag the Sample Folder bin from inside the Bin 1 bin to the bottom of the **Bin** window in the left panel of the **Project** window.

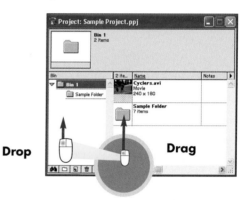

Drop   Drag

3 Display the List View

The **Project** window provides several different views of the clips in each bin. Use the three buttons below the clip panel to switch between **Icon**, **Thumbnail**, and **List** views. Click the rightmost **List View** button to see a list of the clips in the Sample Folder bin.

④ Create a New Bin

Premiere displays the list of clips with information about their format. Click the **New Bin** folder button under the left bin pane to create a new bin folder. Premiere then displays the Create Bin dialog. Enter **Bin 2** as the name, and click **OK**. You can also rename a bin by selecting it, and then clicking the name and typing new text.

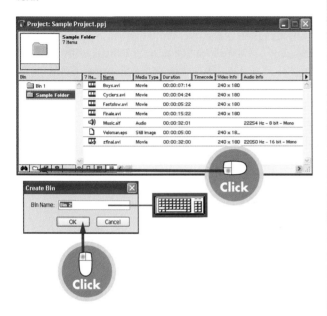

⑤ Delete a Bin

Premiere adds the new bin to the Project window. To delete the new bin, select it, and then click the **Delete** button below the bin pane, or press the **Delete** key. Deleting a clip, or an entire bin full of clips, does not delete the actual clip files from your disk; it just deletes the references to them from your project.

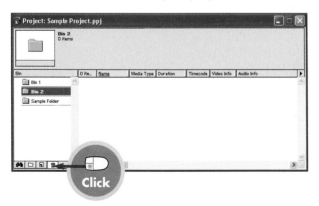

⑥ Save Your Project

Before going on, this is a good time to save your project again. Choose **File**, **Save**. The current project bins and settings will be saved so that you can continue working with them later.

How-to Hint

Importing Multiple Files

Besides opening individual files and importing an entire folder of clips, you can use the standard operating system conventions to select a group of files from the Open dialog. In the **Import** dialog, click to select a first file, and then (**Command+click**) [**Ctrl+click**] to select multiple files, and then click **Open**.

Window Menus

Premiere provides several different ways to access the available menu options for each window. Click the triangular **window menu** button near the upper-right corner of each window or palette to access the common commands and display options for that window.

Pop-Up Context Menus

For quick access to the most useful menu options available for a specific window, or to an object within a window, (Control-click) [right-click] on the window or object to display a pop-up context menu.

How to Play Clips in a Clip Window

Now that you have organized the clips for your project into bins, you can view individual clips and prepare them for inclusion in the Timeline. Clips are displayed in individual Clip windows with controls for playback and editing.

1 Open a Clip Window

To view a clip, such as the zfinal clip in the Sample Folder bin, double-click it, such as the zfinal clip in the Sample Folder bin (or select it in a bin and choose **Clip**, **Open Clip**). You can open multiple **Clip** windows and switch between them by clicking them or by selecting them from the **Window** menu.

2 Play the Clip

Premiere opens the clip in a separate **Clip** window, with the name of the clip in the title bar. To play through the clip, use the playback control buttons at the bottom of the Clip window. Click the **Frame Back** and **Frame Forward** buttons to step backward and forward through the clip, respectively. Click and hold a **Frame** button to scan through the clip, or press **Shift** as you click to jump five frames at a time.

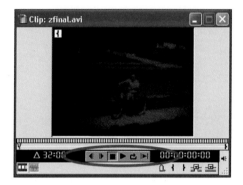

3 View the Timecode

The Clip window displays the total Clip Duration (in seconds and frames) to the left of the play controls. The Current Clip Location *timecode* appears to the right. This shows your current location in the clip, corresponding to the Set Location triangular *shuttle* slider.

④ Jog and Shuttle in the Clip

To jump to a general area of the clip, click the corresponding point along the shuttle slider area under the video. To *shuttle* rapidly through the clip, click and drag the **Set Location** blue triangular shuttle slider to the left (backward in clip) or right (forward). To *jog* through the individual clip frames, click in the striped **Frame Jog** tread area and drag the cursor right or left.

Drag

Click

⑤ Adjust the Volume

To quickly adjust audio volume during playback of the clip, click the **Set Volume** button on the bottom right of the window. Clicking the button cycles through medium and high volume and mute.

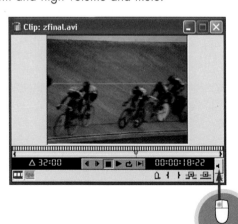

Click

⑥ View Audio Controls and Images

Besides video files, the Sample Folder bin contains two other types of files: Audio and Still Image. Double-click the Music.aif clip to open a **Clip** window that displays the audio file with the audio waveform and playback controls. Double-click Veloman.eps to open a second **Clip** window that displays the still image file.

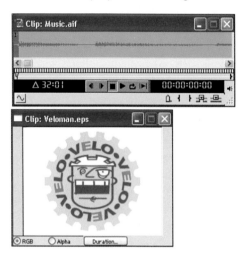

How-to Hint

Using Keyboard Shortcuts

Premiere provides many keyboard shortcuts to simplify playing back clips. Simply press the **spacebar** to start and stop playback. Use the **Left** and **Right** cursor control keys to step through frames, and the **Up** and **Down** cursor keys to jump to the beginning and end of the clip.

Entering a Timecode

To move to a specific timecode, click the **Current Clip Location** display, type in a new time, and press (**Return**) [**Enter**]. You can also enter the time on the numeric keypad as consecutive digits without colons.

How to Add Clips to the Timeline

After you have imported and organized your clips in bins in the Project window, you can begin arranging the clips into a sequence in the Timeline window. You then can enhance your production by adding other components such as transitions, effects, titles, overlays, and background audio.

① Add a Video Track

To start building your production, open a project with clips, such as the Sample Project you saved in Task 3. Open the **Sample Folder** bin and then click the icon for the Boys video file and drag it to the shaded Video 1A row in the Timeline window.

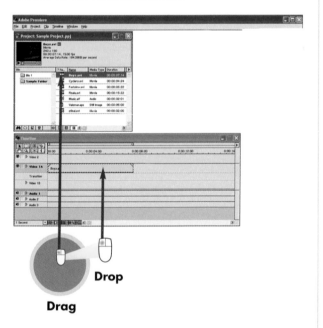

② Add a Second Video Track

To add a second video clip to be played in sequence after the first clip, click the Cyclers video file, drag it to the Video 1A row in the Timeline window, and place it immediately after the Boys clip.

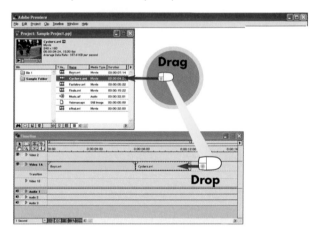

③ Add an Audio Track

To add an audio music track to play with these silent video clips, click the Music audio file and drag it to the start of the Audio 1 track.

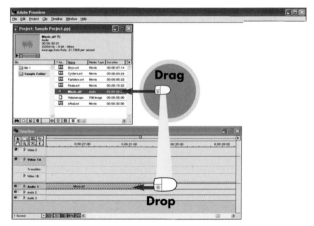

4 Scroll the Timeline

The video files have disappeared! The music file is much longer than the video clips, so the Timeline window scrolled to the end of the full production. Use the scrollbar at the bottom of the window to scroll back to the beginning of the production.

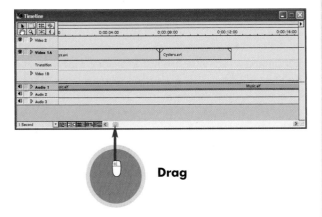

Drag

5 Zoom the Timeline

To change the Timeline so that the entire production fits in the window, use the **Zoom** menu at the bottom left of the window to zoom the Timeline display out to **2 Seconds**.

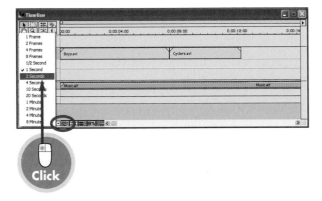

Click

6 View the Full Timeline

After zooming out, the entire contents of the Timeline now are visible in the window.

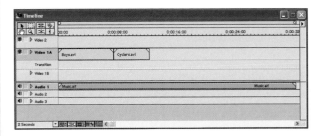

How-to Hint

Quick Scrolling

To quickly scroll through the Timeline, use the Hand tool button (hand icon) in the tool area at the top left of the Timeline window. To select the Hand tool, click it, or press the **H** key. Click and drag the hand cursor to scroll in the Timeline.

Quick Zooming

To quickly zoom the Timeline in and out, just press the "+" or "-" keys, or use the Zoom tool button (magnifying glass icon) in the tool area at the top left of the Timeline window. To select the Zoom tool, click it, or press the **Z** key. The cursor changes to a magnifying glass with a plus sign ("+"), and you can then click on a clip to zoom in on the Timeline. To zoom out and see more, hold down the (**Option**) [**Alt**] key to change the cursor to a minus sign ("-"), and then click to zoom out.

How to Preview a Program on the Timeline

After you have started editing your production on the Timeline, you also can play it in its current form in the Program Monitor window at the top center of the Premiere work area. The Monitor window and the Timeline are synchronized so that they move together as you play or shuttle in either area.

❶ Playing the Program

The Monitor window has much the same play controls and time displays as the Clip window (see Task 4). To play the current program on the Timeline, use the **play control** buttons at the bottom of the Monitor window.

❷ Using the Edit Line

As the program plays in the Monitor window, the corresponding position is displayed in the Timeline by the vertical *edit line*. The *time ruler* along the top of the Timeline window shows the current time of the edit line. Move the edit line in the Timeline and note the changes to the corresponding frame displayed in the Monitor window.

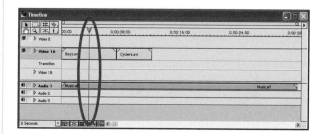

❸ Dragging the Edit Line

To move the edit line, first position the cursor in the time ruler; the cursor changes to a triangle. Click anywhere in the time ruler to jump the edit line to that position, or click and drag the triangle to the left or right to shuttle through the program. By dragging the triangle off either side of the window, you can shuttle to the beginning or end of the program.

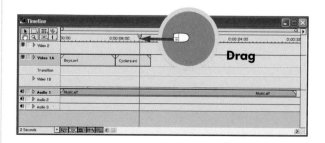

4 Using the Navigator Palette

Premiere provides another method for displaying and moving around in the Timeline layout. The Navigator palette to the right of the work area offers a graphical view of the entire Timeline. The Current View box (in green) shows the area currently visible in the Timeline window, and the edit line (in red) shows the current position of the edit line. If the Navigator palette is not currently visible, click the **Navigator** tab in the Palette window, or choose **Window**, **Show Navigator**.

5 Scrolling in the Navigator Palette

You can use the Navigator palette not only to view the Timeline but also to move the Timeline and Monitor window displays. Click and drag on the **Current View** box (in green), using the hand cursor to scroll the view in the Timeline window to the corresponding area of the project. Or hold down **Shift** to display the triangle cursor and click and drag the edit line (in red) to move through the Timeline.

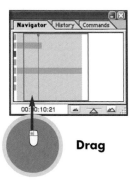

Drag

6 Zooming in the Navigator Palette

You also can zoom the Timeline display from the Navigator palette. Click the **Zoom Out** and **Zoom In** buttons at the bottom of the palette to zoom the Timeline. You can also click and slide the **zoom slider** between the buttons to adjust the zoom level.

Click

How-to Hint

Current Timecode

To keep track of where you are in the program, Premiere displays the corresponding *timecode* in both the Program Location of the **Monitor** window and the **Timecode** area at the bottom left of the **Navigator** palette. You also can jump directly to a timecode by typing in either of these fields.

Current Zoom Level

To keep track of your zoom level as you zoom in and out in the **Timeline** window, watch the **Zoom** menu at the bottom left of the **Timeline** window. Premiere displays the zoom level, with the **Timeline** displaying a period ranging from 1 Frame to 8 Minutes.

Task

Importing and Organizing Clips

As you saw in Part 1, "Getting Started with Adobe Premiere," Premiere organizes your editing activity into a project. This includes the media clips you are working with (organized in bins in the Project window), the edits that you have performed on them (sequenced on the Timeline window), and even your current arrangement of windows in the Premiere work area (saved as a workspace).

The first step in working with a project is to import and organize your source media clips, including video, audio, and images. To assist in the editing process, it is useful to build a library of your clips, organized in whatever way is helpful for you—perhaps by topic, theme, or date. Your clip libraries can then be saved and shared among different projects.

The Project window provides powerful organization capabilities, including multiple ways of viewing clips and clip information, and the capability to import and collect clips into bins as a hierarchy of nested folders. As you organize your clips, you can also add your own text notes and labels, and then use Premiere's search tools to find clips matching the specific characteristics.

The tasks in this part take you through using the Project window to import, organize, view, and search clips. They also demonstrate the wide variety of user interface options provided by Premiere, including program, window, and pop-up menus; command buttons; and text input.

The final task also introduces the Premiere Undo capability and History palette so that you can feel free to experiment with the different features as you work on a Project, try different operations, and then easily back them out and start over.

How to Use the Project Window

In the Project window, you can import, organize, and view the clip files that you plan to edit together into your production. After you assemble the clips, you can then trim, edit, and view them in the Clip, Timeline, and Monitor windows.

❶ Open a Project

Open a recent project, such as the project you saved in Part 1. Choose **File**, **Open Recent Project**, and then open the Sample Project name that you saved (or choose **File**, **Open**).

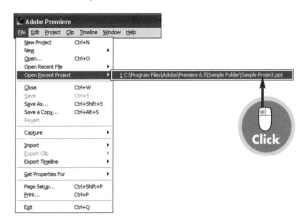

❷ Select a Bin

The bin area on the left side of the **Project** window displays a hierarchical view of the bin folders that you have imported and added to your project. Click the **Sample Folder** bin to select it.

❸ Select a Clip

The clip area on the right side of the **Project** window displays the media clip files contained in the currently selected bin. Click on the **Cyclers** movie file to select it.

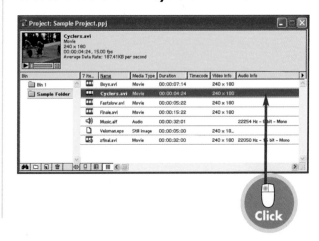

④ Preview the Clip

The preview area at the top of the **Project** window displays information about the current clips and provides a thumbnail viewer for playing through the clip. Click on the triangular **Play** button to play through the clip, or drag the slider.

⑤ Open a Window Menu

Premiere provides several different ways to access the available menu options for each window and pane within a window. Click the triangular **window Menu** button near the upper-right corner of the **Project** window to access common commands and options.

⑥ Pop Up a Context Menu

Premiere also provides pop-up context menus for quick access to the most useful menu options available for a specific area within a window. (**Control+click**) [**Right+click**] on the preview and bin areas to see the available options. Some of the common commands also are available as buttons at the bottom of the bin and clip areas.

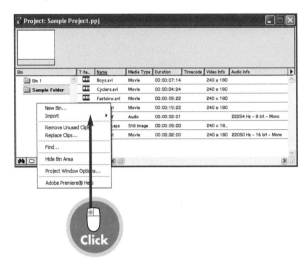

How-to Hint

Resizing and Hiding Panes

You can resize the bin and clip areas by clicking and dragging the **Resize Bin Area** button (two arrow icons) at the bottom of the **Project** window. You also can use the window or context menus to **Hide** or **Show** the entire preview or bin areas.

Poster Frames

By default, Premiere uses the first frame of a clip for the thumbnail icon. You can choose a different poster frame to visualize the clip, especially if the clip begins with a fade up from black. In the preview thumbnail, click the **Set Poster Frame** button to the right of the slider, or select it from the pop-up context menu.

How to View Clip Information

As you assemble your clips in the Project window, Premiere provides several options for displaying information about the clips. These include summary information in the clip lists, detailed clip Property information, and even a Data Rate graph to show how the frames in the clip are compressed.

❶ Preview a Clip

To see basic information about a clip in the **Project** window, view the clip in **List** view, or click on the clip so that it is displayed in the preview area, with the thumbnail viewer and clip information.

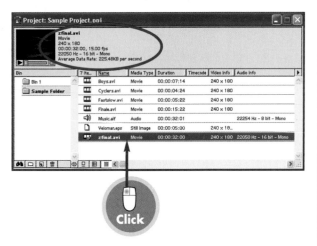

❷ Display the Info Palette

Premiere also displays summary information about the currently selected object in the *Info palette* along the right side of the work area. If the palette is hidden, click on the **Info** tab in the **Palette** window, or choose **Window**, **Show Info**. The Info palette is especially useful for viewing information about clips in the **Timeline**.

❸ Display Clip Properties

To see more detailed information about a clip, select it in the clip or preview area, and choose **Clip**, **Properties**, or choose **Properties** from the pop-up context menu.

④ View the Properties Window

The clip **Properties** window displays details on the clip file on disk, and the audio and video tracks in the file. To display a graph of the clip *data rate*, click the **Data Rate** button at the bottom left of the **Properties** window.

⑤ View the Data Rate Graph

The **Data rate graph** window shows the data rate of each frame in the file (as individual bars) and the average data rate (as the white line). Use this to verify that your clip can be played at a specific target data rate.

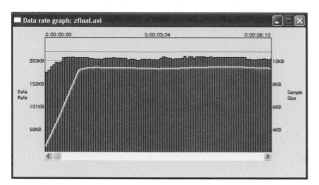

⑥ Display File Properties

To find out information about a file even before you open it, choose **File**, **Get Properties For**, **File**. Premiere then opens the Properties dialog for that file.

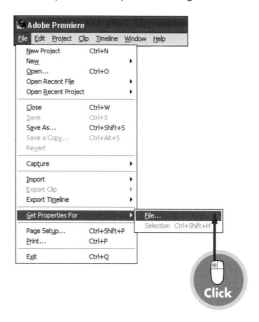

How-to Hint

The Data Rate Graph

The **Data rate graph** can be useful in understanding how well your clips will play on different computer systems, and over the Internet, at different data rates. The graph lets you study in detail how well each individual frame of the clip was compressed. For files compressed with independent keyframes, and difference frames between the keyframes, the keyframe sizes are in red, and the difference frame sizes are in blue.

How to Import Clips

Premiere offers several options for importing clips into your project and organizing them into bins. You can import clips individually, in groups, or as an entire folder at one time.

① Import a Clip

To import an individual clip file into your project, first select Bin 1 as the destination bin, and then choose **File**, **Import**, **File** (or choose **Import** from the pop-up context menu). Premiere displays the Import dialog.

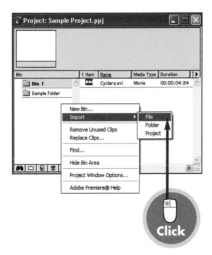

② Select a Clip

Browse to the Premiere Sample Folder (from Task 1), click to select the Fastslow file, and then click **Open**.

③ View the Clip

Premiere adds the clip to the currently selected bin. Click the clip to display the video and its properties in the preview area.

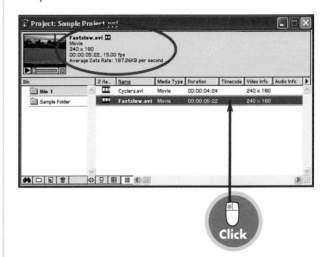

④ Import Different Clip Types

Premiere can import a wide variety of different video, audio, and image media types and file formats. In the Import dialog, click the **Files of Type** drop-down menu to view and select the specific media file formats that you can import into projects.

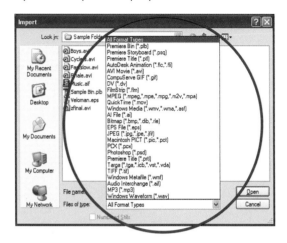

⑤ Import a Group of Clips

Besides opening individual files, you can use the standard operating system conventions to select a group of files at one time. In the Import dialog, click to select a first file, and then (**Command+click**) [**Ctrl+click**] to select multiple files. Click **Open**.

⑥ Import a Folder

To import an entire folder of clip files into your project, first select Bin 1 as the destination bin; then choose **File**, **Import**, **Folder** (or use the pop-up context menu). In the **Browse for Folder** dialog, navigate to the Sample Folder, click on the folder name to select it, and then click **OK**.

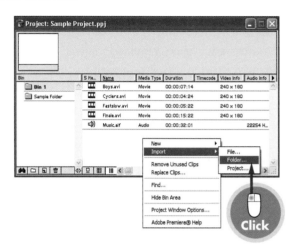

⑦ Delete Some Clips

Click on the triangular icon to expand Bin 1 to see the imported clips. To delete clips, (**Command+click**) [**Ctrl+click**] the clip's icons to select them, and then click on the **Delete** button below the bin pane (or press the **Delete** key). Deleting a clip only removes it from the project; it does not delete the actual clip file from disk.

How to Organize Bins

As you import clips into the Project window, you can organize them into bins. Bins act like file folders and can be moved, copied, renamed, nested, and otherwise rearranged to help you organize your clips.

1 Create a New Bin

To add a new bin folder to a project, click the **New Bin** button (folder icon) under the bin area (or use the **Project window** menu). In the Create Bin dialog, type the name **Bin 2** for the new bin, and click **OK**.

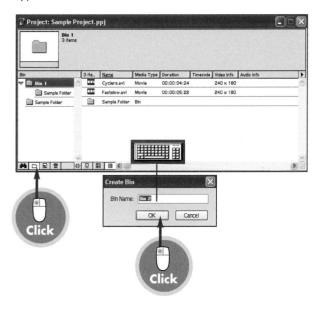

2 Rename a Bin

To rename a bin folder, click the Sample Folder name nested under Bin 1 in the bin area, and enter a new name as **Sample 2** by editing the name field in place.

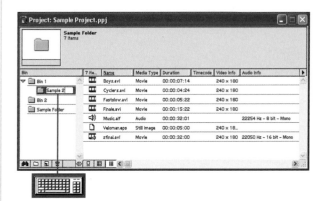

3 Select Clips

To select an individual clip, click the clip icon or thumbnail in the clip list. To select multiple clips in the Sample 2 bin, click the Cyclers clip name and drag the cursor down and over as a selection rectangle to select and highlight a group of three clips.

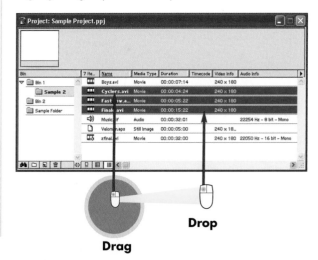

Drag

Drop

④ Move Clips

After you select an individual clip or group of clips, you can move the selected item between bins. Click the icon area to the left of the clip names and drag the clips to the Bin 2 folder.

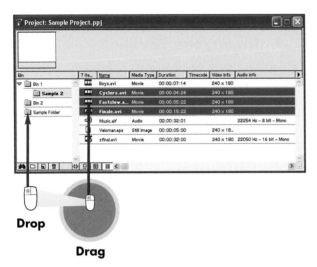

Drop

Drag

⑤ Move a Bin

Similarly, you can move entire bins, along with their contents to nest them hierarchically. To move the Sample 2 bin, click on the folder icon for the bin, and drag and drop it onto the Bin 2 folder.

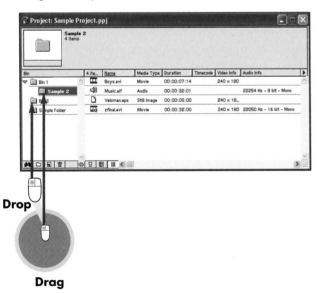

Drop

Drag

⑥ Delete a Bin

To clean up your project, delete the new bins. Click on the Bin 2 folder to select it, and then click on the **Delete** button below the bin pane (or press the Delete key). Or select **Clear** from the pop-up context menu.

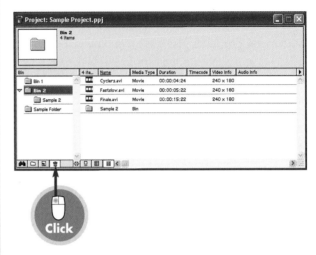

Click

Cleaning Up

An easier way to clean up your project after you have been experimenting is to simply close the project, throw away any changes, and reopen it to the last saved version. Or choose **File**, **Revert**. When the warning dialog asks whether you want to discard your changes to this project, click **Yes**.

Cut, Copy, and Paste

Another way to move and copy both clips and bins is through the **Clipboard Cut**, **Copy**, and **Paste** commands. You can select these from the **Edit** or pop-up context menus, or use the normal keyboard shortcuts.

How to Reuse Bins

After you organize your clips into bins in the Project window, you can save the bins to use with other projects. You also can open multiple bin windows to help organize clips.

1 Export the Bin

After you organize a group of clips into a bin, you also can save the bin for use in other projects. Click on the **Sample Folder** bin icon to select it, and choose **Project**, **Export Bin from Project**. In the Save File dialog, navigate to the folder where you want to save the bin, enter **Sample Bin** as the name, and click **Save**.

2 Import the Bin File

To use the saved bin file in a project, choose **File**, **Import**, **File**. In the Import dialog, select the Sample Bin saved bin file, and click **Open**.

3 View the Bin

Premiere adds the saved bin to the currently selected bin in the **Project** window. You now have the same clips available in two different bins. With Premiere, you are free to organize your clips as you want, even with copies in multiple bins.

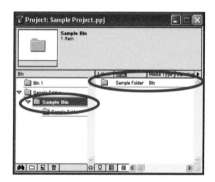

④ Open a Bin Window

To open a bin in a separate window, click on the **Sample Folder** bin icon to select it and choose **Open Bin in New Window** from the pop-up context menu.

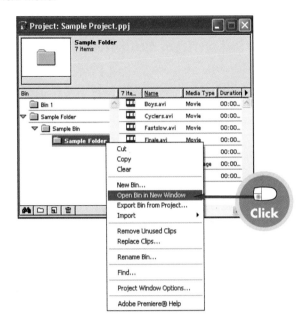

⑤ View the Bin Window

Premiere opens the bin in a separate bin window. You now can drag and drop between windows to organize and access the clips in your project.

⑥ Open an External Bin

To access clips in a bin file from another project, choose **File**, **Open**. Select the bin file, and Premiere opens the bin in a separate external bin window, with the hierarchical folder view. You then can copy clips or even the entire bin into your project.

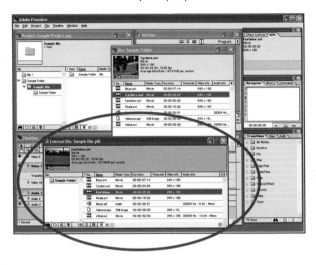

Multiple Bin Windows

You can open multiple bin windows for the bins in your project, which can be helpful when you are organizing clips across multiple folders. The bin windows provide an alternate view of the bins in the project, so changes in one view are reflected in the other.

Hiding the Preview Area

To save screen space when you are working with bin windows, click in the window and choose **Hide Preview Area** from the pop-up context menu. Premiere hides the top part of the window, with the thumbnail preview and clip information.

How to View Clips

As you organize your clips in bins, Premiere provides three different ways to view the contents of the bins and additional options to customize the views. Select from the available views in the Project window menu or click on the view buttons below the clip area.

1 Select the Icon View

To view and organize your clips as icons, select the Sample folder, and then click the **Icon View** button. You can drag the icons around to organize them, or select **Clean Up View** from the **Project window** menu to move them back into a grid layout.

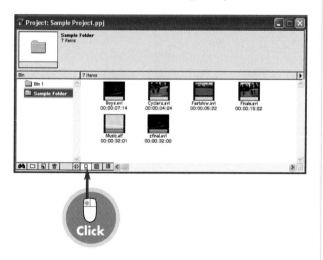

2 Select Icon Options

To customize the Icon view, select **Project Window Options** from the **Project window** menu. From the **Size** list, choose the size to display each icon, and select **Snap to Grid** to force the icons to line up in a grid layout. To make the **Project** window display faster, deselect **Draw Icons** to not display a thumbnail of each clip.

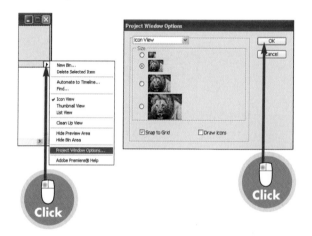

3 Select the Thumbnail View

To view your clips as thumbnails in a list with additional information, click the **Thumbnail View** button. You then can sort the list according to the entries in each column by clicking on the column headings.

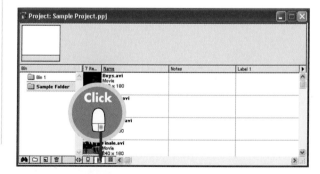

④ Select Thumbnail Options

To customize the thumbnail view, select **Project Window Options** from the **Project window** menu. From the **Icons** list, choose the size to display each icon, or deselect **Draw Icons** to not display a thumbnail of each clip.

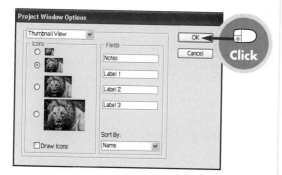

⑥ Select List Options

To customize the List view, select **Project Window Options** from the **Project window** menu. From the **Fields** list, select the information about each clip that will be displayed in the List View.

⑤ Select the List View

To view your clips in a terse list with descriptive information about each clip, click the **List View** button. Click on the column headings to sort the list.

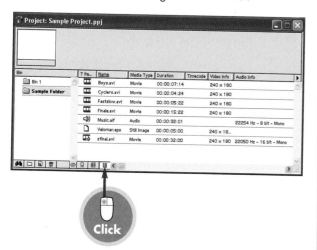

Using Clip Views

Use the List view to review all the information about your clips, including attributes such as media type and duration, as well as user information in the **Notes** and **Label** fields. Use the Thumbnail view to see a thumbnail of each clip along with some basic information and to enter additional notes and labels. Use the Icon view to organize and reorder your clips before moving them to the **Timeline**.

How to Label and Search Clips

Organizing your clips with bins makes them more useful for later work as you use them with other projects. Add your own annotations by entering text notes and labels for the clips. Sort your clips using the annotation text, or search the clip information with the Find command.

① Display the Thumbnail View

To enter notes and labels about your clips, first click on the **Thumbnail View** button to display the clips.

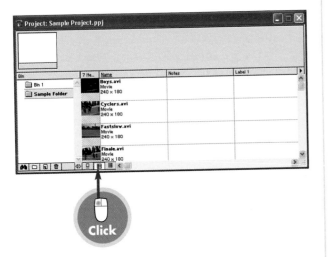

② Enter Clip Notes

Click in the **Notes** field for the clip and type your notes or comments about the clips.

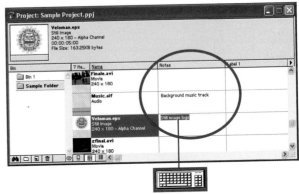

③ Enter Clip Labels

Premiere also provides three other **Label** fields in which you can enter additional information to help identify and organize your clips. To enter a label, click in the **Label 1** field and type **My Label** as the text of the label.

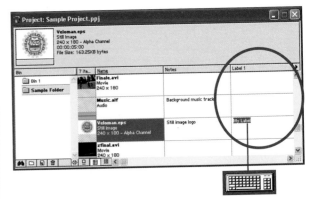

4 Rename Notes and Label Fields

To change the names of the **Notes** and **Label** fields when using the Thumbnail View or List View, select **Project Window Options** from the **Project window** menu and type new names into the Fields area.

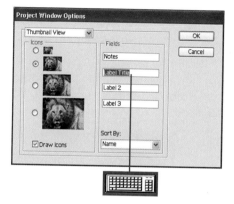

5 Search for Clips

To search for clips in a project, choose **Edit**, **Find** (or use the **Project window** menu). You can also click on the **Find** button (binoculars icon) at the bottom left of the **Project** window.

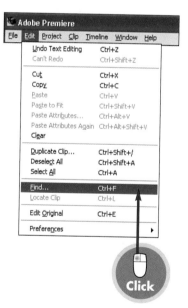

6 Select Find Options

In the Find dialog, use the left drop-down **Find** menu to select the field to search. Use the middle menu to search for matches to the specified text, or to search for fields that do not match the text. Enter the text to search for in the right field. You can enter a second search field in the **And** line. Click **Find** to begin the search, or **Find Again** when continuing a search for the next matching item.

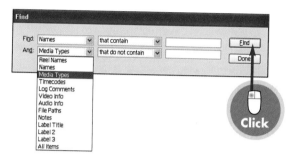

Notes and Labels

You can use the **Notes** and **Labels** fields in any way that is helpful to you. Enter long notes into any of the fields to annotate the clip for later use. Enter a series of keywords to help search for specific clips, or just enter one word to sort the clips in the list displays. In this way, you can organize and annotate collections of clips into bins that can be reused in many different projects.

How to Undo and Change History

Now that you have used Premiere to import and organize clips into bins and have seen how easy it is to move and delete clips and even entire bins, it is time to learn how to recover from mistakes. Premiere offers a variety of ways to undo and roll back a series of actions, which also makes it easy to experiment with changes.

1 Undo and Redo

To undo your last action, choose **Edit**, **Undo**. The name of the action also appears in the menu, such as **Undo Text Editing**. Premiere remembers up to your last 99 actions across all open windows, so you can undo them step by step. You also can choose **Redo** to undo your last undo, and so on.

2 Display the History Palette

Even better, Premiere displays the list of your recent actions in the *History palette* along the right side of the work area. If the palette is hidden, click on the **History** tab in the **Palette** window, or choose **Window**, **Show History**.

3 Go Back in History

The History palette displays each action that has been performed on the project, with the most recent at the bottom. To jump back to a previous state, click the name of the tool or command used in that state. All the more recent states below it in the list are then dimmed.

4 Change History

After you step back to a previous state, you can still move to a different state, whether older (above) or newer (below, and dimmed). You also can start working again at that previous state, in which case the dimmed history list is discarded, and a new list starts.

5 Delete History

You can step back in the History palette to a previous state and delete the states that followed it. Click on the most recent state that you want to preserve, and then open the **Palette window** menu and choose **Delete**, or press the **Delete** button at the bottom-right corner.

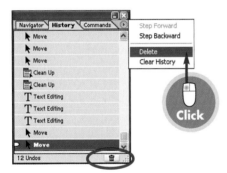

6 Set Undo Properties

To review your Undo and Save setting options, choose **Edit**, **Preferences**, **Auto Save and Undo**. You can set the number of Undo levels (and the number of levels in the History palette).

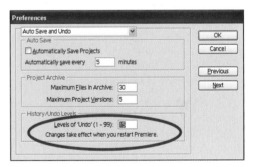

Save and Revert

Even with Undo and the History palette, it still is useful to save a copy of your project when you complete a set of actions. You can use **File**, **Save As** (or **Save a Copy**) to save a copy of your project under a new name so that the older copy you saved previously is still available. You then can experiment from that point, and later discard any changes since the last saved checkpoint, simply by closing the project without saving it and then reopening it. To do this in one step, choose **File, Revert**.

Task

3

Assembling Clips Using the Storyboard and Timeline

After you have imported media clips into your project and organized them into bins, it is time to begin assembling your production on the Timeline. The easiest way to lay out your clips on the Timeline is to make a *rough cut*, in which you first arrange the clips in order, and then fine-tune your production by positioning and trimming them more precisely.

You can get started quickly with Premiere by just clicking and dragging clips into position on the Timeline. You can also use the Storyboard window to arrange the clips into sequence before moving them into the Timeline. Premiere also provides an Automate to Timeline command to automatically lay out a group of clips on the Timeline, and even overlap them with a default transition.

In this part, you'll insert clips into the Timeline individually and in groups, move and delete them, and automate the layout with the Storyboard. In Part 4, "Adding Transitions Between Clips," you can learn more about inserting transitions. This is all you will need to know to make your first video productions.

See Parts 9, 10, and 11 for more on trimming clips and advanced editing techniques.

How to Add Clips in the Timeline

The most direct way to add and organize individual clips in the Timeline window is just to click and drag them. You can drag clips from a *bin* in the Project window, from a Clip window, and within the Timeline window.

1 Open the Sample Project

To start working with a clean slate, choose **File**, **Open Recent Project**, and then choose the Premiere Sample Project file. Or, if the project is already open, choose **File**, **Revert**.

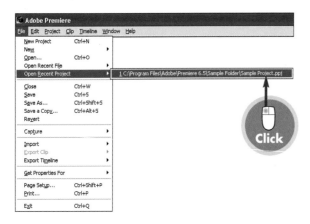

2 Drag from the Project

Select the Sample Folder bin in the **Project** window, and then click and drag the Cyclers clip icon to the Video 1A track in the **Timeline**.

3 Drag from a Clip Window

You can also drag to the **Timeline** from a **Clip** window. Double-click to open the Fastslow clip in a **Clip** window, and then drag from the video area to drop the clip after Cyclers in the Video 1A track. Premiere snaps the second clip into position after the first.

④ Play the Timeline

To view the program on the **Timeline**, close the **Clip** window and click the **Play** button on the **Monitor** window (or select the **Timeline** window and press the **spacebar**). Because the second clip immediately follows the first, the playback shows a simple cut from one to the other.

⑤ **Overlap the Clips**

To stagger a pair of clips in the Video 1 track, drag the Fastslow clip down to the Video 1B track and position it to the left slightly to overlap with the end of the Cyclers clip in Video 1A. This will be used in Part 4 to add transitions between each pair of clips.

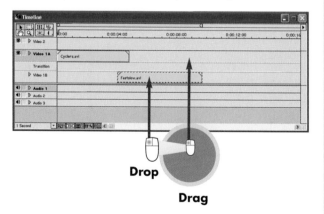

⑥ **Open a Gap**

As you assemble clips on the **Timeline** and insert new clips, you may temporarily introduce gaps in the program. Drag the Fastslow clip to the right beyond the end time of the Cyclers clip. When you play through the **Timeline**, the gap appears as a black screen.

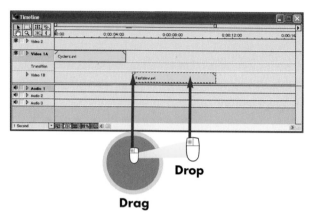

How-to Hint

Locating Clips

As you add more clips to the **Timeline**, you can lose track of which clip came from where. To find the source of a clip in the **Timeline**, select it, and then choose **Locate Clip** from the pop-up context menu. Premiere displays the bin the clip was added from in the **Project** window and highlights the clip in the bin area.

How to Insert and Delete Clips from the Timeline

You can edit a Timeline by inserting new material between existing clips or by deleting material from the middle. The other clips can then automatically adjust to fit. This is called *ripple* editing, because a change in the program ripples through all the clips as they move to make room for new material or close up to fill a gap.

① Insert and Ripple

Drag and hold the Veloman still image clip from the **Project** window bin over the front of the **Fastslow** clip in the **Timeline**. Premiere displays a right arrow icon over the Fastslow clip that will be shifted over, and highlights the size of the new clip. Drop the new clip into place.

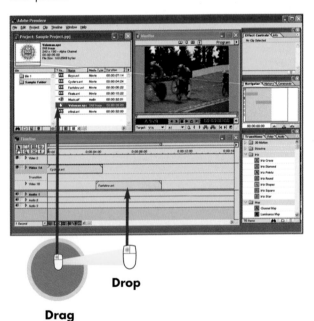

Drop

Drag

② View Ripple Insert

After the ripple insert, the new Veloman clip now starts at the time where Fastslow used to start, and the Fastslow clip is shifted to the end of the new clip to make room for it.

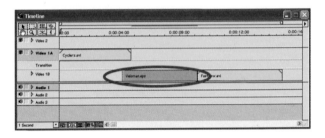

③ Delete a Clip

To delete the Veloman clip in place, select the clip and press the **Delete** key (or choose **Clear** from the pop-up context menu).

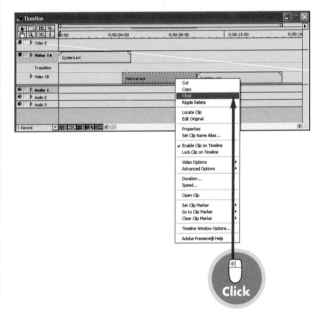

Click

④ View the Delete

Simply deleting the clip does not affect the rest of the program, so there is now a gap in the **Timeline**.

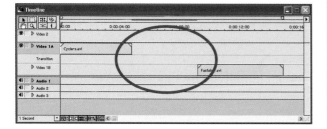

⑥ View Ripple Delete

After the ripple delete, the end of the program on the **Timeline** is shifted back to the left to fill the time period of the deleted clip.

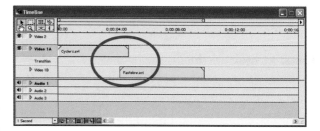

⑤ Ripple Delete Clip

Choose **Edit**, **Undo** to restore the Veloman clip. Now, select the Veloman clip and choose **Ripple Delete** from the pop-up context menu.

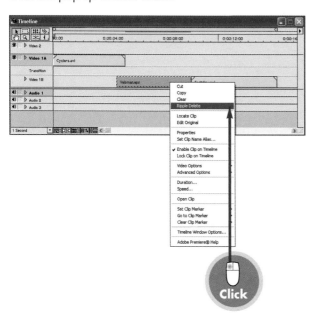

How to Add a Group of Clips to the Timeline

Dragging individual clips to the Timeline to assemble a program can quickly become tedious. Instead, you can select and drag a collection or group of clips all at once. The trick is to have Premiere understand in what order you want them placed in the Timeline.

1 Open the Sample Project

To start working with a clean project, choose **File**, **Open Recent Project**, and then choose the Premiere Sample Project file. Or, if the project is already open, choose **File**, **Revert**.

2 Drag a Group of Clips

Select a few clips from the Sample Folder bin in the **Project** window by clicking and dragging a selection rectangle over their names. Click with the hand cursor from the icon area to the left of the names and drag to the Video 1A track in the **Timeline**.

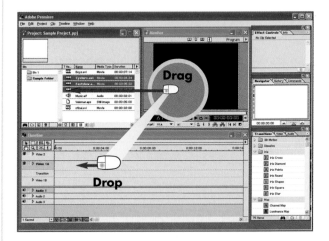

3 View Timeline

Premiere then lays out the selected clips in alphabetical order on the destination track. Scroll back in the **Timeline** to see their order.

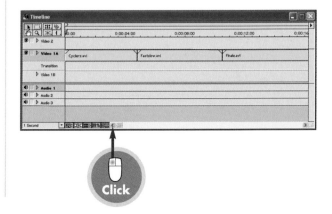

④ Arrange in Icon View

Choose **Edit**, **Undo** to empty the **Timeline**. For more control over selecting clips, click on the **Icon View** button below the bin area. Then rearrange a few clips in the desired order, left to right and top to bottom.

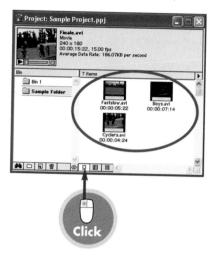

⑥ View Timeline

This time, Premiere lays out the clips in the order that they were organized in the bin.

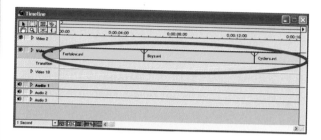

⑤ Drag from Icon View

Select three clips by clicking and dragging a selection rectangle around them, and then click and drag them down to the Video 1A track in the **Timeline**.

How to Automate to the Timeline

To simplify assembling clips on the Timeline, Premiere also provides an Automate to Timeline feature. Automate to Timeline not only adds a group of clips but also arranges them alternately on the A and B tracks, with a default transition between each pair.

1 Open the Sample Project

To start working with a clean project, choose **File**, **Open Recent Project**, and then choose the Premiere Sample Project file. Or, if the Project is already open, choose **File**, **Revert**.

2 Automate to Timeline

Select the **Boys**, **Cyclers**, and **Fastslow** clips from the Sample Folder bin in the **Project** window by clicking and dragging a selection rectangle over their names. Pull down the **Project window** menu and choose **Automate to Timeline** (or select it from the **Project** menu).

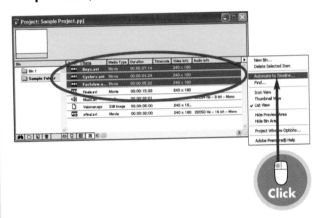

3 Select Contents

Premiere displays the Automate to Timeline dialog. In the **Contents** drop-down menu, choose **Selected Clips** to add to the **Timeline** only the clips you selected (or select **Whole Bin** to add the entire bin).

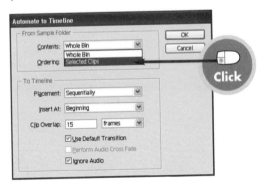

④ Select Insertion Point

In the **Insert At** drop-down menu, select **Beginning** to insert the clips at the front of the **Timeline** (or select **Edit Line** or **End** to insert them at the current edit line position or at the end of the **Timeline**).

⑥ View Resulting Timeline

Scroll in the **Timeline** and look at the **Navigator** window to view the resulting layout. The specified clips have been laid out alternating on the A and B tracks. The ends have been overlapped, and a default transition has been inserted between them.

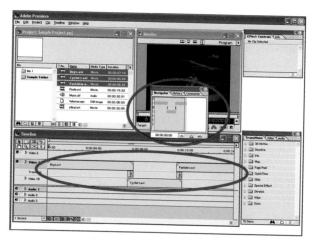

⑤ Select Clip Overlap

In the **Clip Overlap** drop-down menu, enter the number of frames or seconds that each clip should overlap the adjacent clips for a *transition*. Select **Use Default Transition**, and click **OK**.

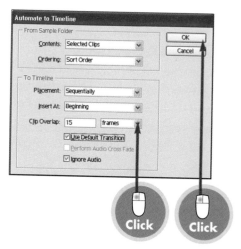

Play, Real-Time Preview, and Rendering

If you play through the **Timeline** in the **Monitor** window or by pressing the spacebar, you will not see any transition effect; instead, the playback simply cuts whenever an A track clip overlaps a B clip below it. The red colored bar above the time ruler at the top of the **Timeline** window warns that this portion of the **Timeline** still must be *rendered* to create the frames showing the transition effect. (See Part 4 for more on previewing and rendering transitions.)

Automating Slide Shows

You can use **Automate to Timeline** to create slide shows too. Just use the storyboard to import and arrange your still image files, and then add them to the **Timeline**, complete with a default transition.

How to Use the Storyboard

An even better way to organize a collection of clips before adding them to the Timeline is to use a story-board layout to arrange the individual clips in sequence. In addition to the Project and Bin windows, Premiere also provides a Storyboard window for arranging the order of a group of clips into a *rough cut*.

1 Open the Sample Project

To start working with a clean project, choose **File**, **Open Recent Project**, and then choose the Premiere Sample Project file. Or, if the Project is already open, choose **File**, **Revert**.

2 Open a Storyboard Window

Choose **File**, **New**, **Storyboard**. Premiere opens a new empty **Storyboard** window.

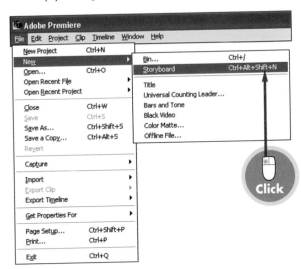

3 Import Clips

To add clips to the **Storyboard** window, select and drag the Sample Folder from the **Project** window to the **Storyboard** window. You can also use the **File** menu to choose **Import File** or **Import Folder**.

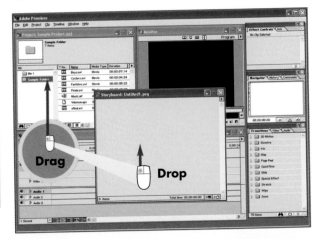

④ Delete Clips

The clips are numbered to show their sequence and also have arrows connecting them to show the flow from one to the next. Each clip is displayed with a thumbnail icon, along with its duration. Click the zFinal clip and then press the **Delete** key to delete it from the storyboard.

⑤ Reorder Clips

Drag the Fastslow clip earlier in the sequence to insert it in front of the preceding Boys clip. Then drag the Cyclers clip later in the sequence to insert it after the Finale clip.

⑥ Automate to Timeline

Choose **Project**, **Automate to Timeline** (or choose it from the **Storyboard** window menu or the pop-up context menu). Or click the button at the bottom right of the **Storyboard** window. Set the **Storyboard** and **Timeline** options in the **Automate to Timeline** dialog, and Premiere automatically lays out the clips on the **Timeline**.

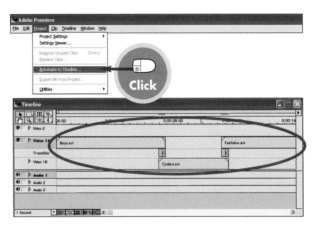

How-to Hint

Icon Sizes

Choose **Storyboard Window Options** from the **Storyboard window** menu or the pop-up context menu to set the size of the clip thumbnail icons in the window.

Save the Storyboard

After you organize your clips in a **Storyboard** window, you can save your work for later use. Choose **File**, **Save**.

Print Storyboard

You can also print the **Storyboard** window display for use as a reference. Just choose **File**, **Print**.

Task

4

Adding Transitions Between Clips

After you have organized your clips in the Project window and laid them out in a sequence in the Timeline window, you can start to think about what happens when you move or transition from clip to clip during the playback of your production. The simplest visual effect is to *cut* from one clip to the next, with the last frame of the first clip immediately followed by the first frame of the next clip.

Although a cut is often the best and most direct transition, you have arranged the clips to tell a story, and might find that the visual effect of a cut is too abrupt. Instead, you might want to use a visual transition between the clips to help advance the story or set a mood—for example, to suggest the passage of time, or movement in location, or a switch to a different part of the story.

Premiere offers more than 75 transitions, including wipes, dissolves, stretches, zooms, 3D motion, and masks, that provide you a range of creative freedom. Each transition also can be customized in duration, speed, direction, and other ways. In addition, you can use transitions in Premiere to show two clips at the same time with a split-screen or inset. Just don't get too carried away with your creative freedom so that you detract from your story!

How to Use Automated Transitions

As you saw in Part 3, "Assembling Clips Using the Storyboard and Timeline," Premiere's Automate to Timeline command greatly simplifies building a production from a group of clips by automatically laying them out on the Timeline window. It also can insert a default transition between each pair of clips, which you then can modify and customize.

❶ Open the Sample Project

Open the Premiere **Sample Project** and select the **Sample Folder** bin. Click and drag a selection rectangle to select the first three clips. From the pop-up **Project window** menu, choose **Automate to Timeline**, or select it from the **Project** menu.

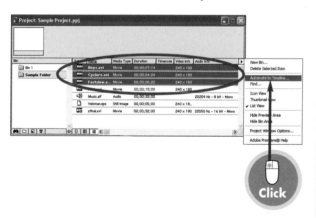

❷ Automate to Timeline

In the **Automate to Timeline** dialog, choose **Contents**, **Selected Clips**. Verify that **Use Default Transition** is checked, and then click **OK**.

❸ Review the Transitions

Premiere then automatically lays out the three clips in the Timeline window, alternating between the Video 1A and Video 1B tracks. Premiere also adds a default transition on the Transition track between the video tracks. To view the settings for the first transition (between the **Boys** and **Cyclers** clips), simply double-click the **transition** (or click the transition and select **Transition Settings** from the pop-up context menu).

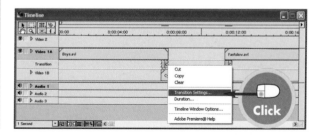

④ View Transition Settings

The title area of the Transition Settings dialog shows that this default transition is a Cross Dissolve. The animation in the bottom-right corner shows that the transition starts with the A track and dissolves to the B track.

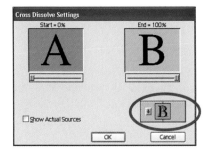

⑤ Show Actual Sources

Click the **Show Actual Sources** check box to view the actual clips from the Timeline. Drag the **Start/End slider** under the **Start** window to preview the effect of the transition. Then click **Cancel** to prevent any changes to the default transition settings.

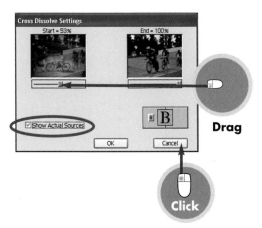

Drag

Click

⑥ View the Second Transition

Double-click the second transition (between the Cyclers and Fastslow clips) to show its settings. Notice that Premiere has automatically set the transition to dissolve back from the B to the A track. You can click the **Track selector arrow** button to the left of the animation to reverse the direction of the transition.

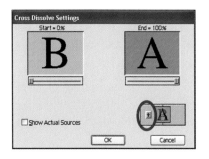

How-to Hint

Clip Overlap

Use the Clip Overlap option in the Automate to Timeline dialog to adjust the amount of overlap between adjacent clips. You can specify the amount of overlap in frames or seconds, or specify no overlap for simple cut transitions.

Setting the Default Transition

You can set the default transition and its properties in the Transitions palette (see Task 4).

Audio Cross-Fade

The Automate to Timeline dialog includes the option to Ignore Audio or include the audio with each clip. You also can select Perform Audio Cross-Fade to have Premiere include a transition between the audio track of each clip (see Part 14).

How to Preview Transitions

Transitions require creating new frames by combining, manipulating, and overlapping regions from the ends of two adjacent clips.

Before exporting your final project, Premiere must first render it, or generate the frames for these transitions and other effects. You can render these sections of the Timeline as you work, or Premiere can display a real-time preview.

❶ Play the Timeline

Select the **Timeline** window, and then press the **Spacebar** to play through the Timeline (or click on the **play controls** in the **Monitor** window). Premiere just plays through the video clips, cutting directly between the A and B tracks. Premiere is not previewing the program because the final frames for the two transitions have not been rendered for playback, as indicated by red bar above them in the time ruler.

❷ Render-Scrub Through Video

To preview the visual effect of the transition, *render-scrub* through the video by pressing the (**Option**) [**Alt**] key and then dragging the edit line in the time ruler. The cursor changes from a triangle to an arrow, and the **Monitor** window shows the transition effect.

❸ Select the Real-Time Preview

Premiere 6.5 supports real-time preview from the Timeline. It is the default for some project settings, or you can select it for your projects. Choose **Project**, **Project Settings**, **Keyframe and Rendering**. In the Project Settings dialog, under **Rendering Options**, select (**Preview to Screen**) [**Real Time Preview**]. Click **Save**.

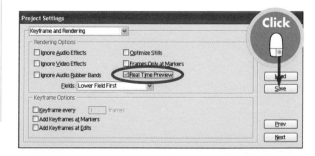

④ Play the Real-Time Preview

Press (**Return**) [**Enter**] to play the preview in the **Monitor** window, complete with transitions and other effects. Premiere simulates the actual frame rate and appearance of the final program as close as possible, depending on your system resources and the complexity of the Timeline.

⑤ Set the Work Area

Double-click on the **work area bar** to select only the currently visible area of the **Timeline**. The end markers move to the edges of the window. Then drag the two ends of the **work area** to cover just the first transition. Use the pop-up context menu to Preview, or Render the work area.

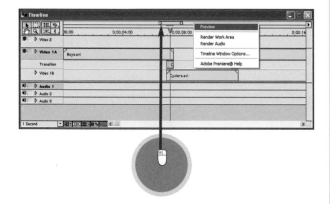

Drag

⑥ Render to Disk

To generate a preview of the work area, press **Shift** and the (**Return**) [**Enter**] key. (**Shift** reverses the current setting of the **Real Time Preview** option.) After Premiere builds the preview, the colored bar above the Timeline changes to green.

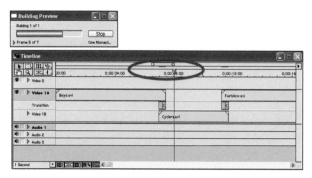

Playing and Previewing and Rendering

To Play through the clips on the Timeline, press the Spacebar or use the Monitor window controls.

To Scrub slowly through sections of the Timeline, drag the edit line.

To Render-Scrub and preview effects, press (**Option**) [**Alt**] and drag the edit line. For a Real-Time Preview of transitions and effects, press the (**Return**) [**Enter**] key (if enabled).

To Render the current work area on the Timeline, press **Shift** and the (**Return**) [**Enter**] key. After rendering, the transitions will be displayed when you play the clip.

If the Real-Time Preview option is not set, the use of the **Shift** key is reversed for rendering and previewing.

How to Set Transition Durations

You can adjust the length or duration of a transition by adjusting the extent that the clips overlap, and then shrinking or lengthening the transition to match.

1 Change the Clip Overlap

To increase the overlap of the first two clips, drag the Cyclers clip to the left. Because the transition area has changed, the area above the time ruler is red to show that it needs to be re-rendered.

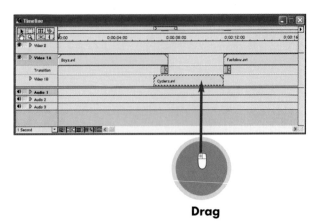

Drag

2 Move the Transition

You can drag transitions in the Timeline just like clips. Drag the transition clip to the left to align with the start of the Cyclers clip.

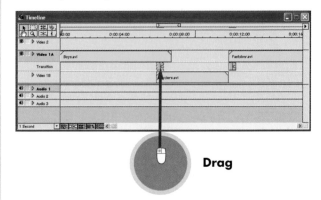

Drag

3 Adjust the Transition Duration

Adjust the length of transitions by dragging from the edge. Extend the transition to the end of the **Boys** clip by clicking and dragging the right edge of the transition clip. The cursor changes to a bar with arrows pointing left and right.

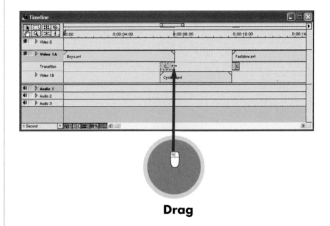

Drag

④ Check the Duration

To set or check the duration length, choose **Clip**, **Duration** (or choose **Duration** from the context menu). Premiere displays the Clip Duration dialog with the length of time of the transition.

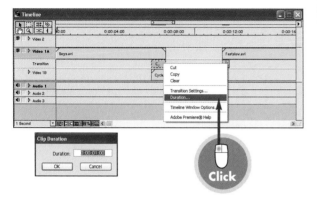

⑤ Set the Work Area

To render the transition, remember to first set the work area by double-clicking the **work area bar** above the Timeline to extend the work area to cover the entire visible area in the Timeline window.

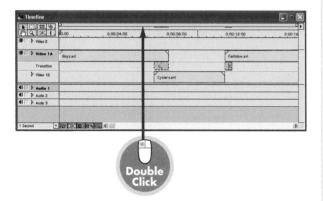

⑥ Preview the Transitions

Press (**Return**) [**Enter**] to preview the project with both transitions. Premiere plays a real-time preview of the project with the transition effects, or, if needed, builds a preview and then plays through the entire window work area.

How-to Hint

Easy Fade to Black

You can use a dissolve transition to create a fade up from black or fade down to black. The second transition in step 6 actually fades up from black because there is no clip in the second track.

Preview Files

When you render a transition and create a preview, Premiere actually saves the frames for the transition in a preview file on the hard disk. You can change the defaults for rendering in the **Project** menu, under **Project Settings**, **Keyframe and Rendering**.

How to Use the Transitions Palette

Task 4

To make it easier to select and modify transitions, Premiere organizes them into the Transitions palette. Like other Premiere elements, the Transitions palette is organized into a hierarchy of folders and can be customized to match your work style.

1 Show the Transitions Palette

To show the **Transitions** palette, click on the **Transitions** tab in the **Palette** window, or choose **Window**, **Show Transitions**.

2 Expand the Transitions Palette

Click on the triangle to the left of the **Page Peel** folder to expand the folder to show all the included transitions. Scroll through the list of transitions. Open the **Transitions** palette menu to choose **Expand all Folders** or **Collapse all Folders**.

3 Animate the Transitions

For a visual preview of the effect of the transitions, open the **Transitions** palette menu and choose **Animate**. Each of the transition icons now animates to show the effect of the transition.

④ View Transition Information

For a brief explanation of each transition, click the **transition** and then look at the **Info** palette. To show the Info palette, click the **Info** tab in the **Palette** window, or choose **Window**, **Show Info**.

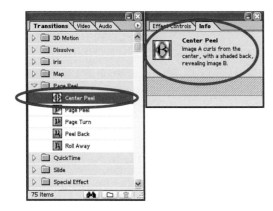

⑤ Set the Default Transition

Double-click on the **Dissolve** folder to show its contents. The Cross Dissolve transition (outlined in red) is the current default transition, used by the Automate to Timeline command. To change the default transition, select a transition, and then choose **Set Selected as Default** from the **Palette** window menu.

⑥ Set the Default Properties

Premiere then displays the **Default Effect** dialog. Set the default duration of the default transition and its alignment relative to the cut point. Click **OK** to accept the current settings.

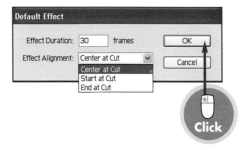

How-to Hint

Customizing the Transitions Palette

You can reorganize and customize the **Transitions** palette by dragging your favorite transitions to the front of the list and by using the palette menu to add new folders and even hide transitions to simplify the list.

Finding Transitions

You can also search for transitions by name; choose **Find** from the pop-up palette menu, or click the **Find** button (binoculars icon) at the bottom of the window.

How to Insert and Modify Transitions

Inserting and modifying transitions with Premiere is as easy as working with any other kind of clip. Just drag to move transitions and double-click to change settings.

① Insert a Push Transition

To replace the default Cross Dissolve transition, open the **Slide** folder in the **Transitions** palette, select the **Push** transition, and drag it on top of the first transition in the **Timeline**.

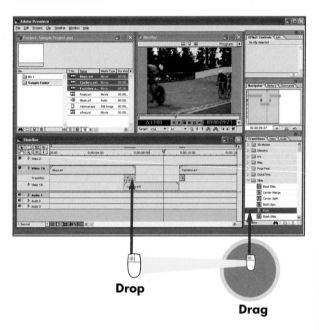

Drop

Drag

② Set the Edge Direction

Double-click the new **Push** transition clip to display the **Push Settings** dialog. The transition defaults to pushing the old clip out left to right, as shown by the red Edge Selector arrow next to the animation in the bottom-right corner of the window. Click on the edge at the top center of the animation to change the transition to push from top to bottom.

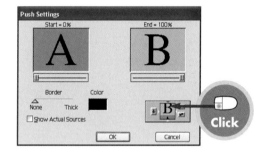

Click

③ Show the Sources

For a better understanding of the visual effect of the transition, click the **Show Actual Sources** check box to display the corresponding frames of the two clips. Drag the **Start** and **End** sliders under the two windows to preview the transition.

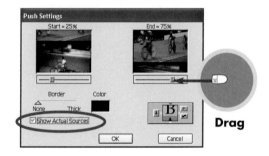

Drag

④ Set the Border

Drag the **Border** slider to add a border between the frames and adjust its thickness. Click on the **Color** rectangle to display the **Color Picker** dialog and select yellow. Then click **Cancel** to close the dialog and experiment with another transition.

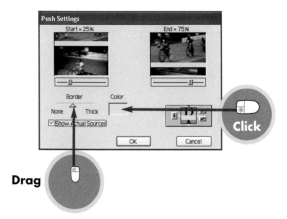

Drag

⑤ Set the Zoom Transition

Open the **Zoom** folder in the Transitions palette, and double-click the zoom transition to display the Zoom Settings dialog. Drag the small rectangle in the **Start** window to change the center point of the zoom effect to the top-left corner of the frame. Drag the Start slider to preview the effect.

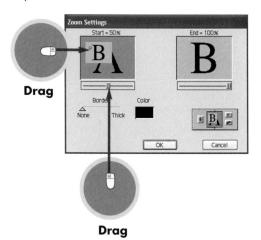

Drag

Drag

⑥ Set the Play Direction

To change the play direction of the transition from Forward to Reverse, click the small **F** button to the right of the animation. The button marking changes to R. The transition now zooms A out to reveal B, instead of zooming B in to cover A.

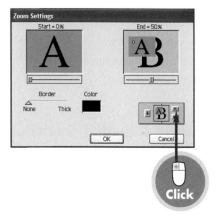

Click

How-to Hint

Anti-Aliasing

Click the **Anti-Aliasing** selector button under the Forward/Reverse button to adjust the smoothness of the edges of the transition.

Local and Global Settings

When you double-click a transition clip in the Timeline and change the Settings dialog, you are setting the options only for that specific instance of the transition between two clips. When you change the Settings dialog in the Transitions palette, you are changing the global default settings for that transition, which will then be applied each time you use it thereafter.

How to Choose Transitions

Premiere provides many transitions and organizes them into categories as folders in the Transitions palette to help you make sense of them. This task provides a brief tour of the different types of transitions.

❶ Using Dissolve Transitions

Double-click the **Dissolve** folder in the **Transitions** palette. Then double-click the **Additive Dissolve** transition to view its controls. The dissolve transitions fade one clip into another so that the first fades away and the second gradually appears. Click **Cancel** to view the next group of transitions.

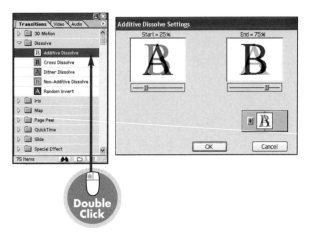

❷ Using Wipe Transitions

Double-click the **Wipe** folder, and then double-click the **Barn Doors** transition. The wipe transitions push away the first clip to reveal the second, using various geometric patterns. You can control the starting location and direction of the wipe.

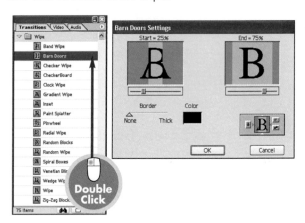

❸ Using Slide and Stretch Transitions

Double-click the **Slide** and **Stretch** folders, and then double-click the **Funnel** transition. The slide transitions move the second clip in to cover the first, and the stretch transitions distort the clips as they slide in. Some also break the clips into pieces, or rotate the clips as they slide.

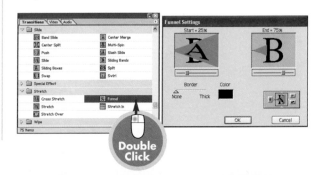

④ Using Iris and Page Peel Transitions

Double-click the **Iris** and **Page Peel** folders, and then double-click the **Iris Star** transition. The iris transitions perform wipes in geometric shapes from the center of the display. The page peel transitions curl the first clip away to reveal the second.

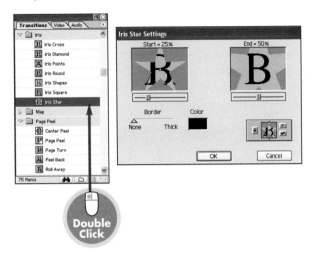

⑤ Using Zoom Transitions

Double-click the **Zoom** folder, and then double-click the **Zoom Trails** transition. The zoom transitions zoom down the first clip and zoom up the second clip into place.

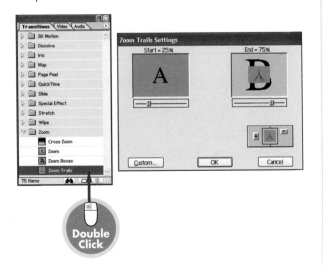

⑥ Using 3D Motion Transitions

Double-click the **3D Motion** folder, and then double-click the **Curtain** transition. The 3D transitions move away the first clip in 3D perspective to reveal the second clip.

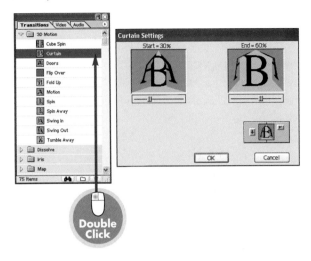

Special Effect Transitions

Check out the Special Effect and Map transitions for more complex effects. Use Direct and Take to force the use of the B track even when it is overlapped by an A track. Use Image Mask to design your own transition effect based on a user-supplied mask image.

Fades and Flashes

To fade to (or from) black, or any other color, use a Cross Dissolve transition between the video and a still image of that color. To quickly create colored mattes, use the Bin window pop-up context menu to choose New, Black Video or Color Matte. You also can use mattes to tint your video and to simulate quick flashes.

Multiple Transitions

You can also create more complex effects by chaining multiple transitions, one after another, or by applying multiple transitions at the same time, for example, to dissolve a wipe effect.

How to Create Split-Screens and Insets

You also can use transitions to create an effect showing two clips playing on the display at the same time by using a split-screen or inset. The trick is to set the transition at a specific point and have it not change while the clips are playing.

❶ Align the Clips

Clear the Timeline by choosing **File**, **Revert**. Select the Premiere **Sample Folder** bin and drag the Boys and Fastslow clips into the Video 1A and Video 1B tracks so that they are aligned at the beginning of the window.

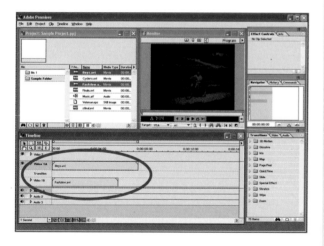

❷ Add a Wipe Transition

To create a split-screen effect, open the **Wipe** folder in the **Transitions** palette and drag the **Wipe** transition to the **Transition** track in the **Timeline** between the two clips. Premiere automatically sets its duration to match the shorter clip.

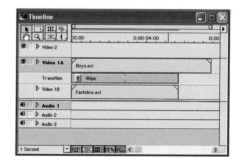

❸ Set Up the Split-Screen

Double-click the **Wipe** transition to open the Wipe Settings dialog. Hold down the **Shift** key while moving the **Start** slider to 50%. This sets the same Start and End point for the transition, so it does not change as the clips play. Click **Show Actual Sources** to preview the split-screen effect.

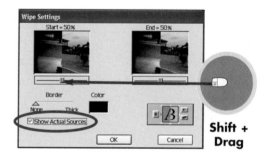

Shift + Drag

④ Add an Inset Transition

Similarly, to create an inset effect, replace the Wipe transition by dragging and dropping the **Inset** transition from the **Wipe** folder over the **Wipe** transition in the **Timeline**.

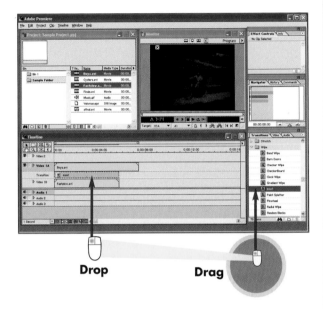

Drop　　　　**Drag**

⑤ Set Up the Inset

Double-click the **Inset** transition to open the Inset Settings dialog. Hold down the **Shift** key while moving the **Start** slider to 50%. Click **Show Actual Sources** to preview the inset effect.

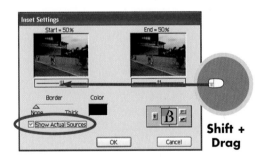

Shift + Drag

⑥ Get Creative

Click on the edges of the animation to move the Edge Selection red triangle and show the inset in another corner. Or get creative by using a different transition such as Iris Round (in the Iris folder) to create a circular inset, and then drag the center point to a corner.

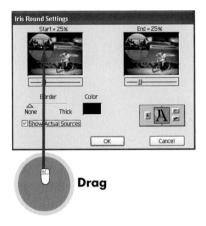

Drag

More Splits and Insets

You can use a **Stretch** transition to show a split-screen effect with the entire width of both frames squeezed into the display, or a 3D Motion effect such as **Cube Spin** to show both frames in perspective. Or use the **Zoom** transition to control the size and position of a rectangular inset in the frame. Look through the Transitions palette for more ideas.

More Effects

For different approaches for creating similar split-screen and inset effects, use the Transform video effect (see Part 15) and Motion Settings (see Part 16).

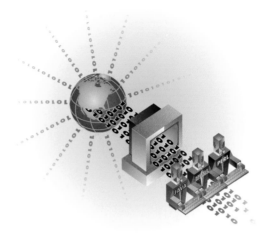

5

Exporting Clips and Projects

Now that you have imported and organized clips and laid them out in a production on the Timeline, it is time to export your work, saving it to a movie file that you can keep and share with others. Premiere provides built-in support for exporting to common desktop video and audio formats, including Microsoft Video for Windows (.avi) and Apple QuickTime (.mov), and for exporting in Web and DVD formats (see Part 7, "Exporting to Web and DVD Formats").

Premiere provides a wide range of options for the exported file format, including video and audio compressors, video resolution and frame rate, audio size and sample rate, and other special processing options. To help manage all these options, Premiere includes preset project settings to use while editing the clips and export settings to define the output format. You can also define and save your own settings. Premiere also provides a Settings Viewer to help ensure that all these different settings are consistent.

In this part, you'll apply the export settings to save individual clips in a variety of different formats. You can use Premiere in this way to quickly convert clips to new formats, and even trim and resize clips, all without importing them into a project. You'll also explore the most useful video and audio compression options for the QuickTime and AVI file formats. In the Part 6, "Exporting to Video and Audio Formats" you will move on to exporting an entire production from the Timeline, and using other video and audio file formats.

For much more information on file formats and compressors, see the Tutorials and other information on the Adobe Web site (www.adobe.com).

How to Export a Video Clip

To start making sense of all the export options in Premiere, you will first step through the process by exporting a single video clip. For the moment, you will not set any of the export options, so Premiere will export the clip in the default video file format. You will check the results in the next task by looking at the clip properties.

① Open the Sample Project

Choose **File**, **Open Recent Project**, **Sample Project** to open the project that you saved in Part 1. If you have just launched Premiere, click the **Open** button in the initial Load Project Settings dialog, navigate to the Sample Folder, and select the **Sample Project** file.

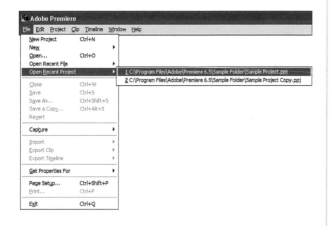

② View the Cyclers Clip

Click on the Sample Folder in the bin to show all the clips, and then double-click the Cyclers clip to open a **Clip** window and view the clip.

③ Export the Clip

To export the clip to a new video file, choose **File**, **Export Clip**, **Movie**.

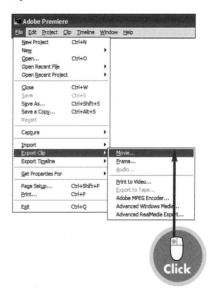

4   Name the Clip

Premiere displays the Export Movie dialog. Navigate to the Sample Folder, click the **File name** field, type Cyclers Copy as the name of the clip, and click **Save**.

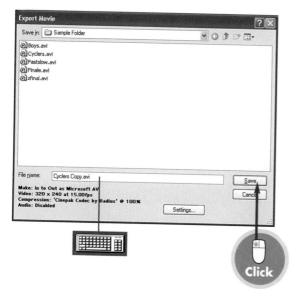

5   Save the Clip

Premiere then displays the Exporting dialog as it processes the clip and saves it to disk as a new clip file. The dialog includes a meter to indicate progress as it counts through the frames in a clip. Click **Stop** if desired to abort the export.

6   View the New Clip

When the export completes, Premiere displays the saved Cyclers Copy clip in a new **Clip** window. Oddly, the new clip appears to be larger than the original. Go on to the next task to see what happened to it.

How to Check Clip Settings

In Task 1, you saved a copy of the Cyclers clip using the default settings. However, it now appears that the new clip is larger than the original. In this task, you will look at the clip properties to understand what happened.

1 Resize the Cyclers Clip Window

Premiere automatically shrinks a video clip to fit in a **Clip** window. Click on the triangular area at the bottom right of the original Cyclers clip window. Premiere displays the clip size (240×180) at the top left, and also shows the extent of the full clip as a rectangular outline. Drag the window down and to the right so that the clip expands to full size in the window.

Drag

2 Resize the New Clip Window

Click on the corner of the new Cyclers Copy clip window. The copied clip (320×240) is indeed larger than the original. Resize the window to also expand it to full size.

Drag

3 Open the Clip Properties

To find out more about the clips, click on each clip window and choose **Clip**, **Properties** (or (**Control+click**) [**Right+click**] to display the pop-up context menu, and then choose **Properties**).

Click

④ View the Clip Properties

Premiere displays the Properties dialog for each clip. Both files have the same **Total Duration** (4:24, or under five, seconds) and the same **Frame Rate** (15.00 fps). Both are compressed with the same **Compressor** (Cinepak). However, the Cyclers Copy clip has a larger resolution or **Frame Size** (320×240 versus the original's 240×180) and therefore has a larger **File Size** on disk (1.57MB versus 899.60KB).

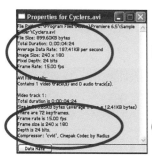

⑤ Open the Project Settings Viewer

To understand why the new Cyclers Copy clip has a different size, check the default settings for the project. Close the **Clip** windows and Properties dialogs, and then choose **Project**, **Settings Viewer** to review the current project settings.

⑥ View the Project Settings

The Settings Viewer is a great way to check that your capture, project, clip, and export settings are consistent. Premiere highlights the Frame Size row in red to show the problem: The **Project Settings** and **Export Settings** use a size of 320×240, but the sample clip files imported into the project were created at 240×180. As a result, Premiere expanded the Cyclers clip to the larger size before exporting it. Click **OK** to close the dialog.

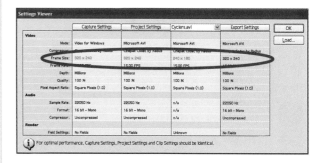

How-to Hint

Clip Properties

You can check the properties for a clip without opening it. Just choose **File**, **Get Properties for File**, and select the file.

Project Settings

Typically, you want use the same settings to capture, process, and export your clips to avoid any extra conversions or processing. You can use different export settings to save in several different file formats. And, when doing a rough edit, you can set the project settings to a lower resolution to save processing time and storage.

Changing Settings

Premiere provides several different ways to change settings. You can change capture, project, and export settings from the Settings Viewer dialog; you can change project settings from the **Project** menu and the initial Load Project Settings dialog; and you can change export settings from the Export dialog.

How to Use Export Settings

There is a great deal of flexibility in Premiere for exporting your clips and productions. Use the Export Settings dialog to customize the file type, video and audio properties, and other special processing. In this and the following tasks you will first step through the options in the Export Settings dialog, and then save the clips in several different formats.

1 Export a Clip

Open the Sample Project, and open the zfinal clip in the Sample Folder. Premiere displays it in a Clip window. Then choose **File**, **Export Clip**, **Movie**.

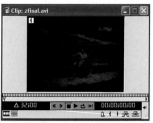

2 Open the Export Settings

Premiere displays the Export Movie dialog, with the default export settings listed at the bottom left of the window. Click the **Settings** button to review and change the export settings.

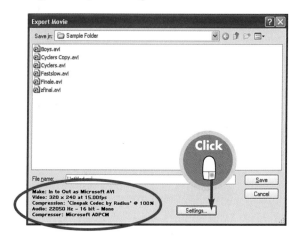

3 Review the Export Settings

Premiere displays the Export Movie Settings dialog. Click the drop-down list at the top left to switch between the different panels, or click the **Prev** and **Next** buttons at bottom right to cycle through the panels in order.

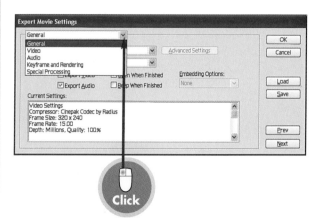

④ Review the General Settings

The General panel displays a summary of the current settings. Make sure that both **Export Video** and **Export Audio** are checked, if you want to save a file with both video and audio. Also check **Open When Finished** to have Premiere automatically open the exported clip to play.

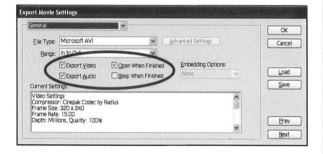

⑤ Set the Export Range

Click the **Range** drop-down list and choose **Entire Clip** so that the full clip is exported. You also can select **In to Out** to export only a part of the clip.

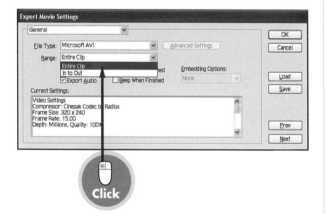

⑥ View the File Type

The **File Type** setting in the General panel determines the available compression and processing options for the Video and Audio panels. Premiere can export to the common desktop video formats, Apple QuickTime and Windows AVI, as well as to a sequence of image files. Go on to Task 4 to choose video settings.

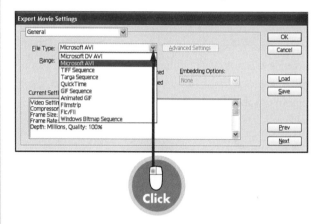

Choosing the File Type

Select the **File Type**, and video and audio compressors, that will be compatible with the systems where the file is to be played. Typically, choose **Microsoft AVI** if the file is to be played on Windows machines, and **QuickTime** for use on Macs or on both platforms. If in doubt, check the properties of an existing file that works well and use the same settings for your files.

Load and Save

Premiere provides **Load** and **Save** options in the Project and Export Settings dialogs. Use these to save your preferred settings and then reload them when you need them, so you won't have to click through all the dialog options to set and verify the settings.

How to Choose Video Settings

The Video panel of the Export Movie Settings dialog provides options to specify the compression format, color depth, frame size, frame rate, and other attributes of the output file. After you choose the basic file type, these settings determine the file size and visual quality of the file that you export.

❶ Review the Video Settings

In the General panel of the Export Movie Settings dialog, click the **File Type** drop-down list and choose the **QuickTime** format. Then click **Next** to move to the Video panel.

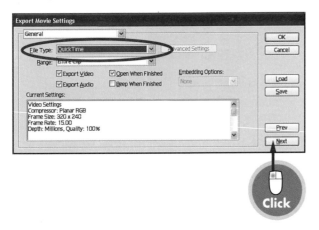

❷ Select the Video Compressor

In the Video panel, click on the **Compressor** drop-down list and choose **Sorenson Video**. Sorenson Video is a widely used compressor for the QuickTime format.

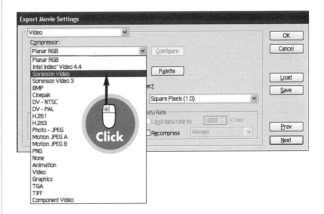

❸ Select the Video Depth

The **Depth** option with Sorenson compression defaults to **Millions** for full-color video. If you choose other formats, and especially uncompressed formats such as **None**, they will provide the **Depth** option to specify the amount of color detail.

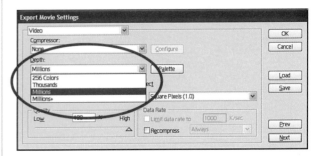

④ Select the Frame Size

Because the clip you are exporting is smaller than the default frame size, click the **Frame Size** field and type the new horizontal size (h) as **240**. Notice that the vertical size (v) is automatically changed to 180. This is because 4:3 Aspect is checked to maintain the 4 to 3 ratio between the width and height of the frame.

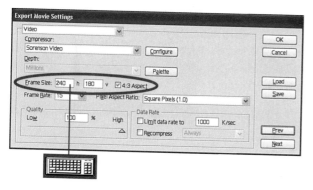

⑥ Select the Quality

Finally, click and drag the **Quality** slider to **90%** to set the desired video quality. (Low is 0%, and High is 100%.) Depending on the compressor, you can typically reduce the output file size significantly with only a small apparent reduction in quality.

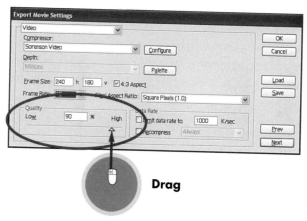

Drag

⑤ Select the Frame Rate

Click the **Frame Rate** drop-down list to review the available frame playback speed. Leave the setting at **15** frames per second (fps) to maintain the setting of the original file.

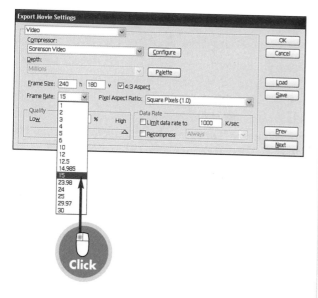

Click

How-to Hint

Choosing a Compressor

Many video compressors are available, and even more compressor-specific options are available. Typically, it is best to use the common settings so that your files are playable on the widest variety of systems.

Quality Versus File Size

Compressing video involves a difficult trade-off between the output file size and the quality of the video frames. For best results, capture video clips in a format with as little compression as possible (that is, **None**, **Motion JPEG**, or **DV**), and also edit them in that format to minimize damage from continually decompressing and then recompressing. Then use heavier compression when the final production is exported to a file for later playback.

How to Choose Audio Settings

The Audio panel of the Export Movie Settings dialog provides options to specify the data rate, format, compressor, and other audio attributes of the output file. Again, you will leave most of the settings from the original file unchanged.

① Select the Audio Compressor

Click the **Compressor** drop-down list and choose **QDesign Music 2**, a common QuickTime audio compressor for music tracks. Although the audio data size is much smaller than the video size in the final exported file, it is still worth compressing the audio. The quality loss from this compression is often imperceptible to human ears, especially when the clip plays on low-end consumer speakers.

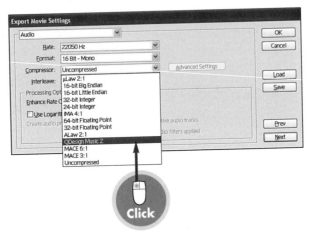

② Select the Audio Rate

Select the **Audio** panel, and then click the **Rate** drop-down list to select the audio sampling rate. Choose **22050** Hz (Hertz), which should provide good quality for a background music soundtrack.

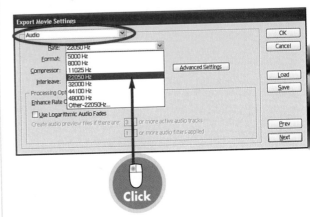

③ Select the Audio Format

Click the **Format** drop-down list and choose **16 Bit - Mono**. Use Stereo only if you are working with true stereo clips because it can double the size of the audio data. Some compressors also offer an 8 bit format which can be used to reduce the audio data size, but typically with a noticeable loss of quality.

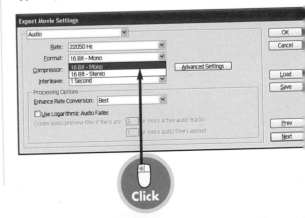

④ Select Advanced Settings

Click the **Advanced Settings** button to display the compressor-specific settings dialog. The QDesign Music Encoder dialog provides a **Bitrate** drop-down list to set the target data rate for the compressed audio. Click **Cancel** to use the default rate.

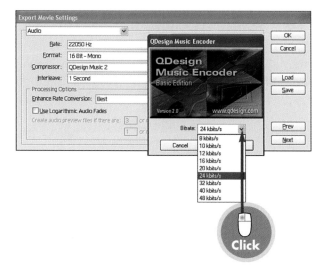

⑤ Select the Interleave

Click the **Interleave** drop-down list to select how often blocks of audio data are interleaved, or inserted, among the video frames in the exported file. A setting of **1/2 Second** or **1 Second** is typical, but might need to be increased if audio is breaking up during playback.

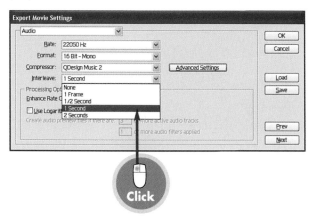

⑥ Select the Rate Conversion

Click the **Enhance Rate Conversion** drop-down list to select the amount of processing to be used when converting the input clips to a different sample rate for export. Select **Best** for highest quality results, although these come at the expense of additional processing time.

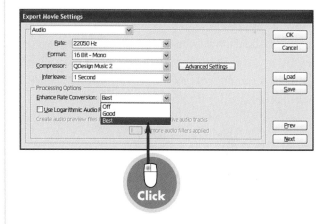

Controlling the Data Rate

Depending on the compressors, you might be able to set a target data rate for the audio and video data using the **Advanced Settings** in the Audio panel and the **Data Rate** settings in the Video panel. This limits the amount of bandwidth required to play the file over a network or from a slow disc like an older CD-ROM drive.

How to Use Special Processing Settings

Beyond all the editing functions and effects available when working with clips in the Timeline, Premiere also provides Special Processing functions during export that can be applied to the entire clip or production. You can crop or scale the frame size and deinterlace television video for display on computer monitors.

1 Review the Special Processing Settings

Select the **Special Processing** panel from the Export Movie Settings dialog to review the summary of current processing settings. Then click **Modify** to change the settings. Premiere displays the Special Processing dialog.

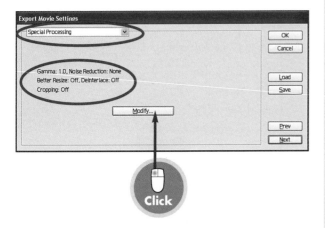

2 Define a Cropping Region

To crop the exported video, drag the corner handles of the cropping rectangle, or type specific values for the **Left**, **Right**, **Top**, and **Bottom** margins. Click and drag within the rectangle to position it over the frame.

3 Select Scaling

Click **Scale to 240×180** to have the cropped video enlarged to the original frame size specified in the Video panel. Otherwise, the video will be exported at the cropped size.

④ Use Noise Reduction

Select the **Noise Reduction** check box to reduce video noise in the movie being exported and to improve compression quality. Noise reduction blurs images by smoothing large changes between pixels. Select **Blur** for a subtle blur, **Gaussian Blur** for a stronger blur, or **Median** for a blur that keeps edges sharp.

⑤ Select Better Resize

Check the **Better Resize** box if you have selected cropping and scaling. Premiere will then use its own high-quality resizing method. Otherwise, the video will be resized by the method built in to the selected compressor, which might be faster but produce lower quality.

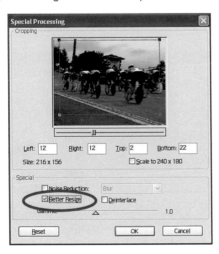

⑥ Use Deinterlacing

Select the **Deinterlace** check box if you are processing *interlaced* television video, in which each frame contains alternating pairs of lines, which can cause visible tearing when displayed on a computer monitor. Use *deinterlacing* for video intended to be displayed on computers.

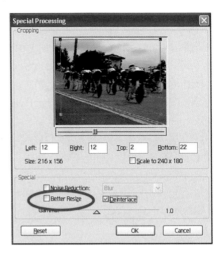

⑦ Select the Gamma

Click and drag the **Gamma** slider to adjust the brightness of the middle tones of the image while preserving the darker and lighter areas. This adjustment compensates for the differences between various display devices. Set the value to around 0.8 for use across multiple platforms, from PC to Macintosh. Then click **OK** to save the Special Processing options.

How to Load and Save Export Settings

To save and reuse your export settings, Premiere provides Load and Save options on each panel of the Export Movie Settings dialog. Built-in preset settings provided with Premiere can be used as a starting point for customizing your own settings.

① Save the Export Settings

Select the **General** panel of the Export Movie Settings dialog and review the settings defined in the previous tasks, as displayed in the **Current Settings** area. Click the **Save** button.

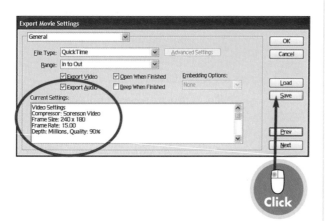

② Name the Export Settings

Premiere displays the Save Export Settings dialog. Type **QuickTime Sorenson QDesign 240x180** as the name for your settings in the **Name** field and additional information in the **Description** field, if desired. Then click **OK**.

③ Load Export Settings

Click **Load** in the Export Movie Settings dialog to review the available settings, including the presets provided with Premiere and additional settings you have saved.

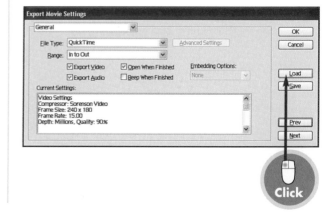

4 View Multimedia QuickTime Settings

Premiere displays the **Load Export Settings** dialog. Your new QuickTime setting now appears at the bottom of the **Available Presets** list, with the corresponding Description on the right. Click **Multimedia QuickTime** to review the preset settings for the Apple QuickTime format when used as a cross-platform format for desktop video playback.

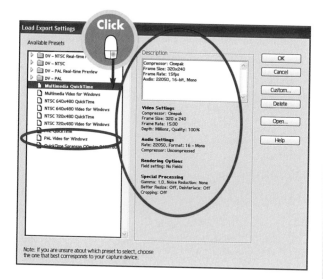

5 View Video for Windows Settings

On Windows, click **Multimedia Video for Windows** to review the preset settings for the Microsoft AVI format for desktop video playback.

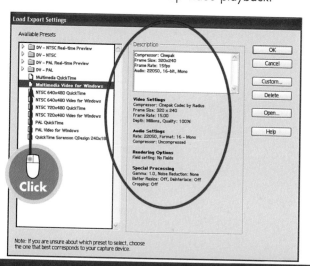

6 View Full-Screen QuickTime Settings

Click **NTSC 640×480 QuickTime** to review the preset settings for the QuickTime format when used for full-size, full-rate video.

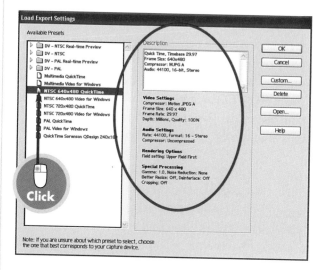

7 View DV Settings

Open the DV - NTSC Real-time Preview folder, and then click **Standard 32kHz** to review the preset settings for the DV camcorder digital video format. The video uses standard DV video compression at full 720×480 frame size and full 29.97fps frame rate, and the audio uses uncompressed audio at 32,000Hz. When you have finished reviewing the export presets, click **Cancel** to exit.

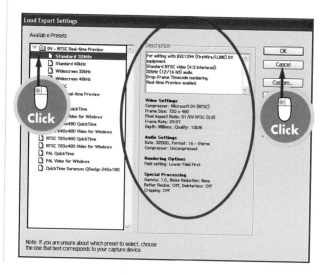

How to Set Project Settings

When starting a new project, project settings need to be compatible with the input clips and output export formats. In earlier parts, you used the presets for Multimedia QuickTime or Multimedia Video for Windows. Now you can create your own project settings to match the format and frame size of your clips.

① Launch Premiere

Launch Premiere to display the Load Project Settings dialog. At this point, you could click **Custom** to set up a new custom project setting. Instead, click **Open** to open the Sample Project to review its settings.

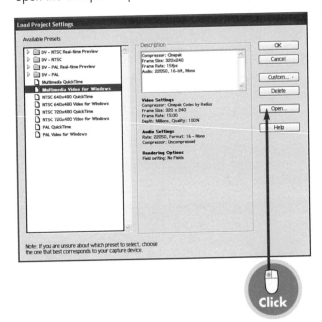

② Open the Project

Premiere displays the Open dialog. Navigate to the Sample Folder installed with Premiere, click to select the Sample Project, and then click **Open**.

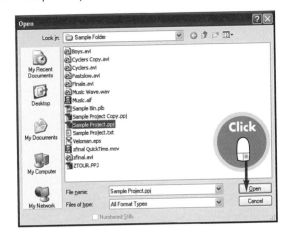

③ Open the Settings Viewer

Premiere opens the saved project. To check the current settings, choose **Project**, **Settings Viewer**.

4 Open the Project Settings

Premiere displays the Settings Viewer dialog. The **Frame Size** row is highlighted in red to show that the Project Settings are inconsistent with the clip and Export Settings. Click **Project Settings** to change them.

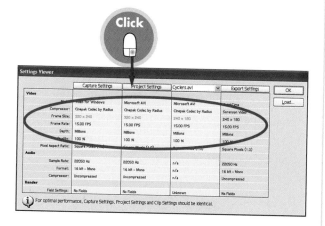

6 Change the Video Settings

In the **Video** panel, click the **Frame Size** field and type the new horizontal size (h) as **240**. The vertical size (v) automatically changes to 180 when 4:3 Aspect is checked to maintain the 4 to 3 ratio between the width and height. Click **Save**.

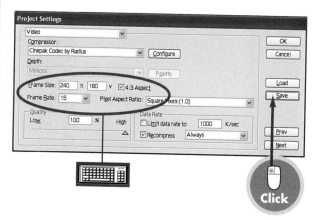

5 Review the General Settings

In the Project Settings dialog, scroll the **Current Settings** area of the **General** panel to review the settings. Click **Next** to display the Video panel.

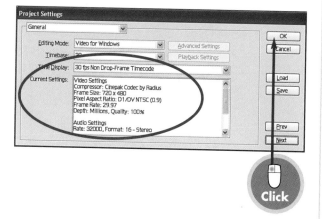

7 Save the Project Settings

Premiere displays the Save Project Settings dialog. Click the **Name** field and type **Multimedia AVI 240x180** (or **QuickTime** for Macintosh) as the new project preset name. Click **OK** to save the settings. Premiere returns to the Project Settings dialog (see step 5). Click **OK** to apply these settings to the current project.

⑧ Review the Project Settings

In the Settings Viewer dialog, the **Frame Size** row is still highlighted in red to warn you that the Capture Settings are not consistent. But the frame size for the project and clip settings now all match. Click **OK** to close the dialog.

⑨ Change the Project Settings

While you are working on your project, you can access the Project Settings dialog to change individual project settings and capture settings. If needed, choose **Project**, **Project Settings** to select one of the panels of the Project Settings dialog.

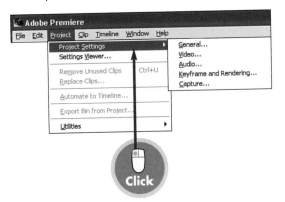

⑩ Save the Project

To save the project with its new settings, click on the **Project** window to select it, and then choose **File**, **Save**.

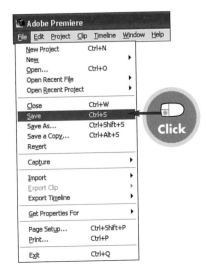

⑪ Name the Project

Premiere displays the Save File dialog. Navigate to the Sample Folder, click the **File name** field, and type `Sample Project 240x180` as the new project name. Then click **Save**.

⑫ Open the Project Presets

Now check the new Project Settings. Choose **File**, **New Project**.

How-to Hint

Project Settings

Premiere uses the Project Settings for previewing your production from the **Timeline**. Typically, settings are determined by the format of the video and audio that you are editing, either from clips on disk or input from a video capture card. However, it can be useful to change them—for example, to temporarily reduce the frame size or frame rate so that your edits and previews can be processed faster.

Export Settings

The Export Settings are independent of the Project Settings, so you can edit a project once, and then export it in a variety of different formats. You can set the export settings from the Settings Viewer dialog at any time, or from the Export Movie dialog when you export.

⑬ Review the Project Presets

Premiere displays the Load Project Settings dialog again. Click on the new preset that you saved, **Multimedia AVI 240x180** (or **QuickTime**), to verify that it is set up properly.

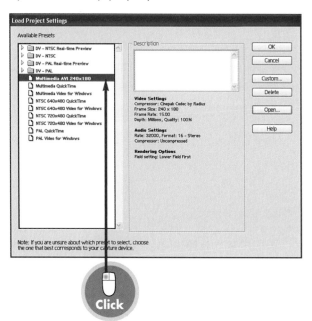

How to Export a Project

In this task, you will step through the entire process of importing, editing, and exporting a project. You will use the new sample project that you saved in Task 1 and the export settings you saved earlier. These are compatible with the clips in the Sample Folder installed with Premiere.

1 Launch Premiere

Close Premiere if it is already running so that you can start from the beginning. Launch Premiere, and it displays the Load Project Settings dialog. Click **Open** to open the new Sample Project to review its settings.

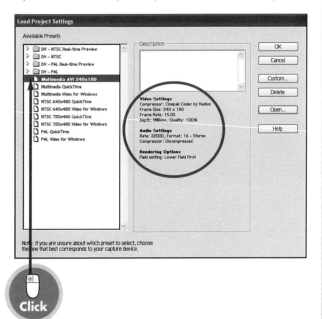

2 Open the Saved Project

Premiere displays the Open dialog. Navigate to the Sample Folder installed with Premiere, click to select the new **Sample Project 240x180** that you saved in the previous task, and then click **Open**.

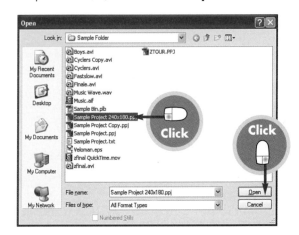

3 Open the Settings Viewer

Premiere opens the saved project. To check the current settings, choose **Project**, **Settings Viewer**.

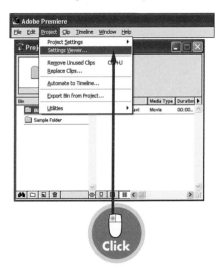

4 Review the Project Settings

Premiere displays the Settings Viewer dialog. Some rows may still be highlighted in red to warn you that the Capture Settings are still not consistent. The fields for the project and clip match, so you can begin editing. (You will set the Export Settings below.) Click **OK**.

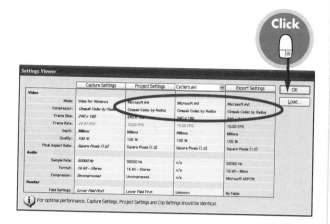

5 Automate to Timeline

Select the Sample Folder in the **Bin** area of the **Project** window, and then select the first four clips (Boys, Cyclers, FastSlow, and Finale) by clicking and dragging a selection rectangle over them. Click the **Project window** menu and choose **Automate to Timeline**.

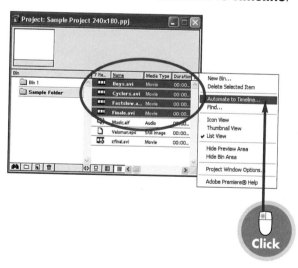

6 Select Automation Settings

Premiere displays the Automate to Timeline dialog. Click the **Contents** drop-down list and choose **Selected Clips** (and not Whole Bin). Use the default transition settings, and then click **OK**.

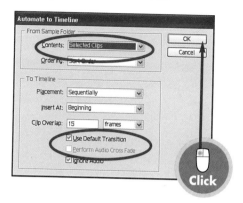

7 Zoom the Timeline

Premiere automatically lays out the four clips on the **Timeline** window, with default transitions between them. Click the **Time Zoom Level** pop-up menu in the bottom-left corner to change the zoom to 2 Seconds so that the entire production is visible.

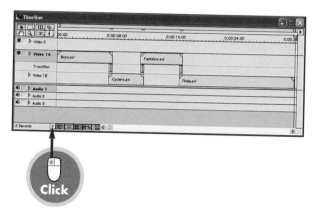

8 Add Background Music

Click and drag the Music clip from the Sample Folder bin to the Audio 1 track in the **Timeline**.

9 Export the Production

You now have a full video and audio production on the **Timeline**. To export the production, choose **File**, **Export Timeline**, **Movie**. You could accept the current settings displayed in the bottom left of the Export Movie dialog. Instead, click **Settings** to change the settings or load a new preset to match the project settings.

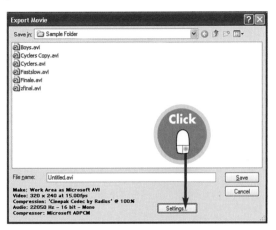

10 Review the Export Settings

Premiere displays the Export Movie Settings dialog. As in Task 3, you can review and change the settings to make sure that they are correct. Instead, click **Load** to load a preset.

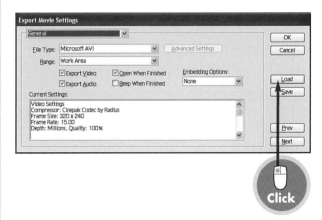

11 Load the Preset Settings

Premiere displays the Load Export Settings dialog. Click to select the **QuickTime Sorenson QDesign 240x180** preset you saved in Task 7, or choose similar settings. Then click **OK**.

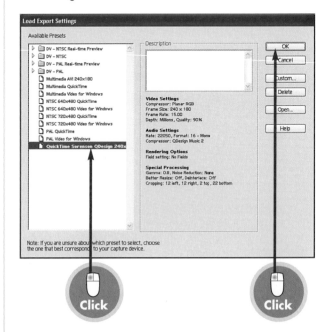

⑫ Review the Settings

Premiere returns to the Export Movie Settings dialog. Review the settings in the **Current Settings** scroll box, and then click **OK**.

⑬ Name and Save the Clip

Premiere returns to the Export Movie dialog. Navigate to the Sample Folder, click the **File name** field and type `zfinal QuickTime` as the name of the clip to be saved as a QuickTime Movie file (.mov in Windows). Then click **Save** to begin the export.

⑭ Review the New Clip

Premiere displays the Exporting dialog as it processes the clip and saves it to disk as a new clip file. When the export completes, the saved clip is displayed in a new Clip window. (**Ctrl+click**) [**Right+click**] and choose **Properties** from the **Clip** window pop-up context menu to view the clip properties.

⑮ Review the Clip Properties

Premiere displays the **Properties** window for the clip. Verify that the clip contains both video and audio tracks, compressed with the Sorenson Video and QDesign Music compressors, with a 240×180 frame size.

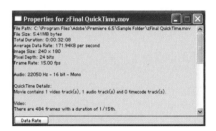

Task

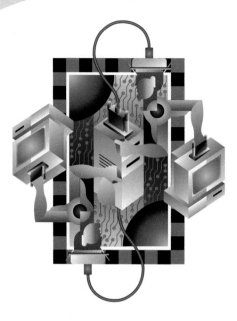

6

Exporting to Video and Audio Formats

In Part 5, "Exporting Clips and Projects," you saw how to save both individual video clips and entire projects. You used the Premiere Export Settings to save and reuse the appropriate settings, including different file format, compressor, and frame size information. You also used the Settings Viewer to check that all these values were consistent for capture, project, clip, and export settings.

In this part, you will explore using Premiere to export clips and projects to common video, audio, and still image file formats. Premiere can save video and audio clips to the common QuickTime and AVI multimedia file formats, with a variety of video and audio compression options. You also can export clips to audio-only formats such as Macintosh AIFF and Windows Wave. Premiere can export individual frames as a still image file and video clips as an animation or sequence of still image files.

Finally, Premiere can "print to video" to provide a full-screen video playback that you can record directly to tape.

Premiere also can export to a variety of Web and DVD formats (see Part 7, "Exporting to Web and DVD Formats.").

How to Export in QuickTime Format

The Apple QuickTime format is the native multimedia format on the Macintosh and is also available under Windows. You can export clips using a desired size and format by loading a preset (as shown in Part 5).

① Export a Clip

Open the Sample Project, open the zfinal clip, and choose **File**, **Export Clip**, **Movie**.

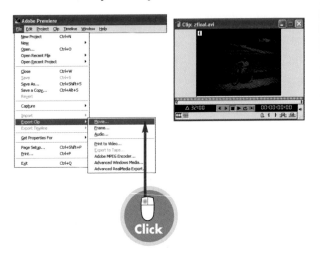

② Open the Export Settings

Premiere displays the Export Movie dialog. Check the current export settings listed at the bottom left. Then click **Settings** to change the settings.

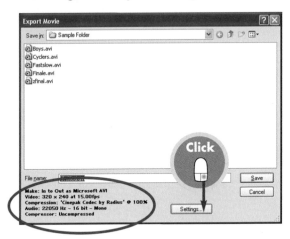

③ Load New Settings

Premiere displays the Export Movie Settings dialog. Instead of clicking through the dialog to check and verify the settings, click **Load** to load a QuickTime preset.

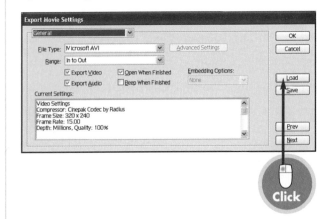

④ Select Export Settings

Premiere displays the Load Export Settings dialog. Select **Multimedia QuickTime**, or choose the preset you saved in Part 6, and then click **OK**.

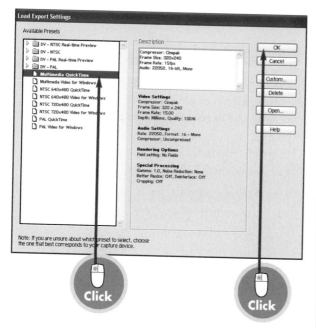

⑤ Confirm the Export Settings

Premiere returns to the Export Movie Settings dialog. Click **OK** to use the preset you just selected.

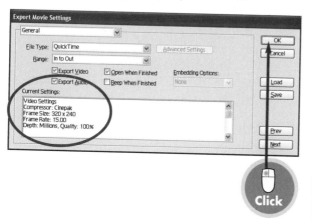

⑥ Name the Clip

In the Export Movie dialog, navigate to the Sample Folder installed with Premiere, click the **File name** field, and type `zfinal QuickTime` as the name of the clip to be saved as a QuickTime Movie file (.mov under Windows). Then click **Save** to begin the export.

⑦ View the New Clip

Premiere displays the Exporting dialog as it processes the clip and saves it to disk as a new clip file. Click the triangle icon to see more detail about the export process. When the export finishes, Premiere displays the saved clip in a new **Clip** window.

How to Export in AVI Format

You also can export the clip in a different format, such as Microsoft AVI for Windows, by using the Export Settings dialog to modify an existing preset.

1 Open the Export Settings

Open the Sample Project and then open the zfinal clip. Choose **File**, **Export Clip**, **Movie**. In the Export Movie dialog, click **Settings** to change the settings.

2 Select the General Settings

Premiere displays the Export Movie Settings dialog. In the **General** panel, click the **File Type** drop-down list and select **Microsoft AVI**. Scroll the **Current Settings** list to review the export settings. Check that Export Video and Export Audio are both selected. Click **Next** to display the **Video** panel.

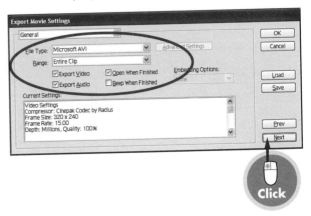

3 Select the Video Settings

In the **Video** panel, click the **Compressor** drop-down list to select **Intel Indeo Video 4.5**. Verify that the **Frame Size** is 320 x 240, and the **Frame Rate** is 15 fps. Click **Next** to display the **Audio** panel.

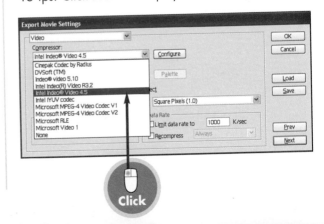

④ Select the Audio Settings

In the **Audio** panel, click the **Compressor** drop-down list to select **Microsoft ADPCM**. Verify that the sample **Rate** is **22050 Hz**. Then click **OK** to keep the settings.

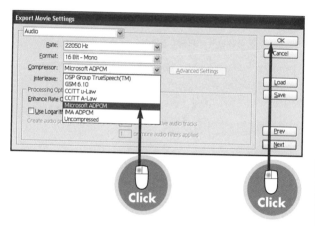

⑥ View the New Clip

Premiere then displays the Exporting dialog as it processes the clip and saves it to disk as a new clip file. When the export finishes, Premiere displays the saved clip in a new **Clip** window.

⑤ Name the Clip

Premiere returns to the Export Movie dialog. Navigate to the Sample Folder, click the **File name** field, and type **zfinal AVI** as the name of the clip to be saved as a Microsoft Video for Windows file (.avi under Windows). Then click **Save** to begin the export.

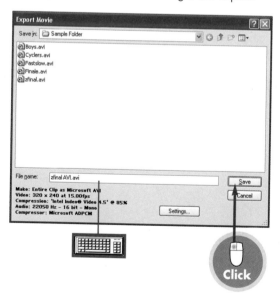

Save the Export Settings

How-to Hint

You can save the export settings that you just used. Repeat the first steps of this task to display the Export Movie Settings dialog. Premiere retains the settings from your last export. Click **Save** to save the export settings as a new preset, with a name like **AVI Indeo ADPCM 320x240**.

How to Export to Audio Formats

Premiere can export audio to other formats besides Microsoft AVI and Apple QuickTime multimedia files. Under Windows, Premiere can export audio-only files to the Windows Wave audio format (.wav). On the Macintosh, Premiere can export audio-only files to the AIFF audio format.

1 Open an Audio Clip

To open an audio clip, choose **File**, **Open**. Premiere displays the Open dialog. Navigate to the Sample Folder installed with Premiere, click to select the Music clip file, and click **Open**.

2 Export the Clip

Premiere opens a new **Clip** window to play the clip, with the audio waveform. Choose **File**, **Export Clip**, **Audio**.

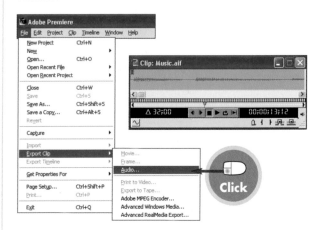

3 Open the Export Settings

Premiere displays the Export Audio dialog. Click on **Settings** to change the export settings.

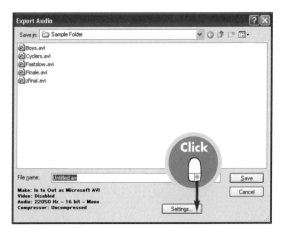

4 Select the Audio Format

Premiere displays the Export Audio Settings dialog. Click the **File Type** drop-down list and select **Windows Waveform** (or **Macintosh AIFF**). Verify the audio settings in the **Current Settings** field. Use **Rate 32000** and **Format 16 - Stereo** and ignore the Compressor setting. Click **OK**.

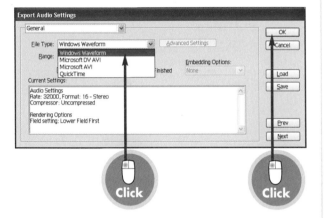

5 Name and Save the Clip

Premiere returns to the Export Audio dialog. Navigate to the Sample Folder, click the **File name** field, and type **Music Wave** (or **Music AIFF**) as the name of the new file. Then click **Save**.

6 Play the New Clip

Premiere then displays the Exporting dialog as it processes the clip and saves it to disk as a new clip file. When the export completes, Premiere displays the saved clip in a new **Clip** window. Choose **Properties** from the **Clip** window pop-up context menu to view the **Clip Properties** (or choose **Clip**, **Properties**).

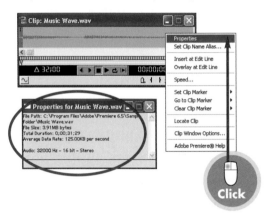

How-to Hint

Audio-Only Files

You can save audio-only clips and productions in the Apple QuickTime and Microsoft AVI multimedia file formats. Even if your clip project includes video, you can export only the audio portion by choosing **File**, **Export Clip** (or **Export Movie**), **Audio**.

How to Export to Still Image Formats

Premiere can export individual frames from video sequences as image files. In this way, you can use stills from your videos for titles or still frames. You also can export a video clip as a sequence of stills or as an animation.

1 Export a Still Frame

Open the Sample Project, open the zfinal clip in a **Clip** window, and then play or scrub to the frame you want to export. Choose **File**, **Export Clip**, **Frame** to open the Export Still Frame dialog.

2 Open the Still Frame Export Settings

Click on **Settings** to change the export settings.

3 Export in Windows Bitmap Format

Premiere displays the Export Still Frame Settings dialog. Open the **File Type** drop-down menu to view the available export file types. To export in the common bitmap image format used in Windows, choose **Windows Bitmap**. Click **OK**.

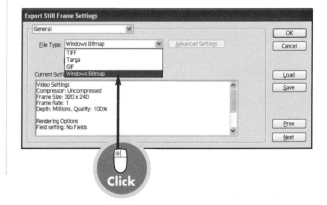

④ Save and View the Still Image

In the Export Still Frame dialog, type a file name and then click **Save**. Premiere saves the selected frame as a still image file, and then opens the file in a **Clip** window. Click **Duration** to set the length of time that this image will be displayed when placed on the **Timeline**.

⑤ Export a Still Sequence or Animation

To export the current clip as a sequence of still images or as an animation, choose **File**, **Export Clip**, **Movie**. Then click **Settings** in the Export Movie dialog. In the Export Movie Settings dialog, click the **File Type** drop-down list to view the available export file types. Select **Animated GIF** to export the video sequence as an animation for use on a Web page. Then click **OK**.

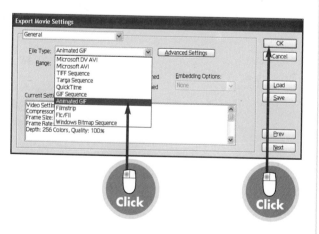

⑥ Save and View the GIF Animation

In the Export Movie dialog, type a file name and then click **Save**. Premiere saves the clip and opens it in a **Clip** window. Notice that the video quality of the animated GIF file is significantly reduced because it is compressed to reduce the size for Web downloading.

How to Print to Video

Premiere can blank the display and play a clip or the contents of the Timeline on your display or on a television screen. This is useful for previewing your work and for recording to videotape. If your computer or laptop has an option to output the display as a television signal, you then can record your productions directly to tape.

1 Print to Video

Open the Sample Project, and open the zfinal clip in a **Clip** window. Then choose **File**, **Export Clip**, **Print to Video**.

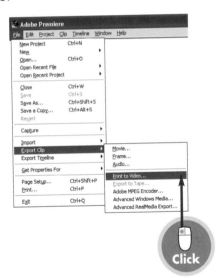

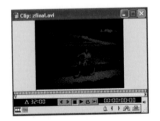

2 Select the Print to Video Settings

Premiere displays the Print to Video dialog. If desired, enter times for **Color bars for** and **Play black for** to display color bars or black before playing the movie. This gives you time to start recording before video is displayed. Select **Loop Playback** to have the playback repeat continuously. Then click **OK**.

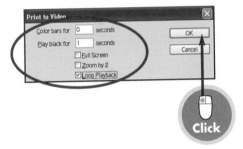

3 View the Video

Premiere blanks the display and plays the clip (or Timeline) centered on the screen. Press **Esc** to stop the playback.

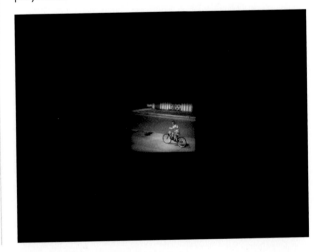

4 Select the Full-Screen Settings

In the Print to Video dialog, you also can select **Full Screen** (Windows) or **Zoom Screen** (Macintosh) to have the video enlarged to fill the entire display. Depending on your system and display hardware, you also can select the display screen and zoom amount. Then click **OK**.

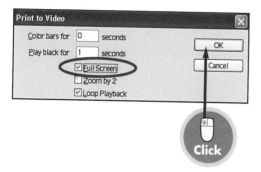

5 View the Full-Screen Video

Premiere blanks the display and plays the clip (or Timeline) full-screen. If the original material is low resolution, the full-screen enlarged playback may look blocky. Press **Esc** to stop the playback.

6 Export a File List

To export information about the clips used in a project, choose **File**, **Export Timeline**, **File List**. In the Save File List dialog, enter a file name and click **Save**. Premiere saves the plain text file, and then opens it in a **Text** window, listing the bins and clip files.

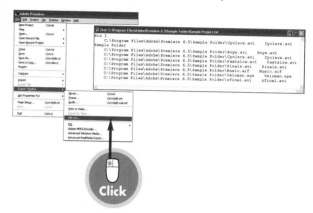

How-to Hint

Exporting Edit Decision Lists

For professional editing, Premiere can export an Edit Decision List (EDL) with information about the project assembled on the Timeline for use in a post-production studio.

Viewing DV Video

When editing a project with DV settings, Premiere can preview and play the video out the FireWire connection to your DV camcorder. You then can cable the analog video out from the camcorder to view on a television or record on a VCR. See the **Playback Settings** on the **General** panel of the Project Settings dialog.

Task

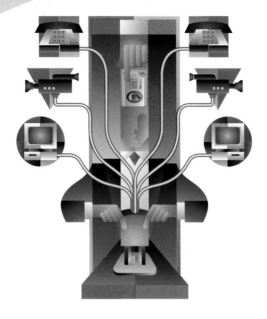

Exporting to Web and DVD

As described in the previous parts, Premiere can export your productions to disk in various media file formats. Beyond those formats, Premiere includes built-in support for exporting directly to a variety of streaming media formats so that you can share your movies over the Web. Premiere also supports exporting directly to MPEG format, ready to be imported into DVD authoring tools.

On Macintosh OS X, Premiere can export your movies to native QuickTime formats for streaming Web video. For DVD authoring, Premiere can export to iDVD in QuickTime DV format, or to DVD Studio Pro using the MPEG exporter installed with DVD Studio Pro. On Mac OS 9, Premiere includes Cleaner EZ to export to Web formats.

On Windows, Premiere includes exporters for Windows Media and RealMedia formats, and the new Adobe MPEG Encoder to export in MPEG-1 and MPEG-2 formats for DVD authoring. Premiere also includes Sonic DVDit! LE to author your clips into DVD productions.

How to Export to Web and DVD Formats

Premiere provides several different ways to export your material to Internet formats. This task provides an overview of these different approaches. The remaining tasks in this part provide more detail on exporting in specific formats.

① Export a Timeline

After you have created your video production in Premiere, you can export the Timeline into a file optimized for Internet viewing. From an open project, choose **File**, **Export Timeline** to select one of the four export options.

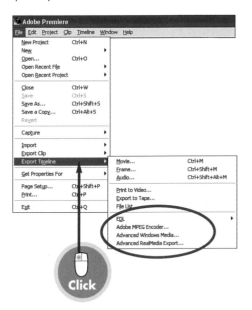

② Export a Clip

You also can export a single clip directly to Internet formats. Open a **Clip** window, or select a clip on the Timeline and then choose **File**, **Export Clip** to select one of the export options.

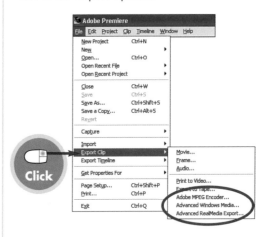

③ Create Windows Media Files

Use Advanced Windows Media (Windows only) to create Windows Media files that can be played using the Microsoft Windows Media Player application. See Task 2 to export in Windows Media streaming formats.

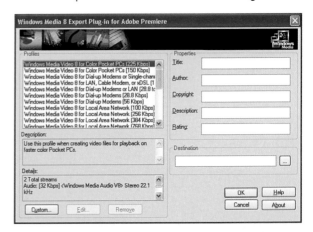

④ Create RealMedia Files

Use Advanced RealMedia Export (Windows only) to create RealMedia files that can be played using the RealNetworks RealPlayer application. See Task 3 to export in RealMedia streaming formats.

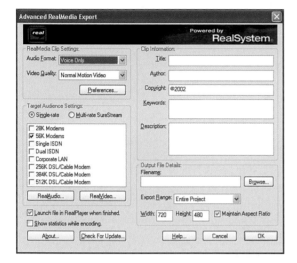

⑥ Create QuickTime Movie Files

Use the QuickTime File Exporter (Macintosh only) to create QuickTime Movie files that can be played using the Apple QuickTime Player application. See Task 5 to export to QuickTime streaming formats.

⑤ Create MPEG Files

Use the Adobe MPEG Encoder (Windows only) to create MPEG files to use for DVD authoring. See Task 4 to export in DVD, VCD, and other compatible MPEG formats for use in DVDit! LE.

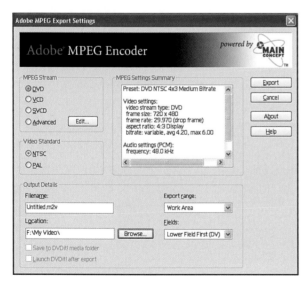

⑦ QuickTime MPEG Encoder

Use the QuickTime MPEG Encoder (Macintosh only) to create MPEG files for use in DVD authoring. See Task 6 to export to MPEG format for use with DVD Studio Pro.

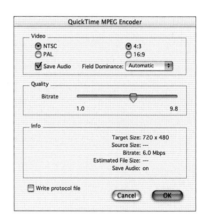

How to Use Windows Media Export

Use the Advanced Windows Media export option (Windows only) to export your movie in Microsoft Windows Media format. The movie must contain an audio track. Windows Media files can be played back from a local file or over the Web using the Windows Media Player application (see www.microsoft.com/windows/windowsmedia). See the Adobe Web site to upgrade Premiere to support the new Windows Media version 9.

❶ Export to Windows Media

To export to Windows Media format, choose **File**, **Export Timeline**, **Advanced Windows Media**. Or choose **File**, **Export Clip** to export an individual clip. Premiere displays the Windows Media Export Plug-In dialog.

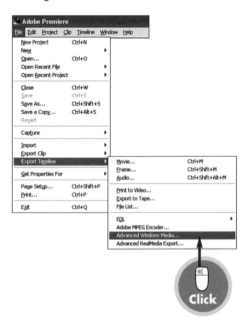

❷ Select the Target Profiles

From the **Profiles** list, select the standard profile that best matches the type of content and your target bandwidth. For example, click **Video for Local Area Network** (768 Kbps) to encode your movie for viewing on your computer or streaming over a network. Review the **Description** and **Details** information below your selection.

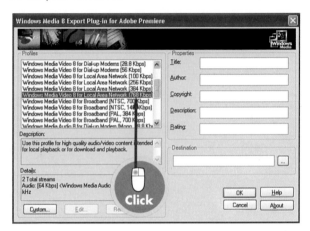

❸ Enter Output File Properties

If desired, you also can enter optional descriptive information about your movie in the **Properties** section.

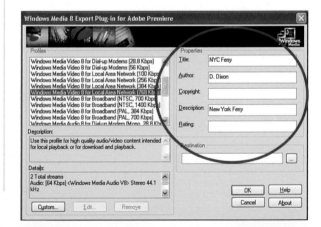

④ Select the Destination

From the **Destination** section, click the "**...**" button to display the Save As dialog to enter the Windows Media filename for export (with a .wma, .wmv, or .asf extension).

⑤ Start the Export

After reviewing your settings, click **OK** to start the export process. When exporting from the **Timeline**, the entire contents are exported, not just from the In to Out point.

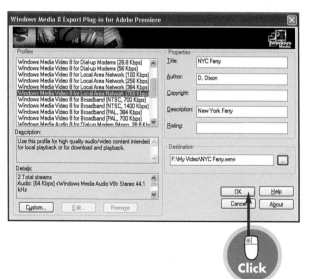

⑥ View Your Movie

The Exporting dialog then is displayed as your movie is encoded to Windows Media format. After the process is complete, you can run the Windows Media Player to view your exported movie.

How to Use RealMedia Export

Use the Advanced RealMedia Export option (Windows only) to export your movie in RealMedia Media format (.RM). RealMedia files can be played back from a local file or over the Web using the RealPlayer application (see www.real.com).

1 Export to RealMedia

To export to RealMedia format, choose **File**, **Export Timeline**, **Advanced RealMedia Export**. Or choose **File**, **Export Clip** to export an individual clip. Premiere displays the Advanced RealMedia Export dialog.

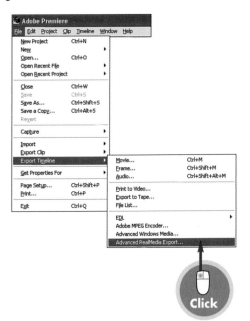

2 Select the Clip Settings

In the **RealMedia Clip Settings** section, use **Audio Format** to select the quality that best matches your movie's audio content, and **Video Quality** to specify the amount of motion in your movie.

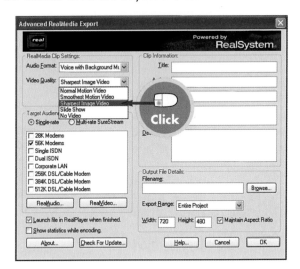

3 Select the Target Audience

In the **Target Audience Settings** section, click the **Single-rate** and choose **512K DSL/Cable Modem** to encode your movie for viewing on your computer or streaming over a network.

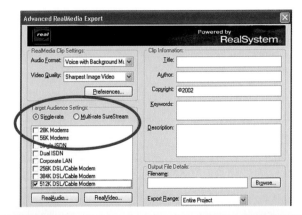

④ Enter Output File Details

Enter descriptive information in the **Clip Information** section. Under **Output File Details**, click **Browse** to display the Export file dialog to enter the output filename (.rm). Use **Width** and **Height** to set the output pixel resolution.

⑥ Play Movie in RealPlayer

The Exporting dialog is then displayed as your movie is encoded to RealMedia format. After the process completes, Premiere can automatically launch the RealPlayer to play your movie.

⑤ Start the Export

From **Export Range**, choose how much of your current project you want to export: the **Entire Project** or the current **Work Area**. Click **Launch file in RealPlayer when finished** to play the file after the export is finished. Then click **OK** to start the export.

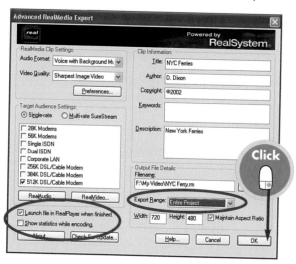

How-to Hint

Encoding Options

Use **Preferences** under **Clip Settings** to specify advanced compression settings. Use **RealAudio** and **RealVideo** under **Target Audience** to specify compression rates.

Multi-Rate SureStream

You can support a wider audience with the **Multi-Rate SureStream** option. Unlike single-rate files that can play from any Web site, multi-rate requires using a RealNetworks RealServer.

Compression Statistics

Click **Show statistics while encoding** to display a statistics window with performance data for your file.

How to Use the Adobe MPEG Exporter

On Windows, Premiere includes the Adobe MPEG Exporter, with presets to export MPEG-1 and MPEG-2 files in a variety of DVD-compatible formats, including VCD (Video CD) and SVCD (Super Video CD). You then can import these files into DVDit! SE to author onto DVD.

1 Export to MPEG

To export to MPEG format, choose **File**, **Export Timeline**, **Adobe MPEG Encoder**. Or choose **File**, **Export Clip** to export an individual clip. Premiere displays the Adobe MPEG Export Settings dialog.

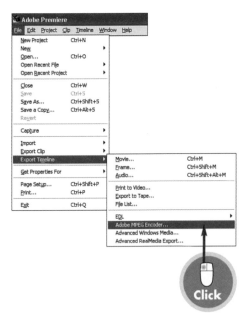

2 Select the Format

Select the MPEG compression format under **MPEG Stream** to use a preset for **DVD**, **VCD**, or **SVCD**. To set **Advanced** settings, click the **Edit** button. Premiere displays the Advanced MPEG Settings dialog.

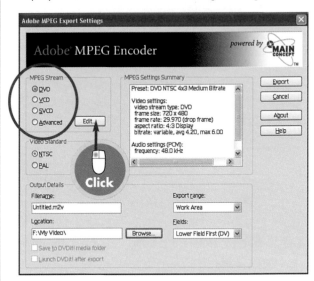

3 Select Advanced Presets

Under the **Basic Settings** tab, click the **Presets** drop-down menu to select a preset for the DVD type, aspect ratio (4x3, 16x9), TV format (NTSC or PAL), and bitrate (Low, Medium, High, or Standard).

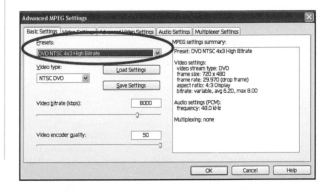

4 Select Advanced Settings

Click the **Video Settings** tab and the other tabs to set individual MPEG compression options. Click **OK** to exit the dialog.

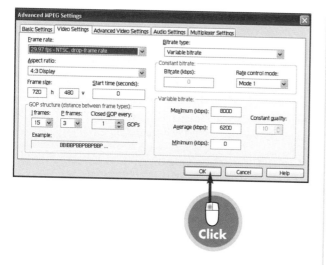

6 Export to MPEG

Your movie is exported as separate MPEG video (.m2v) and Wave audio files. You can view these files in Premiere and then import them directly into DVDit! LE to author onto a DVD.

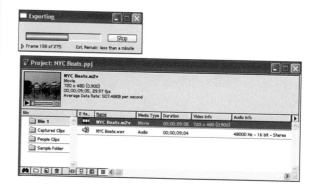

How-to Hint

Encoding Options

If you specify inconsistent MPEG compression settings, an error message explaining the problem is displayed in red in the **MPEG Setting Summary** area under the **Basic Settings** tab.

Editing MPEG Video

Although you can import MPEG files back into Premiere, it's not a good idea to perform more editing on them because they are heavily compressed. Instead, go back to the original clips (such as those in DV format) in your project to edit them further.

5 Start the Export

In the **Output Details** section, click **Browse** to select the destination file, and set the **Export range** to **Entire Project** or **Work Area**. Then click **Export** to compress and save the MPEG file. Premiere displays the Exporting dialog.

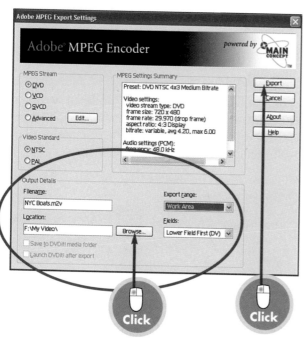

How to Use QuickTime File Export

As shown in Part 5, "Exporting Clips and Projects," Task 8, Premiere can export directly to QuickTime format (.mov) on Macintosh and Windows. Macintosh also uses the QuickTime File Exporter to prepare files for streaming. QuickTime files can be played from a local disk or over the Web using the Apple QuickTime Player application, which is preinstalled on Macintosh or available as a free download for Windows (see www.apple.com/quicktime).

① Export to QuickTime

To export to QuickTime, choose **File**, **Export Timeline**, **Movie**. Or choose **File**, **Export Clip** to export an individual clip.

② Open the Export Settings

Premiere displays the Export Movie dialog. Enter a destination filename and then click **Settings** to set the export format. Premiere displays the Export Movie Settings dialog.

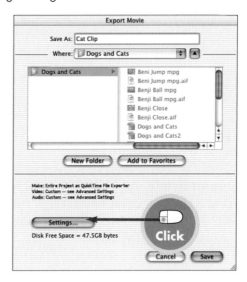

③ Select the QuickTime File Exporter

Under the **General** panel, click **File Type** and select **QuickTime File Exporter**. Under **Range**, select **Entire Project** or **Work Area**. Then click **Advanced Settings** to configure the export format.

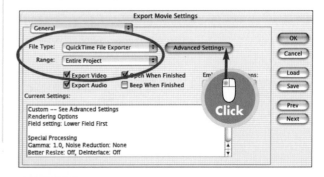

④ Select QuickTime Format

Premiere displays the QuickTime File Export Settings dialog. Click the **Export** drop-down menu and select **QuickTime Movie**.

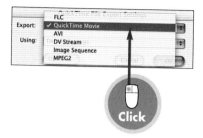

⑤ Select the Streaming Format

Click the **Using** drop-down menu and select a preset setting, such as **Streaming 100kbps - Voice - Low Motion**. Then click the **Options** button.

⑥ View the Streaming Settings

Premiere displays the Movie Settings dialog showing the **Video** and **Sound** compression settings, and the Prepare for Internet Streaming option. Click the **Settings** buttons to examine and change the specific options in each area.

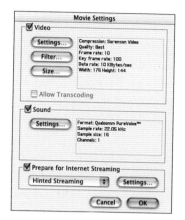

⑦ View Movie in QuickTime Player

Finally, click **OK** to close the Settings dialogs, and then click **Save** in the Export Movie dialog to export the movie. The Making Movie dialog is displayed as your movie is exported. You then can view your exported movie using the QuickTime Player.

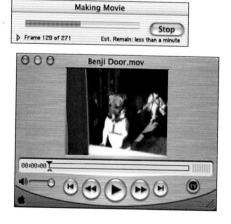

How to Export to iDVD and DVD Studio Pro

On Macintosh, Premiere can export movies to both of the Apple DVD authoring tools. You can export to iDVD in QuickTime DV format, or compress files in MPEG-2 format for DVD Studio Pro, including using Timeline markers as DVD chapter points (requires the DVD Studio Pro QuickTime Export module).

① Choose the Export Format

Choose **File**, **Export Timeline**, **Movie**. Or choose **File**, **Export Clip** to export an individual clip. Premiere displays the Export Movie dialog. Enter a destination filename and then click **Settings** to set the export format. Premiere displays the Export Movie Settings dialog.

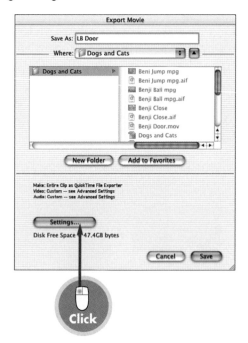

② Export DV Format to iDVD

To export movies to iDVD, choose QuickTime DV format. Click the **File Type** drop-down menu and select **QuickTime**.

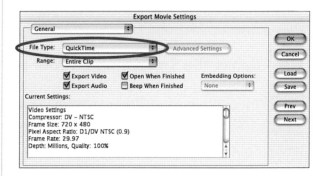

③ Select DV Video Format

Click **Next** to step to the Video tab, and pull down the **Compressor** menu and select **DV - NTSC**. (See Part 5 for more on setting file export formats.)

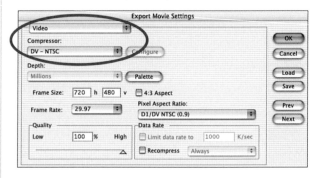

④ Export MPEG Format to DVD Studio Pro

Or, to export movies to DVD Studio Pro, use **MPEG** format. As in Task 5, click the **File Type** drop-down menu and select **QuickTime File Exporter**. Set the export **Range**, and then click the **Advanced Settings** button to configure the export format.

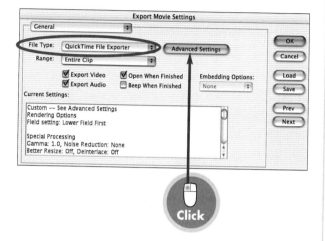

⑤ Select MPEG Format

Premiere displays the QuickTime File Export Settings dialog. Click the **Export** drop-down menu and select **MPEG2**. Then click the **Options** button.

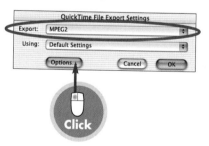

⑥ Select the MPEG Options

Premiere displays the QuickTime MPEG Encoder dialog. Set the **Video** and **Quality** options as appropriate for your DVD Studio Pro project.

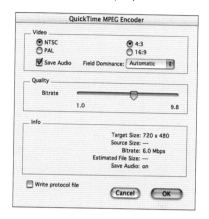

⑦ Start the Export

Finally, click **OK** to close the Settings dialog, and then click **Save** in the Export Movie dialog to export the movie. The MPEG Encoder dialog is displayed as your movie is exported. Your movie is exported as separate MPEG video and AIFF audio files. You then can import these files directly into DVD Studio Pro to author onto a DVD.

Task

Capturing and Using DV

The advent of the DV (Digital Video) format for consumer camcorders has brought dramatic improvements in the capability to conveniently edit good-quality video on personal computers:

- DV is "real" video, high-quality, full-resolution, full-rate video and audio.
- DV is a digital format, so copies are exactly the same as the original and no longer suffer the losses of converting back and forth to and from analog.
- DV is compressed lightly, so it is reduced enough in size to be feasible to transfer and store on personal computers, but still high enough quality to edit and manipulate without damage.
- DV camcorders use the FireWire digital interface (also called IEEE-1394 and i.Link by Sony), so devices such as camcorders can communicate with your computer using a single, consistent interface.
- The FireWire interface is two-way, so you not only can capture video from your camcorder to Premiere, but you also can export your clips and productions back out to the camcorder.
- The FireWire interface also supports *device control*, so you can operate your DV camcorder directly from Premiere, and even schedule automated capture and recording.
- DV keeps a timecode with the recorded video, so you can organize clips on a tape with their exact time-code and keep the timecode with the captured clips in Premiere.

Premiere provides strong built-in support for DV, with presets for specific camcorder models and capture and editing presets for the DV format. You can use the Movie Capture window to control your camcorder from your computer and then capture clips into your project. You also can log a list of clips for automated capture using the Batch Capture window. And when you have finished editing your production, you can export it back to DV tape to save and share.

Of course, if you do not have a DV camcorder, Premiere still can edit clips in DV format and also can capture audio and video clips using analog capture devices.

How to Connect Your DV Camcorder

To start working with your DV camcorder, connect it to your computer with a FireWire cable and then configure Premiere to work with DV video. Premiere depends on the FireWire support in your system to interface to your camcorder.

1 Check Your DV Capture Board

DV-enabled Macintosh systems have DV support built in. On a Windows PC, an add-in board typically provides the FireWire interface. To check your hardware, choose **Control Panel** under the **Start** menu and then open the **System** control panel. Select **Device Manager** (under the **Hardware** tab on Windows XP), and open the **1394 Bus** entry to check that your hardware is listed as OHCI Compliant.

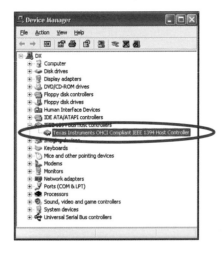

2 Connect Your DV Camcorder

Plug the smaller connector on the FireWire cable into the DV interface on your DV camcorder (typically marked DV IN/OUT or IEEE 1394). Plug the larger connector to the FireWire connector on your computer. Then plug in your camcorder, turn it on, and set it to VCR or VTR mode (tape player), and not Camera mode.

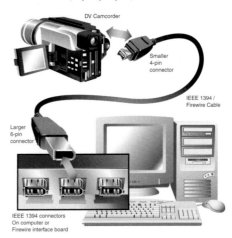

3 Select DV Preset

Launch Premiere. On the initial Load Project Settings dialog, select **DV-NTSC Real-time Preview** (or **DV-PAL**) and choose **32kHz** or **48kHz** audio depending on the formats provided by your camcorder. Click **OK**.

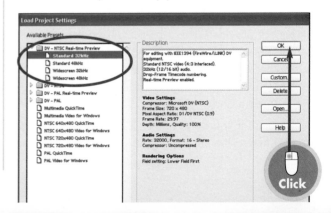

④ Open Project Settings

Premiere opens a new project. Choose **Project**, **Project Settings**, **General** to verify the playback settings.

⑤ Open Playback Settings

Premiere displays the Project Settings dialog, with the General options. Because you selected the DV project preset, the editing mode is set to DV Playback for Windows and QuickTime Playback for Macintosh. Click the **Playback Settings** button.

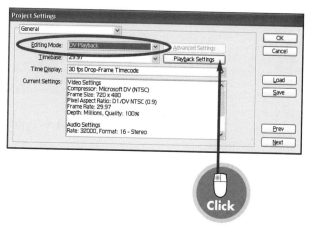

⑥ Set Playback Settings

In the DV Playback Options dialog, use the **Output** settings to specify whether video is played back on the camcorder, on the desktop in the **Monitor** and **Clip** windows, or on both. Use **Render Scrub** to specify whether **Timeline** previews are displayed on the camcorder or desktop. Click **OK** when finished, and then click **OK** again to close the Project Settings dialog.

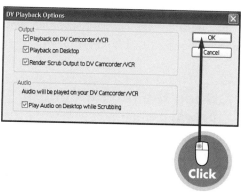

Output to DV

Use the DV Playback Options dialog to output playback over the FireWire cable to your DV device. You then can hook up a TV monitor to see how the video looks on a interlaced display, with the more limited TV color range and safe area (see Part 11 "Editing in the Monitor Window", Task 1).

Display Quality

Remember that television video, including DV, is interlaced, so individual frames can appear ripped on your computer monitor. However, the final DV video still will look fine on a television screen.

Capturing Analog Video as DV

If your DV camcorder supports analog input, you can use it to dub (copy) your old analog videotapes to digital format on a DV tape, and then input the video to Premiere from the DV tape. You also can use some DV camcorders to pass the analog video input directly through the FireWire cable and into Premiere.

How-to Hint

How to Select Your DV Device

Next, configure Premiere for your specific DV camcorder, and test the connection to verify that Premiere can communicate with your camcorder over the FireWire interface.

① Open the Device Control Preferences

To configure Premiere for your DV camcorder, choose **Edit**, **Preferences**, **Scratch Disks and Device Control**.

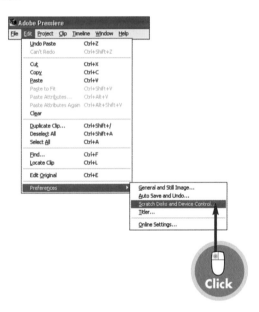

② Open Device Control Options

Premiere displays the Preferences dialog with the Scratch Disks and Device Control options. In the Device Control section, make sure that Device is set to **DV Device Control 2.0**, and then click **Options**.

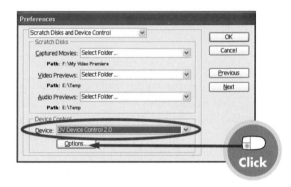

③ Set the DV Device

Premiere displays the DV Device Control Options dialog. Click the **Device Brand** drop-down list and select your camcorder brand. Then click the **Device Type** drop-down list and select your camera model. (If your model is not listed, click **Go Online for Device Info** to launch a browser to connect to the Adobe Web site and search for your device.)

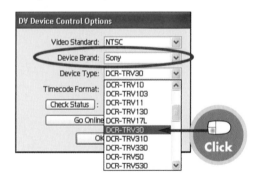

④ Check the Connection Status

Click the **Check Status** button to have Premiere attempt to verify the connection with your camcorder.

⑥ Set Scratch Disks

Premiere returns to the Preferences dialog. In the Scratch Disks section, select the disk and folders to be used for **Captured Movies**, **Video Previews**, and **Audio Previews**. Use a separate, fast disk for capture and for preview files (not just a partition on the same disk). Click **OK** to close the dialog.

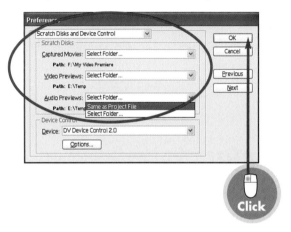

⑤ Verify the Connection Status

Premiere reports the device control status. Offline means that Premiere cannot communicate with your camcorder; check the connections and settings and verify that the camera is turned on in VCR or VTR mode. Detected means that Premiere can communicate with your camcorder but cannot control the tape; check that a tape is inserted. Online means that all is well. Click **OK** to close the dialog.

How-to Hint

Device Control

Although you can capture from a DV device even if Premiere cannot control it, having a full connection with device control is much better. Instead of stopping and starting manually, you can click on the VCR-like controls in the Premiere interface to control it, and automatically capture a group of clips.

Low Disk Space Warning

Premiere can warn you when scratch disk space is running low. Choose **Edit**, **Preferences**, **General and Still Image** to set the Low Disk Space Warning Level.

How to Set Up Movie Captures

The next step in capturing from a DV camcorder is to open the Movie Capture dialog and set up the final settings for capturing. The Movie Capture dialog is used to control the whole capture process, from previewing the video to controlling individual and batch captures.

❶ Open the Movie Capture Window

Choose **File**, **Capture**, **Movie Capture**. Premiere displays the Movie Capture dialog.

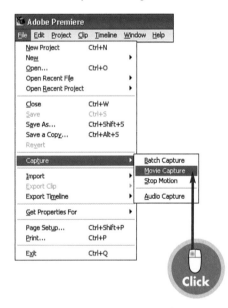

❷ Open the Capture Settings

If the Control Panel is not visible, open the **Movie Capture** window menu and choose **Expand Window**. Click the **Settings** tab to display the current **Capture Settings** and **Preferences**. Then open the **Movie Capture** window menu and choose **Capture Settings** (or click the **Edit** button under the Capture Settings section).

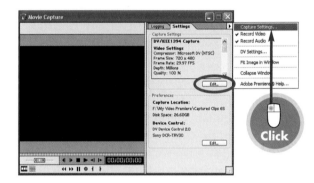

❸ Set the Capture Format

Premiere opens the Project Settings dialog to the **Capture Settings**. Make sure that the **Capture Format** is set to **DV/IEEE 1394 Capture**. Then click the **DV Settings** button. Premiere displays the DV Capture Options dialog.

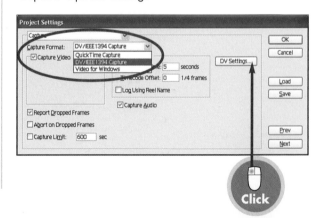

④ Review the DV Capture Options

Leave the **Preview Video On Desktop** and **Preview Audio On Desktop** boxes checked to view the DV input on the computer display. If this causes too much load on your system, uncheck the boxes to view the video only on your camcorder display. Click **OK**.

⑥ Set the Capture Options

You now are ready to capture from your DV camcorder. To change the directory where the captured clips are saved, click the **Edit** button under the **Preferences** section. Use the window menu if needed to change the DV Settings

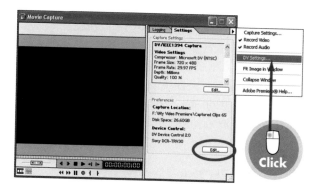

How-to Hint

Close the Movie Capture Window

Close the **Motion Capture** window whenever you are finished with it. While it is open, it has primary focus within Premiere, and any other operations might be slowed accordingly.

⑤ Set the Capture Settings

Click the **Preroll Time** field and enter **5** seconds, so Premiere will back up the tape and roll up to full speed before starting capture. Leave **Report Dropped Frames** checked to display a warning if any input frames were missed. Use **Capture Limit** to specify the maximum number of seconds to record. Click **OK** when finished.

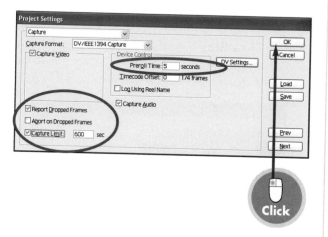

How to Use DV Device Control

With the FireWire interface, you can control your camcorder directly from Premiere. This is great if you have ever tried to coordinate capturing on a computer while working the buttons on a miniature camcorder. With Premiere device control, you can just click the VCR-style controls under the Movie Capture window.

① Open the Movie Capture Window

To start a new capture, choose **File**, **Capture**, **Movie Capture** (as in Task 3).

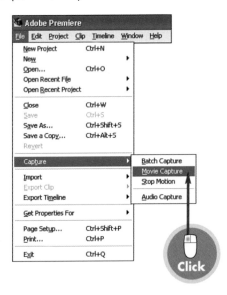

② Play the Tape

Premiere displays the Movie Capture dialog. Use the VCR device control buttons along the bottom of the window: Click **Play** to start playback, **Pause**, and **Stop**. Or press the **spacebar** to start and pause play.

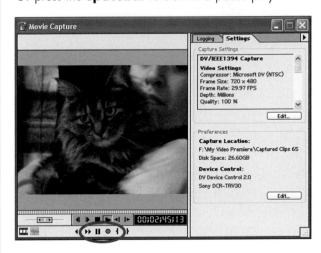

③ Step Through the Tape

Click the **Frame Back** or **Frame Forward** buttons to move a frame at a time. Click the **Reverse Slow Play** or **Slow Play** buttons (to the right of Play) to play at slow speed. The Timecode display to the right of the controls displays the timecode for the current frame.

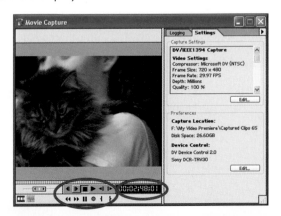

④ Rewind and Fast Forward

To move more quickly through the tape, click the **Rewind** or **Fast Forward** buttons (or press the **R** or **F** keys). If the tape is stopped, these move the tape at full speed. If the tape is playing, these act as a fast scan and will display the video as the tape is moving.

⑤ Jog Through the Tape

To move frame by frame through the tape, click and drag the **Jog** control bar (the dashed line above the controls). As you move it one step to the left or right, it rewinds or advances the tape a single frame at a time.

⑥ Shuttle Through the Tape

To move rapidly through the tape, click and drag the **Shuttle** control, with the speed proportional to the distance of the control from the center point. You also can type a frame time directly into the Timecode display to the right of the controls, and press **Enter**.

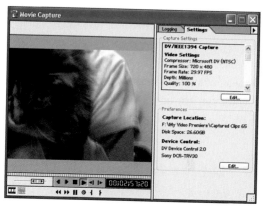

Window Size

The input DV format video is full size, but Premiere displays the **Movie Capture** window in a reduced size. Drag the lower-right corner of the window to resize it and see your input video in much more detail.

Stripe Tapes for Continuous Timecode

It is helpful to have unbroken timecode throughout your entire DV tape. If you record the tape with gaps, you will end up with multiple segments with the same timecode. Avoid gaps when you shoot by always recording for a few extra seconds at the end of each clip, and then later, restart recording after backing up into this "scratch area." Even better, stripe each new tape by prerecording timecode onto it—simply record through the entire tape with the lens cap on.

How-to Hint

How to Capture with Device Control

You can use device control to simplify the process of capturing a clip by marking the In and Out points of the clip that you want to capture. Premiere then automatically controls the tape to capture the clip and even can automate the batch capture of a list of clips (see Task 6).

① Set the In Point

As in Task 4, choose **File**, **Capture**, **Movie Capture**. Then click the **Logging** tab. Use the device control buttons to move to the starting point of the clip. Click **Set In** under the display or in the Logging area (or press the **I** key) to mark the first frame of the clip that you want to capture.

② Set the Out Point

Move to the end of the clip and click **Set Out** under the display or in the Logging area (or press the **O** key) to mark the last frame of the clip that you want to capture. You also can type a timecode directly into the field.

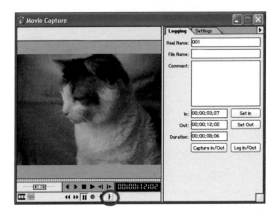

③ Play the Marked Clip

Press the (**Option**) [**Alt**] key and click **Set In** to move the tape back to the In point. Click **Play** (or press the **spacebar**) to play the clip. Press (**Option**) [**Alt**] and click **Set Out** to move the tape to the Out point.

4 Start Capture

To capture the marked clip, click **Capture In/Out** in the Logging area, or press the (**Options**) [**Alt**] key and click the red **Record** button.

6 Name the File

When capture is complete, Premiere displays the File Name dialog. Type the file name and click **OK**. The file is saved in the Captured Movies folder specified in the Preferences dialog under the **Scratch Disks** options. Premiere adds the clip to the current **Project** window, if one is open. Otherwise, Premiere opens a new **Clip** window to display the captured file.

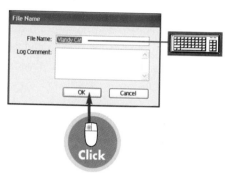

5 Monitor the Capture

Premiere moves to the preroll position before the In point, starts playing the tape, starts capturing at the In point, and stops at the Out point. The current capture status is displayed in the top-left corner of the window. Press the **Esc** key at any time to abort the capture.

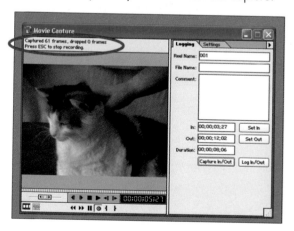

How-to Hint

Manual Capture

As with other Premiere controls, you can type a time-code directly in the **In**, **Out**, or **Duration** fields. You also can capture from the current position in the tape at any time; just click the **Record** button (or press the **R** key).

Capturing Without Device Control

If device control is not available for your camcorder, Premiere displays simplified controls in the Movie Capture window with a Record button. You then can use the VCR controls on your camcorder to queue the tape for capture.

Capture Only Video or Audio

Use the **Capture Video** and **Capture Audio** buttons in the bottom-left of the **Movie Capture** window (or under **Capture** settings in the Project Settings dialog) to capture only video or audio.

How to Create a Batch Capture List

You can use device control not only to simplify the capture of a single clip but also to create a timecode log so that Premiere can perform an automated capture of a collection of clips. The Batch Capture window contains a list of clips, with the timecode value for each In and Out point.

1 Open the Movie Capture Window

Choose **File**, **Capture**, **Movie Capture**. Premiere opens the **Movie Capture** window. Click the **Logging** tab, then click the **Reel Name** field, and type a name to be used to identify this tape when capturing clips.

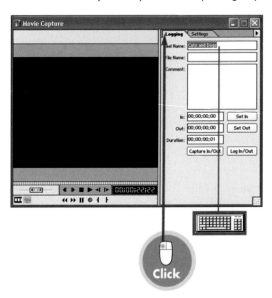

2 Set In and Out Points

As in Task 5, use the device controls to position the tape and click the **Set In** and **Set Out** buttons to mark the beginning and end of the clip you want to capture. Then click the **Log In/Out** button.

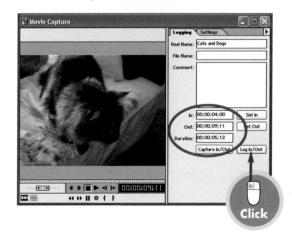

3 Enter the Filename

Premiere displays the File Name dialog. Type the name to be used for the clip file, and then click **OK**.

④ Add More Clips

Premiere displays the Batch Capture window with an entry for the clip. Repeat this process to add more clips to the batch list by setting each In and Out point in the Movie Capture window, and then clicking **Log In/Out**.

⑤ Save the Batch List

After adding all the clips that you want to capture to the batch list, you can save the list. Click the **Batch Capture** window to select it, and then choose **File, Save**.

⑥ Name the Batch List

Premiere displays the Save File dialog. Click in the **File Name** field and type a filename for the batch list file. Then click **Save**.

How-to Hint

Enter the Batch List Manually

You also can enter a batch list manually. Choose **File, Capture, Batch Capture**. Then click the **Add New Item** button at the bottom right of the window to enter timecode values for the In and Out points.

Export the Batch List

The batch list also can be exported as a plain text file, for your records, or to import into another application. Open the **Batch Capture** window menu and choose **Import/Export Settings, Export to Text File**.

How to Capture with a Batch List

After you have created (and saved) a batch list with the clips you want to capture, you can use Premiere to automatically record the clips from your DV camcorder. You can capture the entire list in one operation, or selected clips.

① Open the Handles

Open the **Batch Capture** window menu (from Task 6), and choose **Handles**.

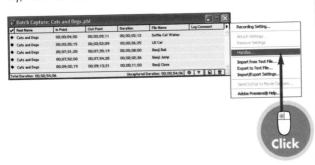

② Set the Capture Handles

Premiere displays the Capture Handles dialog. Type the number of frames to be used as handles, which are captured before the In point and after the Out point of each clip to provide extra frames to use during editing. Click **OK**.

③ Capture a Single Entry

To capture a single entry from the batch list, click the corresponding row in the list and then open the **Batch Capture** window menu and choose **Send In/Out to Movie Capture**. Premiere then sets the Movie Capture window with the In and Out points from the selected clip so that you can record the clip by clicking **Capture In/Out** (see Task 5).

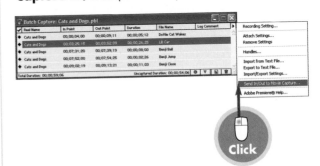

4 Capture Multiple Entries

To capture directly from the batch list, first select the clips to be captured by clicking the **diamond** symbol in the leftmost column. Or click the check box in the heading to select or unselect all the entries. Then click the **Record** button. Premiere displays the Insert Reel dialog to confirm that the correct tape is inserted in your camcorder. Click **OK** to start the batch capture.

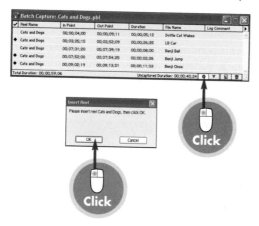

6 View the Clips

Premiere adds the captured clips to the current **Project** window, if one is currently open. The clips now are available for you to play, or to import into your projects.

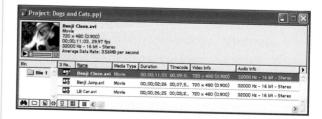

How-to Hint

Edit Batch List Entries

You can edit an individual entry in a batch list by double-clicking it to open the Clip Capture Parameters dialog, or by using Send In/Out to Movie Capture to change the settings in the **Movie Capture** window, and then clicking **Log In/Out** to add the new settings back to the batch list (under a new name).

Redigitizing

With batch lists, you can save processing time and disk space by capturing and editing low-resolution clips, and then recapture only the clips you need for the final edit at full resolution. After you have finished editing the low-res clips, choose **Project**, **Utilities**, **Project Trimmer** to create a trimmed batch list.

5 Watch the Batch Capture

Premiere displays the capture progress for each clip in the **Movie Capture** window. Click the mouse, press the **Esc**, or press **Command+.** (period) on the Macintosh to abort the capture when the camcorder is not seeking.

How to Export to a DV Camcorder

DV camcorders not only provide a wonderfully convenient source for capturing high-quality digital video, but you also can record your clips and productions back out to your camcorder to save and share with others. You also can use your DV camcorder to pass through the video to its analog outputs, to record the video to a VCR.

❶ Connect Your DV Device

Turn on your DV camcorder in VCR/VTR mode and check that it is set up properly for device control (see Tasks 1 and 2). Check the connection status using the DV Device Control Options dialog, accessed from the **Scratch Disks** and **Device Control** options in the Preferences dialog.

❷ Set Playback Options

Choose **Project**, **Project Settings**, **General**. In the Project Settings dialog, the Editing Mode should be DV Playback (Windows) or QuickTime (Macintosh). Click **Playback Settings** to use the DV Playback Options dialog to display on the DV camcorder and the desktop. Click **OK** to close each dialog.

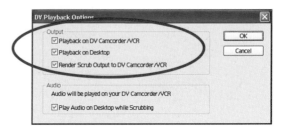

❸ Open a Clip

Open the clip to be exported in a **Clip** window, or click the **Timeline** and select the portion to export. If needed, generate the preview file so that it is ready to play (see Part 4, task 2).

4 Export to Tape

Make sure that the proper tape is loaded and that it is positioned where you want to start recording, with a prerecorded timecode on the tape (see Task 4). Choose **File**, **Export Clip**, **Export to Tape**.

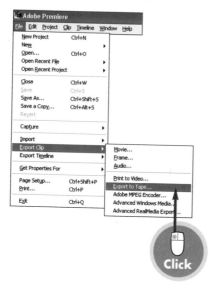

5 Select Export Settings

Premiere displays the Export to Tape Settings dialog. Check **Activate recording deck** to let Premiere control the DV camcorder. Check **Assemble at time code** to enter an In point for the capture; otherwise, recording begins at the current tape location. Set **Timecode offset** to around **150** frames (5 seconds) so that Premiere backs up the tape and rolls up to full speed before starting to record. Click **Record** to begin exporting.

6 Watch the Export

Premiere then exports the clip back to the DV camcorder. Watch the camcorder display to see the video and hear the audio being recorded. Depending on the Playback Settings, the video also is shown on the computer display, although the playback may be jumpy on the display. Press **Esc** to stop recording.

How-to Hint

Export Timeline

Use **Export Timeline**, **Export to Tape** to export a portion of the Timeline to a DV camcorder. Be sure to render the contents of the Timeline first to ensure that it can be played back in real time.

Print to Video

Use **Export Clip** or **Timeline**, **Print to Video** under the **File** menu to play full-screen video out the FireWire connector to manually record to tape or to an attached analog recorder (see Part 6 "Exporting to Video and Audio Formats," Task 5).

Play from the Timeline

The DV Playback Options settings (see Step 2) cause Premiere to play back the contents of the active **Clip** or **Monitor** window out the FireWire connector. You then can view the playback on an attached television, or record directly from a playing clip or from the contents of the Timeline.

How to Capture Analog Video and Audio

Premiere also can capture analog video and audio, and use digital audio from audio CD. However, these are more dependent on your system configuration. See the Premiere documentation for more information.

1 Analog Video Capture

Premiere can capture from analog devices such as 8mm camcorders and VHS video recorders. You typically connect your video equipment to the capture device with a composite or an S-video cable. Then choose **Project**, **Project Settings**, **Capture**.

2 Windows Analog Capture Format

Under Windows, in the Project Settings dialog, click the **Capture Format** drop-down list and select **Video for Windows**. Click **VfW Settings** to display the Video for Windows Capture Options dialog.

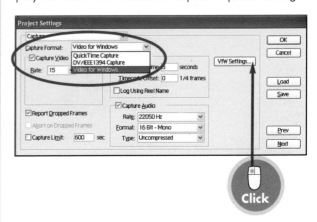

3 Set Windows Capture Options

Use **Video Overlay** for a higher-quality preview during capture. Use the **Driver Settings** buttons to set detailed video capture format options. Click **OK** to close each dialog. Also use the **Settings Viewer** to make sure that you have selected a compatible Video for Windows project format.

4 Set Macintosh Capture Options

Continuing from Step 1 on the Macintosh, in the Project Settings dialog, click the **Capture Format** drop-down list and select **QuickTime Capture**. Use the **Video**, **Audio**, and **Advanced** buttons to set detailed capture options, as supported by your capture device. Click **OK** to close the dialog. Also use the **Settings Viewer** to make sure that you have selected a compatible QuickTime project format.

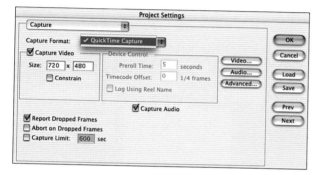

5 Open Movie Capture Window

Choose **File**, **Capture**, **Movie Capture** to open the Movie Capture window. Click the **Settings** tab to check the capture settings. If your capture device does not support device control, click the **Edit** button in the **Preferences** section to display a simplified Movie Capture window. When ready, click the large **Record** button to start recording.

How-to Hint

Analog Audio Capture

Although Premiere provides a separate **Audio Capture** option, you can simply use the **Movie Capture** window but only enable audio capture (by disabling the **Capture Video** button at bottom left).

Video Capture Devices

Video capture card manufacturers provide drivers and Premiere presets to interface with and control their devices.

Check the Adobe Premiere Web site (www.adobe.com/premiere) for a list of compatible capture cards.

Video Capture Checkout

Before trying to capture directly from Premiere, or to resolve problems with capture, check out your capture device, and the connections from your analog video source, using the capture utility software provided with your capture hardware. When you are sure that the device is working, you then can set up Premiere to work with it.

Task

9

Trimming and Reusing Clips

In Part 3, "Assembling Clips Using the Storyboard and Timeline," you took the clips you had organized in bins in the Project window and laid them out into a production in the Timeline window. However, by using the files provided in the Premiere Sample Folder, you took a shortcut in the editing process because the sample files were already segmented and trimmed, with each scene separated into its own individual clip file. When working with captured material, there is an additional editing step in organizing your material in bins. If you have captured several scenes to one media file, you need to go though the file to mark and trim the individual clips that you will want to use on the Timeline. And, even if you have used batch capture with a DV camcorder to capture each scene to an individual clip file, it is a good idea to capture the clips with handles—extra frames at each end, so you can edit them precisely as needed in the final production. Premiere provides tools in the Clip window to mark and trim individual clips. You can even make duplicate copies of clips with different trim settings that can be applied multiple times. Once the clips are laid out on the Timeline window, Premiere also provides an extensive collection of tools for editing and adjusting the clips relative to each other and the overall production, as described in Part 10, "Editing in the Timeline."

How to Trim Clips

The bin folders in the Project window can be used not only to organize clip files but also to segment and trim the clips before they are laid out in the Timeline window. To do this, you set *markers* and *In* and *Out points* associated with the clip in the Premiere Clip window. Even better, you can make duplicate copies of a clip with different trim settings to play in multiple places on the Timeline.

1 Open the Sample Project

Choose **File**, **Open Recent Project**, and select the **Sample Project** file that you created in Part 1, "Getting Started with Premiere." Or start a new project and import the **Sample Folder** included with Premiere.

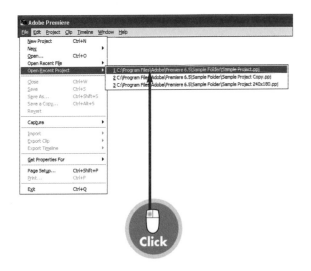

2 Open the zfinal Clip

Premiere opens the Project window and Timeline window for the project. Click the Sample Folder bin and double-click the zfinal clip to open it. You will work with this clip because it is the final result of editing together the other clips—it includes multiple scenes and contains both video and audio.

3 Move Through the Clip

Premiere opens a Clip window with the zfinal clip. You will mark the second scene in the zfinal clip, from 5:18 to the dissolve at 11:18, for a total duration of about 6 seconds. To move through the clip, click and drag the Set Location blue triangular slider to shuttle through the clip, or click and drag in the Frame Jog striped tread area to jog through the frames.

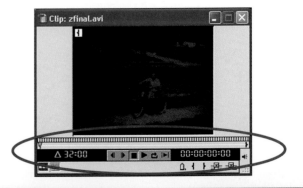

4️⃣ Set the In Point

Move to the beginning of the clip at a timecode of 5:18, as shown in the timecode display. Play and step through the clip with the VCR controls, or press the Left or Right arrow keys on your keyboard to step frame by frame through the clip. Then click the **Mark In** button ("**{**") below the timecode display, or press the **I** key.

6️⃣ Play from In to Out

Premiere sets the **Out point** icon in the slider area under the video. It also displays In and Out icons in the upper corners of the video at the associated frames. Click the **Play In to Out** button at the right of the VCR controls to play through the trimmed sequence.

5️⃣ Set the Out Point

Premiere sets the In point icon in the slider area under the video. Click in the timecode area, type 11:18, and press (**Return**) [**Enter**] to jump directly to the end of the sequence. Then set the Out point: Click the **Mark Out** button ("**}**"), press the **O** key, or click and drag the **Out** icon to the desired time.

How-to Hint — Playing the Trimmed Clip

Press the **Loop** button next to **Play In to Out** button to play the trimmed clip continuously.

Press the (**Option**) [**Alt**] key and click **Play** to play from the current position to the Out point.

How-to Hint — Entering a Timecode

To jump directly to a timecode in the **Clip** window, type the number on the numeric keypad and press (**Return**) [**Enter**]. You can type the time without punctuation. Simply type **518** instead of **5:18**.

How to Mark Clips

You can mark a clip with In and Out points to keep track of a scene, to trim off the ends, or to trim a scene out of a larger clip. When an imported media file contains many different scenes, you can set additional markers to help you quickly jump to specific scenes and easily extract individual clips.

① Go to the Next Scene

Continuing from the previous task, move to the next scene in the **zfinal** clip in the Clip window. Click and drag the **slider**, click the **VCR controls**, or type on the numeric keypad to move to **timecode 15:12**.

② Mark the Next Scene

Open the **Marker** menu and choose **Mark**, **3** to set marker 3 to the beginning of the third scene after the start of the clip (or choose **Clip**, **Set Clip Marker**, **3**).

③ Mark the Remaining Scenes

Using the **Marker** menu, mark the remaining scenes at 17:14, 19:16, and 24:24 as scenes 4, 5, and 6, respectively. Premiere displays the marker number at the top center of the video at the associated frame.

④ Go to a Marker

Now that the markers are set, you can skip directly to any scene. Click the **Marker menu** button and choose **Go To**, **In** to jump back to the In point. Premiere indicates that a marker has been set by a dot to its left in the menus.

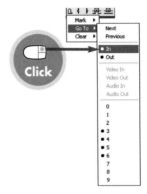

⑤ Move to Markers

Choose **Clip**, **Go to Clip Marker** to jump directly to any defined marker. Hold down the (**Command**) [**Control**] key and press the **Left** and **Right arrow keys** to jump to the previous and next markers, press the **Up** and **Down keys** to jump to the In and Out points, or press a **number key** to jump to a numeric marker.

⑥ Clear Markers

Open the **Marker** menu and choose **Clear** (or choose **Clip**, **Clear Clip Marker**). You can clear the current marker, a specific marker, both the In and Out markers, or all markers at the same time.

How-to Hint

Unnumbered Markers

Besides the In and Out points and the numbered markers from 0 to 9, Premiere also supports up to 999 unnumbered markers for each clip on the Timeline. Open the **Marker** menu and choose **Mark**, **Unnumbered** to set an unnumbered marker. Use the **Previous** and **Next** commands to jump to unnumbered markers.

How-to Hint

Timeline Markers

You also can set markers on the Timeline for important time points that affect multiple clips, such as edit points to synchronize video and audio.

How to Reuse Clips

In Task 1, you set In and Out points for one scene in the zfinal clip. But the clip contains multiple scenes that you could play at different points in the Timeline, each with different trim settings. Premiere can help you keep track of multiple copies of a clip by creating duplicate copies of a *master* clip.

1 Drag the Clip to Timeline

Drag the zfinal clip that you trimmed in the first task from the **Clip** window to the Video 1A track in the **Timeline**. Premiere places the associated audio clip in the Audio 1 track. To show all the clips you are going to use, open the **Zoom** menu in the bottom left corner of the **Timeline** window and set the Timeline display to **1 Second**.

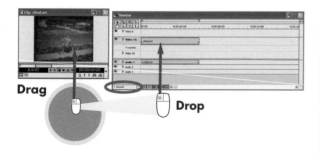

Drag

Drop

2 Change the Trim

Change the trim settings in the Clip window. Slide in both the **In** and **Out markers** to trim the beginning and end of the clip so that it runs from 6:18 to 10:18.

Click

3 Add a Second Instance

Drag the zfinal clip from the **Clip** window to the Video 1B track as a second instance of the clip with a shorter duration. The original instance is still the same, retaining the settings from when it was added to the **Timeline**.

Drag

Drop

④ Add a Third Instance

Close the **Clip** window and drag a third instance of the zfinal clip from the Sample Folder bin to the Video 1A track. The clip copied from the bin retains the most recent trim settings.

Drag

Drop

⑤ Open the Clip from the Project

Double-click the zfinal clip in the **Project** window to reopen it. In the **Marker** menu, jump to the **In point**. The **Clip** window shows that the clip retains the most recent trim settings and markers.

⑥ Open the Clips from the Timeline

Double-click the first and second instances of the zfinal clip in the **Timeline** to open them. The Clip windows do not show the entire master clip with trim settings; instead, they show only the trimmed section of the clip, with the trimmed duration. They retain the timecode from the original master clip.

How-to Hint

Anonymous Instances

Premiere supports trimming and using a clip multiple times, but you can end up with a confusing situation in which the same clip appears on the Timeline in multiple anonymous instances, with very different settings. A better solution is to make explicit, named duplicates of clips so that you can keep track of them, as described in Task 4.

How to Duplicate Clips

Even though Premiere can track multiple instances of the same clip on the Timeline, this can become confusing. Instead, you can create duplicate instances of the clip in the Bin window so that you can keep track of each trim setting individually.

1 Duplicate a Clip

Reopen the Sample Project, or choose **File**, **Revert**. Open the Sample Folder bin, click the zfinal clip to select it, and then choose **Duplicate Clip** from the pop-up context menu (or choose **Edit**, **Duplicate Clip**).

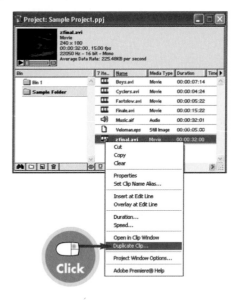

2 Enter the Clip Name

Premiere displays the Duplicate Clip dialog. If desired, click in the **Name** field to type a new name for this clip instance. You can also choose a different project from the **Location** drop-down, if desired. Then click **OK**.

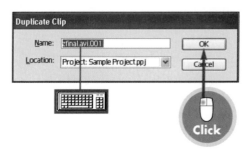

3 View the Duplicate

Premiere creates a duplicate copy of the clip in the Sample Folder bin, with the duration set to the trimmed In and Out points in the master clip.

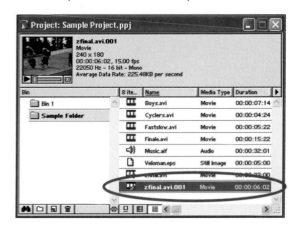

④ Add to the Timeline

Drag the master zfinal clip to the Timeline, and then the duplicate **001** clip. These two clips now are easier to keep track of because they also have different names.

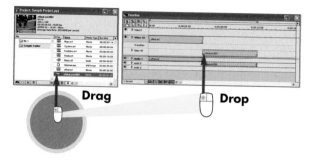

Drag   **Drop**

⑤ Locating Clips

Premiere can also help you keep track of which clip is which on the Timeline. Click the original zfinal clip in the Timeline to select it, and then (**Control+click**) [**Right+click**] the clip and choose **Locate Clip** from the pop-up context menu (or choose **Edit**, **Locate Clip**).

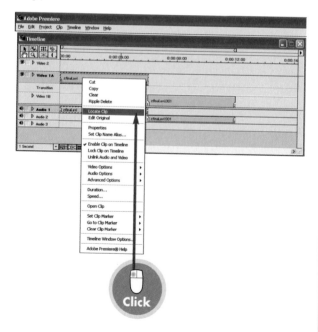

Click

⑥ View Clip in Bin

Premiere displays the Project window and highlights the zfinal clip in the Sample Folder bin as the source for the trimmed clip in the Timeline.

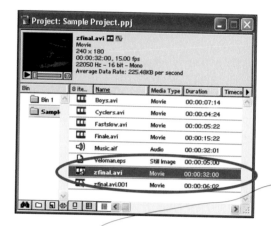

Clip Name Aliases

You can rename your clips in the Bin and Project windows to help keep track of how you are using them. Click on the **clip** to select it, and then (**Control+click**) [**Right+click**] and choose **Set Clip Name Alias** from the pop-up context menu (or choose **Clip**, **Set Clip Name Alias**).

Copy and Paste

You can also make copies of clips by using traditional **Copy** and **Paste** commands. However, explicitly duplicating clips gives you the opportunity to rename them. Copying and pasting in the Project or Bin windows creates a duplicate clip. Copying and pasting in the Timeline creates another instance of the clip.

How-to Hint

How to Trim Clips in the Timeline

Previously, you trimmed clips in the Clip window, made duplicates, and added them to the Timeline window. When you open the resulting clips from the Timeline, they are displayed in their trimmed form, with the remainder of the clip no longer accessible. However, you can still trim the clips in the Timeline.

❶ Duplicate the Clip

Reopen the Sample Project and duplicate the zfinal clip. Give the duplicate a new name. (I added a 002 to the end of the name.)

❷ Add the Clip to the Timeline

Drag the 002 clip to the **Timeline**, part-way into the Video 1A track. Double-click the 002 clip in the **Timeline** to open the **Clip** window.

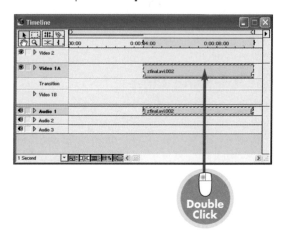

Double Click

❸ Check the Timecode and Duration

The clip was trimmed to have a start time of 5:18 and a duration of 6:02. Premiere displays both an In point icon and any additional markers at the top of the clip.

④ Trim the Clip Shorter

Make sure that the **Selection tool** (arrow icon) is selected in the top-left corner of the **Timeline**. Hold the cursor over the start of the clip in the **Timeline**, and it changes to the red trim tool (square red bracket with double-sided arrow). Click and drag the start of the clip to the right to set the In point later. Premiere also updates the Clip window to show the shorter duration.

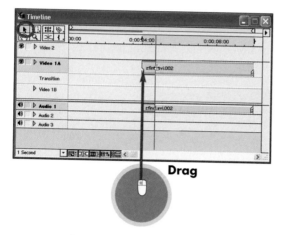

Drag

⑤ Trim the Clip Longer

Because this clip is actually an instance of a longer clip, you can also lengthen the clip to include more of the original material. Click and drag the start of the clip to the left to set the **In point** earlier.

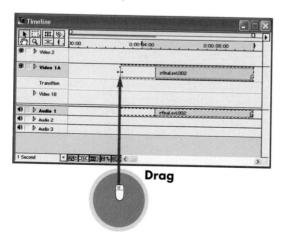

Drag

⑥ Trim the End of the Clip

Click and drag the end of the clip to extend the **Out point** further into the original clip. Premiere shows the numeric markers that you set in the original clip.

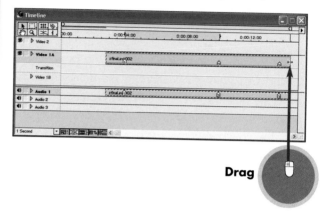

Drag

How-to Hint

Setting Duration

You can also set the duration of a clip directly. Click the clip in the **Project** or **Timeline** window to select it, and then choose **Clip**, **Duration**. Then enter the exact duration time in the Clip Duration dialog.

How to Change Clip Duration and Speed

When you change the length of a clip by setting its In and Out points, this changes the duration of the clip—the number of seconds or frames that are played. You also can change the playback speed of a clip, for slow motion or fast playback. You even can play a clip backward.

① View the Clip Duration

Copy Fastslow or another clip to two tracks in the Timeline. Click the top clip to select it, and then choose **Clip**, **Duration**.

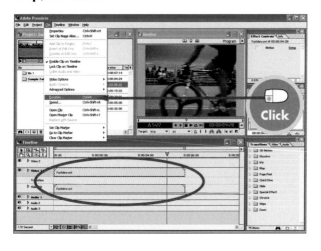

② Set the Clip Duration

Enter a shorter duration in the Clip Duration dialog (such as changing 5:22 to 3:00), and then click **OK**. Premiere adjusts the length of the clip by changing the Out point.

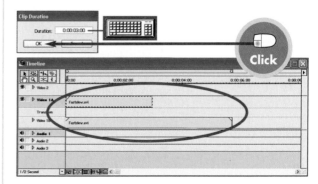

③ View the Clip Speed

Undo the duration change. Then click the top clip to select it and choose **Speed** from the pop-up context menu.

4 Set the Clip Speed Faster

Use the Clip Speed dialog to enter a New Rate of **200%** to speed up the clip to play twice as fast. You also can specify a New Duration and have Premiere adjust the speed to match. Click **OK**.

5 Play the Clip Faster

Premiere adjusts the clip and displays the speed percentage with the clip name. Because the clip is being played faster, its duration is reduced by half. The top clip now plays twice as fast as the bottom clip.

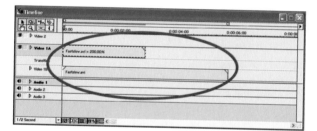

6 Play Slower and Backwards

Use the Clip Speed dialog to set the New Rate to negative 75% to slow down the clip and also play it backward. Premiere increases the duration because the clip now takes longer to play.

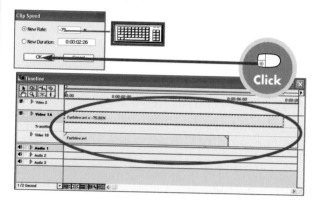

How-to Hint

Dropping or Duplicating Frames

Changing the speed of a clip requires either dropping some frames (to play through it faster) or duplicating frames (for slow motion). If you play a 30 frame per second clip at half speed, it looks like you are playing it at 15 frames per second.

How-to Hint

Rate Stretch Tool

Use the **Rate Stretch Timeline** tool to change the playback speed of the clip by dragging its ends in the **Timeline** (see Part 10, Task 8).

How-to Hint

Changing Speed in Projects and Bins

Choose **Clip**, **Speed** to change the speed of a clip in the **Project** window. Or use **Clip**, **Advanced Options**, **Interpret Footage**.

How to Reuse Projects in the Timeline

Premiere offers several approaches for working with larger projects. You can build a project in several independent pieces and then import them into a master project. You also can reuse portions of the Timeline as virtual clips to nest multiple effects and to reuse a complex edit in multiple places in the Timeline.

① Create and Save a Simple Edit

Open the Sample Project and arrange two clips in the Timeline, and then add a transition between them. Choose **File**, **Save As** to save the project under a new name such as "Work Project."

② Save and Import a Project

Choose **File**, **Import**, **Project**. Select the project to be imported, and then use the Import Project dialog to import at the End of the current project. Premiere inserts the imported project into the **Timeline** at the specified point, and adds a new bin with the clips from the imported project.

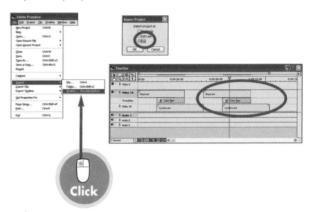

③ Select the Block Select Tool

Undo the imported project. Click and hold the **Block Select** tool (the dashed rectangle) in the top left of the **Timeline** window to display the pop-up menu of selection tools. Choose the second **Block Select** tool (with the two overlapping rectangles).

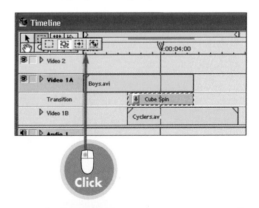

④ Block Select a Region

The cursor changes to a block selection icon (arrow in a dashed rectangle). Click and drag the cursor along the **Timeline** to select the two clips with a transition.

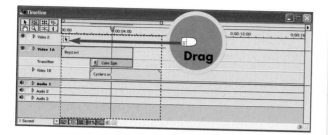

⑤ Copy as a Virtual Clip

The cursor changes to the **Virtual Clip** tool (two clips with a horizontal arrow). Click and drag from inside the selected region to create a virtual clip at a new location on the **Timeline**. Press **Shift** to create a virtual clip with just the video or audio portions of the source area.

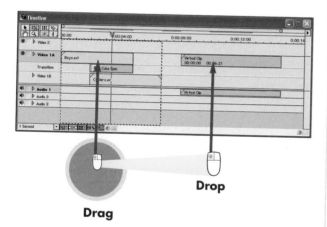

Drag

Drop

⑥ Edit with the Virtual Clip

The entire source area now appears as a single virtual clip in the Timeline. Any new edits you make in the source region of the **Timeline** will appear in any virtual clips. Click the **Selection** tool (arrow) and add a new clip and transition to layer three clips with two transitions into your production.

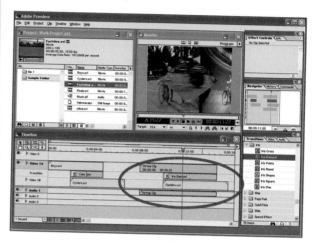

How-to Hint

Organizing Virtual Clips

Because the source areas for virtual clips appear on the same Timeline as your main program, you should create a virtual clip area separate from your main program at the beginning (or end) of the Timeline. You then can exclude the virtual clip area from your program when it is played or rendered.

How-to Hint

Repeating and Nesting Virtual Clips

You can create multiple virtual clips from the same source section of the Timeline—for example, to repeat a sequence, possibly with different effects. You also can create virtual clips that contain nested virtual clips—for example, to build up a series of transitions between more than two clips.

Task

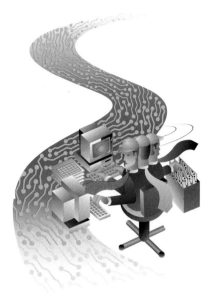

10

Editing in the Timeline

In the early parts of this book, you worked with individual clips in the Timeline window, inserting and deleting clips on the video and audio tracks.

In Part 9, "Trimming and Editing Clips," you trimmed and duplicated clips in the Project window before copying them to the Timeline and performed simple trims on clips in the Timeline.

In this part, you will explore Premiere's tools for editing clips and tracks on the Timeline, operating on groups of clips, and making independent adjustments to the video and audio tracks of a clip. The tasks in this part roughly follow the order of the Premiere tool buttons in the Timeline window.

Premiere provides a tremendous variety of tools for editing on the Timeline. As a result, it accommodates a range of different editing styles and different levels of precision in editing, from drag-and-drop with the mouse to keyboard shortcuts, from simple edits of individual clips to operations across adjacent clips, from edits on a single track to multiple tracks. See Part 11, "Editing in the Monitor Window," for another more professionally oriented editing approach.

To experiment with the Premiere editing commands, set up a collection of clips in the Timeline, save the setup as a new Project file, and then try the commands. As you experiment, use Undo or the History palette to back out changes, or Revert to return to the original layout.

How to Use the Timeline Window

The Premiere Timeline window provides a cornucopia of editing options, accessed from various menus, dialogs, tool buttons, toggle buttons, keyboard selections, and other edit controls. This task provides a quick tour of the components of the Timeline window, before the more detailed tasks that follow.

1 Use the Time Ruler

The Time Ruler area at the top of the **Timeline** window displays the current position in your production. Click the **Hand Tool** (or press **H**) and then click and drag the **Timeline** to move to a different section (or use the scrollbar). The edit line shows the current position in the Timeline, or you can click and drag it to scrub through the clips.

2 Navigate in the Timeline

Open the **Time Zoom Level** menu in the lower left of the **Timeline** to change the time period for the display, and zoom in and out. Select the **Zoom Tool** (or press **Z**) and click to zoom in, or press (**Option**) [**Alt**] and click to zoom out. You also can use the Navigator palette to move and zoom the display.

3 Set the Work Area

The Preview Indicator area above the Time Ruler shows whether a preview needs to be generated or already exists. The yellow work area band above it shows the current working areas for previews. Drag the triangular **Work Area Markers** to adjust the work area. Double-click the bar to set the work area to the entire region currently visible in the window.

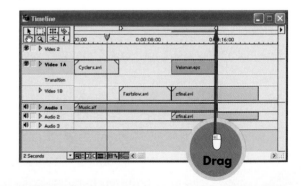

4 Set the Track Options

The Track Heading area on the left side of the **Timeline** shows the names and status of the available tracks. Open the **Timeline window** menu and choose **Track Options**, or click the **Track Options Dialog** button, to display the **Track Options** dialog where you can add, rename, or delete tracks (see Task 3).

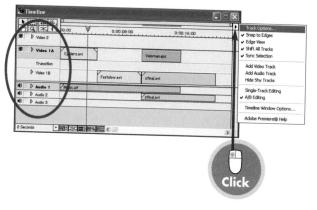

6 Select a Timeline Tool

Click one of the **Timeline Tools** in the upper left of the **Timeline** window to control editing operations in the **Timeline**. Some tool buttons provide access to several related tools, indicated by a small triangle in the bottom-left corner. Click and hold one of these buttons to select an alternate tool.

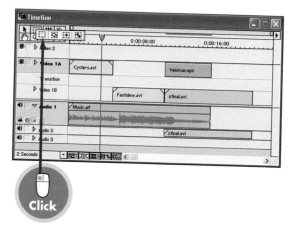

5 Set the Track Display

Use the triangular **Collapse/Expand Track** control and track display buttons to control how the track contents are displayed. Expand the audio track to see the audio waveform (see Part 14, "Mixing Audio Tracks").

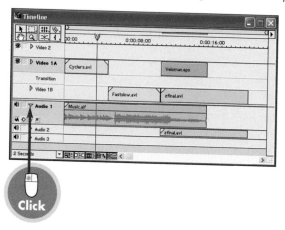

7 Select a Timeline Toggle

Click the **Timeline Toggle** buttons in the bottom left of the window to toggle display and editing operations in the **Timeline**. These toggles, as well as **Timeline** and **Track** options, also can be selected from the **Timeline** menu and the **Timeline window** menu.

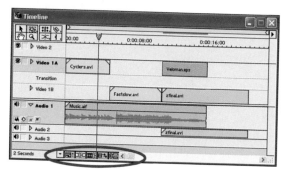

How to Customize the Timeline Window

The Timeline Window Options dialog provides options for controlling the overall Timeline display. Depending on the number of tracks in the Timeline, you can increase the size of the clip icons and display frames from the clips.

1 Open the Timeline Window Options

Open the **Timeline window** menu and choose **Timeline Window Options**.

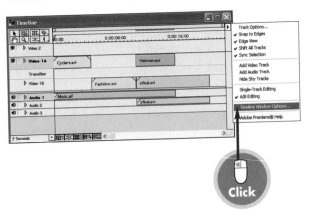

2 Display Timeline Window Options

Premiere displays the **Timeline Window Options** dialog. Use these options to adjust the **Timeline** display to the current window, adding more information when only a few clips are in a large window, or removing detail when you have many clips in the **Timeline**.

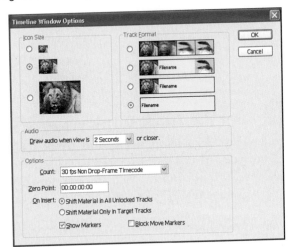

3 Set the Icon Size

In the **Icon Size** section, select the **Icon Size** of the clip icon you want to use in the **Timeline**. Select a smaller size when working with a larger number of tracks.

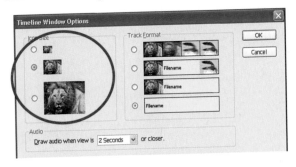

4 Set the Track Format

In the **Track Format** section, select the display format to be used for clip icons in the **Timeline**. The options include displaying the filename, the poster and ending frame, and intermediate frames. The **Timeline** updates fastest when displaying only the filename.

5 Set the Audio Display

In the **Audio** section, select the zoom level at which to start displaying the audio waveform graph when you expand the clip in the **Timeline**.

6 Set the Insert Options

In the **Options** section, set the **On Insert** option to specify which tracks are affected by an insert. Select **Shift Material Only in Target Tracks** to specify that adding new clips will cause only the destination tracks to be shifted to make room for the insertion, or select **Shift Material in All Unlocked Tracks** to adjust all tracks.

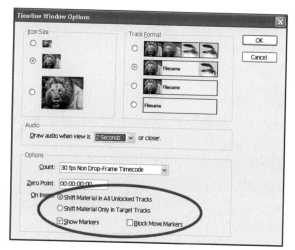

7 Set the Marker Options

In the **Options** section, select **Show Markers** to display clip and Timeline markers. Click **OK** to close the dialog. Premiere updates the **Timeline** window to show the beginning and ending frame of each clip.

How-to Hint

Shifting Tracks When Inserting Clips

You also can control which tracks are shifted on insert using the **Toggle Shift Tracks Options** button at the bottom of the **Timeline** window, or the **Shift All Tracks** command in the **Timeline window** menu.

How to Add and Lock Clips and Tracks

The Track Heading area on the left side of the Timeline shows the names and status of the available tracks. Use the Track Options dialog to add, rename, or delete tracks.

1 Open the Track Options

Open the **Timeline window** menu and choose **Track Options**, or click the first **Track Options Dialog** button under the window.

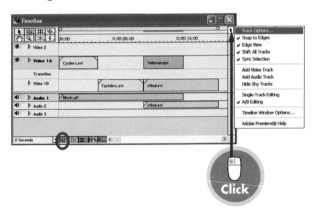

2 Change the Track Options

Premiere displays the Track Options dialog. You can select an existing track to rename or delete it. Click **Add** to add a new track.

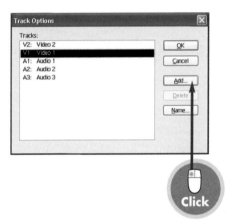

3 Add a Track

Premiere displays the Add Tracks dialog. Enter the number of **Video** or **Audio** tracks to add. Click **OK** to exit each dialog and add the new tracks.

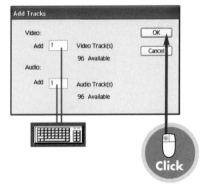

④ Lock an Entire Track

Premiere adds two new tracks to the Timeline: Video 3 and Audio 4. Click the lock icon area next to the track name to lock an entire track so that clips in the track cannot be accidentally selected or edited. The cursor changes to a lock symbol when over a locked track.

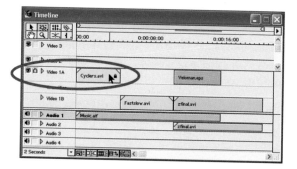

⑥ View a Locked Clip

Premiere marks the locked clips with a hatch pattern of gray slashes and a check mark next to the command in the menus. Choose the **Lock Clip on Timeline** command again to unlock the clip.

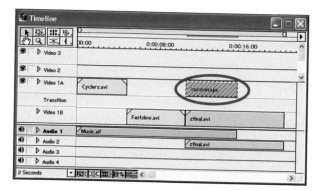

⑤ Lock Individual Clips

Unlock the track, and instead select one or more individual clips on the **Timeline**. Then (**Control+click**) [**Right+click**] and choose **Lock Clip on Timeline** from the pop-up context menu, or from the **Clip** menu.

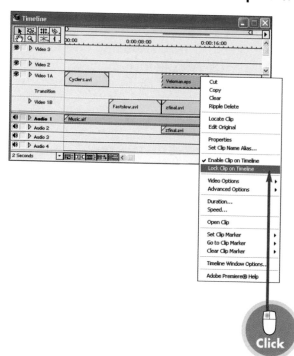

How-to Hint

Adding Tracks When Inserting Clips

You also can add a track when inserting clips in the **Timeline** by dragging and dropping a clip to a point on the Time Ruler.

Preventing Mistakes

Although the History palette and **AutoSave** option can help you recover from mistakes (see Part 2, "Importing and Organizing Clips"), locking individual clips and even entire tracks is a better way to prevent accidental changes to the **Timeline**.

How to Disable and Hide Clips and Tracks

Premiere provides several approaches for focusing your work on a part of a larger production. You can temporarily disable individual clips and even exclude entire tracks so that they will be ignored when playing through the Timeline and exporting to a video file. You also can hide tracks from the Timeline display to reduce the clutter in the window.

1 Disable a Clip

Select one or more clips on the **Timeline**, and then deselect **Enable Clip on Timeline** from the pop-up context menu, or from the **Clip** menu. Premiere marks enabled clips with a check mark next to the command in the menus.

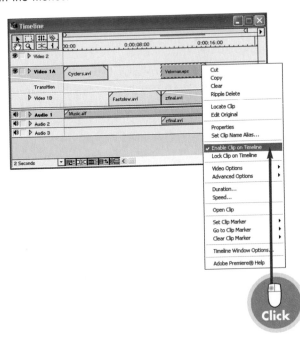

2 View a Disabled Clip

Premiere marks the disabled clips with a hatch pattern of gray backslashes. Choose the **Enable Clip on Timeline** command again to enable the clip.

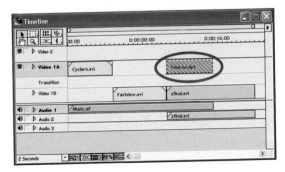

3 Exclude a Track

Click the **eye** (video) and **speaker** (audio) icons at the far left of the **Track Heading** area to mark the tracks as excluded. The icon disappears, indicating that the entire track will be ignored when previewing the **Timeline** or exporting to a file. Click again to include the tracks.

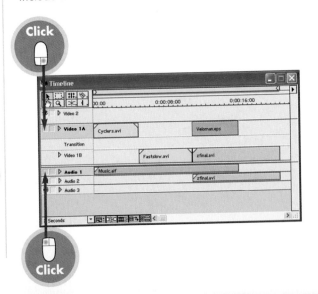

④ Mark a Track as Shy

Press (**Command**) [**Ctrl**] while clicking on the **eye** or **speaker** icon to mark a track as shy. Shy tracks are still included when playing or exporting the **Timeline**, but they can be hidden from view.

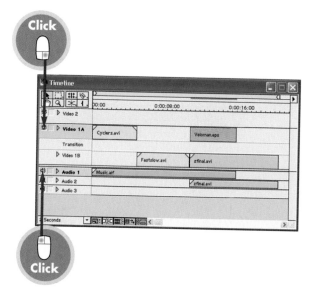

⑤ Hide the Shy Tracks

Premiere displays the eye icons as outlines to mark the shy tracks. Open the **Timeline window** menu and choose **Hide Shy Tracks**, or select it from the **Timeline** menu, to temporarily simplify the **Timeline** display by hiding the shy tracks.

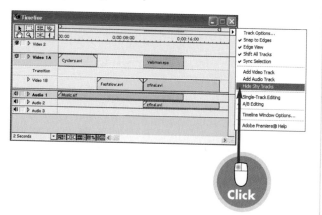

⑥ Show the Shy Tracks

Premiere hides all the shy tracks from view in the **Timeline** window. Choose **Show Shy Tracks** to display them again.

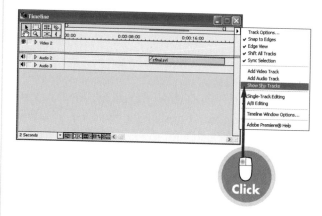

How-to Hint

Locking Hidden Tracks

Disabled clips, and shy and hidden tracks, can still be edited just like any other entry on the **Timeline**. Use the lock option to prevent editing changes to a track, especially a hidden track (see Task 3).

Hiding All Tracks

Press (**Command+Option**) [**Ctrl+Alt**] while clicking an **eye** or **speaker** icon to mark all superimposed video tracks (above Video 1), or all audio tracks, as shy.

How to Select Clips and Tracks

As your productions become larger and more ambitious, the Timeline becomes correspondingly more complex, with many clips, transitions, and effects. Premiere provides a variety of tools for selecting groups of tracks and clips so that they can be moved or edited together.

❶ Select a Clip

Click the **Selection tool** button (or press **V**) to select individual clips in the **Timeline** window. The cursor changes to an arrow icon. Click on a clip to select it. (**Command**) [**Ctrl**] as you click to add or remove additional individual clips to the current selection, or press **Shift** as you click to add a range of clips.

Click

❷ Select All Clips

Choose **Edit**, **Select All** to select all the clips in the Timeline, or **Deselect All** to remove all selections.

Click

❸ Select a Range of Clips

Click and hold the **Selection tool** button and choose the first tool (**Range Select tool**), or press **M**. The cursor changes to a dashed rectangle icon. Click and drag a rectangle over a group of clips to select them. Press **Shift** as you click to add additional clips to the current selection.

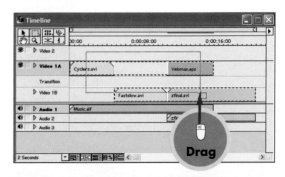

Drag

④ Select a Track

Click and hold the **Selection tool** button and choose the third tool (**Track Select Tool**). The cursor changes to a single right arrow icon. Click a clip to select all the clips in that track from that time forward. Press **Shift** as you click to add additional tracks to the current selection.

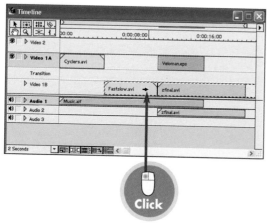

⑤ Select Multiple Tracks

Click and hold the **Selection tool** button and choose the fourth tool (**Multitrack Select Tool**). The cursor changes to a double right arrow icon. Click a clip to select all the clips that occur in all tracks from that time or later.

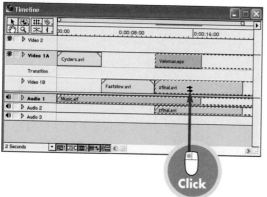

⑥ Select Video and Audio

Click the **Toggle Sync Mode** button at the bottom of the **Timeline** to determine whether linked video and audio clips are selected together or independently (or use the **Sync Selection** command in the **Timeline** menus). When sync mode is enabled, a link icon is visible on the button, and clicking either the video or audio track of a linked clip will select both portions. When disabled, you can select the video and audio tracks independently.

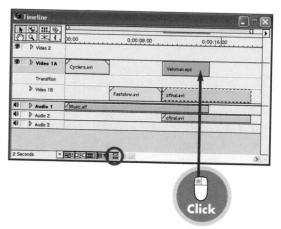

How-to Hint

Block Select Tool

Use the second **Selection tool** button (**Block Select Tool**) to select and duplicate portions of the **Timeline** to reuse as a virtual clip in other portions of the Timeline (see Part 9, Task 6).

How to Split Clips and Tracks

In Part 9, you used the same clip multiple times on the Timeline with different trim settings.

Premiere also provides a Razor tool to split a clip in the Timeline into two parts so that you can insert and delete sections directly on the Timeline.

1 Select the Split Point

Lay out two clips in the Video 1A and Video 2 tracks on the **Timeline**. To help find the exact point where you want to split the top clip, drag the edit line to scrub through the **Timeline**. Position the edit line to mark the point where you want to split the clip.

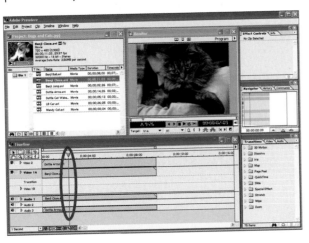

2 Split a Clip

Click and hold the **Razor tool** button and choose the first **Razor Tool**, or press **C**. Move the cursor over the top clip, and it changes to a razor blade icon. Click on the clip at the edit line.

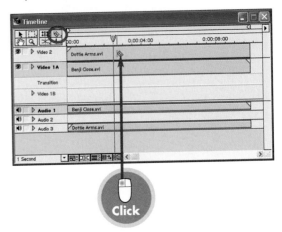

3 View the Split Clip

Premiere splits the clip into two independent instance with the Out point of the first and the In point of the second adjusted to match each other. All linked clips a also split. Use the **Razor** tool again to cut at a secor point.

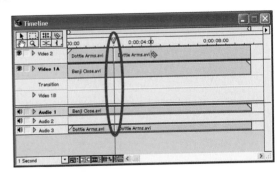

4 Split All Tracks at Once

To split all tracks at a single point in time, position the edit line again to mark a new split point. Choose the second **Razor tool** (**Multiple Razor tool**). Move the cursor over a clip in any track, and it changes to a Multiple Razor icon. Click on the clip at the point where you want to split the tracks.

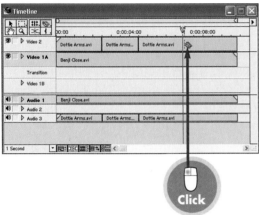

5 View the Split in all Tracks

Premiere splits all the clips at that point on all unlocked tracks. Use the **Multiple Razor tool** again to cut all tracks at a second point.

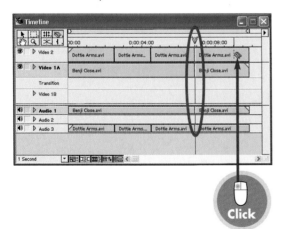

6 Alternate Between Two Clips

Click the **Selection tool** button (or press **V**), and then delete alternating razored sections of the clips. In this way, you can combine two synchronized clips on the **Timeline** and switch between them.

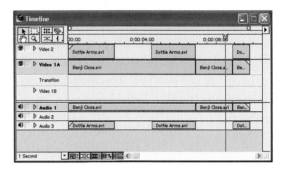

How to Copy Clips and Attributes

You can cut, copy, and paste clips directly on the Timeline, and control how they are adjusted to fit into the available space on a track. You even can copy and paste the attributes of a clip to replicate them across other clips.

1 Open a Gap

Click a short clip to select it. Press **Delete** to remove it from the Timeline in order to make a gap between clips to paste into. Then click a long clip to select it and choose **Edit**, **Copy**.

2 Paste into a Gap

Click the gap between clips to select it as the destination. Choose **Edit**, **Paste**. Premiere inserts the clip at the selected location in the **Timeline** and trims the clip, if needed, by adjusting the Out point to fit the available space in the Timeline.

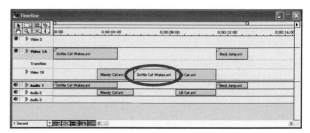

3 Copy and Paste to Fit

Copy the long clip again, and then click to select a smaller clip as the destination. Choose **Edit**, **Paste to Fit**.

In the Fit Clip dialog, select **Change Speed** to slow down or speed up the clip to fit the available space, or **Trim Source** to trim the Out point to fit the available space.

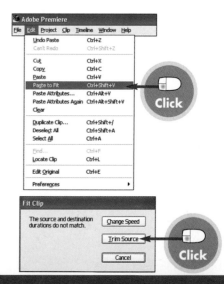

④ View the Timeline

Premiere inserts the clip at the selected location in the **Timeline** and adjusts the clip to fit as specified.

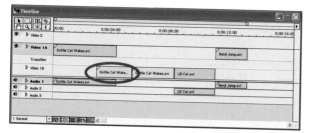

⑤ Paste Attributes

Copy a clip; click a different clip to select it; and then choose **Edit**, **Paste Attributes**. In the Paste Attributes dialog, select **Content** to paste the source clip into the selected destination. The Content section also shows an animation of the effect of the selected option.

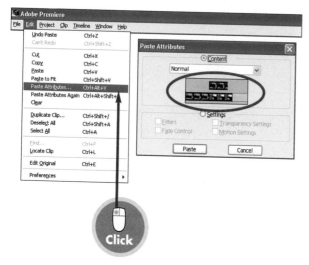

⑥ Specify Settings Attributes

Use the **Content** drop-down menu to choose the type of adjustment to be made to fit the clip into the **Timeline**. Or select **Settings** to transfer filter, fade control, transparency, or motion settings from one clip to another. Click **Paste** to perform the operation.

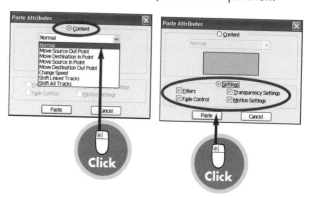

— How-to Hint

Copy Multiple Clips

To copy multiple clips, use the **Block Select tool** (used for virtual clips, see Part 9, Task 6) to select a section of the **Timeline**; then hold down the (**Option**) [**Alt**] while you drag a copy to another section of the Timeline.

Paste Attributes Again

Choose **Edit**, **Paste Attributes Again** to repeat a Paste Attributes operation for additional clips or tracks.

How to Unlink and Unsync Clips

Premiere keeps the video and audio tracks of a clip linked so that they move together, and synced so that they play at the same time. Premiere provides tools to unlink and unsync the clips so that you can edit them independently. When linked clips are moved out of sync, Premiere marks each clip with a red triangle.

1 View the Timeline

Open the **Sample Project** and add different kinds of clips to the **Timeline**: Fastslow (video only), Music (audio only), Veloman (still image), and zfinal (video and audio). Premiere uses different colors for the different types of clips.

2 Unsync Linked Clips

Click the **Toggle Sync Mode** button at the bottom of the **Timeline** to determine whether linked video and audio clips are selected together or independently. Click the button so that the toggle is unlinked (the link icon disappears). Click the **Selection Tool** button in the top left of the **Timeline** window and drag the audio portion of the **zfinal** clip out of sync.

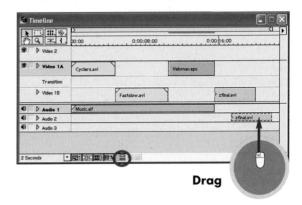

Drag

3 Resync Linked Clips

Click the cursor on the red triangle to display the amount of time that the two tracks of the clip are out of sync. Click and drag the cursor into the time value and then release it to snap the two portions of the clip back into sync.

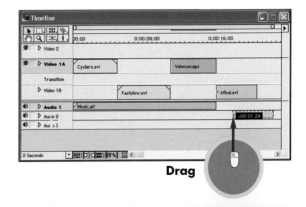

Drag

④ Unlink Video and Audio

Click the **Toggle Sync Mode** button so that the clip tracks are in sync again. Click one of the linked tracks to select both and then choose **Clip, Unlink Audio and Video**.

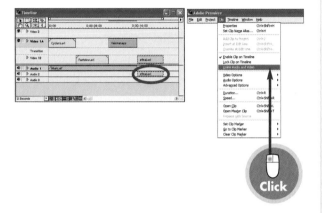

⑤ Realign Unlinked Clips

Premiere recolors the clips to show that they are no longer linked and displays each clip with a white marker. You can then drag the video and audio tracks independently. To realign unlinked clips, click the **Selection Tool** button and click and drag the marker from one clip to the marker in the other clip.

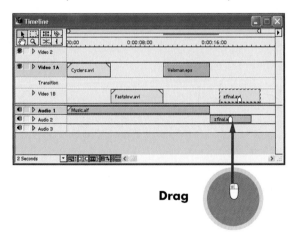

Drag

⑥ Link Video and Audio

Click the **Link/Unlink Tool** button to select it. To link a video and audio clip, or to unlink a linked pair of clips, click the first clip to select it. Move the cursor over the second clip, so that it changes to the **Link/Unlink** icon, and then click on the second clip. Premiere recolors the clips to show the new link status.

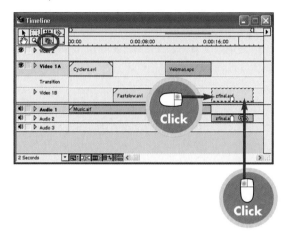

Click

Toggle Sync Mode

Use the **Toggle Sync Mode** button to temporarily unsync the video and audio tracks of a clip so that they can be edited independently. Then click the button again to restore Sync mode.

How to Edit and Trim Adjacent Clips

You can trim an individual clip in the Timeline by simply dragging its ends. You can insert or delete a clip in place, or perform a ripple edit to slide over the adjacent clips.

However, things get more complicated when dealing with a group of adjacent clips on the same or neighboring tracks. Premiere provides Timeline editing tools to provide full control over trimming and editing adjacent clips.

1 Set Up the Timeline

Add a series of clips to the **Timeline**, with at least three clips side by side on the same track, and additional clips on other tracks. Trim the ends of the three adjacent clips to reduce their duration and provide some extra material to work with.

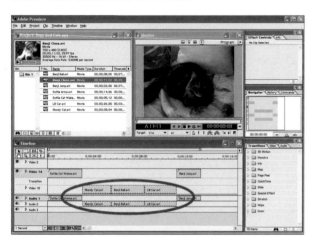

2 Trim in a Clip Window

Double-click a clip in the **Timeline** to display it in a Clip window. Set the In and Out points as desired (see Part 9). Then click the **Apply** button at the bottom of the window to apply the changes to the clip in the **Timeline**.

③ Perform a Rolling Edit

Click and hold the **Edit** tool and choose the first **Rolling Edit Tool** (or press **P**). The cursor icon shows that the edit will trim both clips. In a rolling edit, the Out point of the first clip is adjusted in tandem with the In point of the second clip so that the overall program duration stays the same. As you drag the clip boundary, the **Monitor** window displays a split screen of the two adjacent clips.

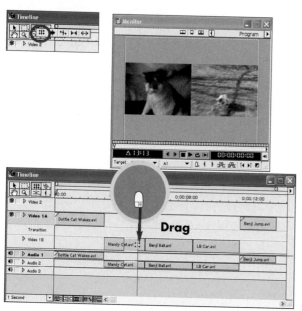

④ Perform a Ripple Edit

Choose the second **Ripple Edit Tool**. The cursor icon changes to show that the edit will trim only one clip. The trimmed clip changes duration, and the rest of the program on the Timeline moves to accommodate the new size.

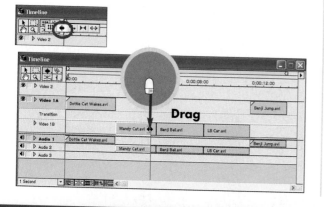

⑤ Perform a Slip Edit

Choose the fourth **Slip tool**. The cursor icon changes to show that the edit will trim only within the one clip. **Drag** to slip the In and Out points earlier or later in the clip, and the duration of the clip remains the same. The **Monitor** window shows the new In and Out Points. The rest of the program on the **Timeline** is unchanged.

⑥ Perform a Slide Edit

Choose the fifth **Slide tool**. **Drag** to slide the clip earlier or later in the program by changing the In and Out points of the neighboring clips. The clip remains unchanged, and its movement trims the adjacent clips. The rest of the program on the Timeline is unchanged.

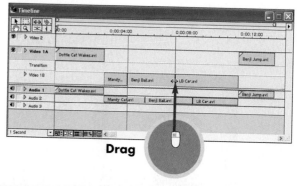

Editing in the Monitor Window

Until now, you have been editing in the Timeline window with a drag-and-drop method, using the mouse to insert, move, adjust, and delete clips. You also have been operating on entire clips or groups of clips. But Premiere supports an alternative editing method with the Monitor window that provides precise placement of clips.

You expand the Monitor window to trim your source clips, specify destination times in the Timeline window, and then make edits using efficient pushbutton (or keyboard) controls. You also can easily edit at arbitrary points in the program, including within and spanning multiple clips.

You can mix and match editing styles at any time, dragging clips to arrange them, and then using the Monitor window controls for precise adjustments. Premiere also simplifies window organization and layout with the Workspace menu options, so you can switch from the A/B Editing organization used throughout this book to this Single-Track Editing organization style more often used by video professionals.

How to Use the Monitor Display

In the A/B Editing workspace layout, the Monitor window displays the Program view so that you can view the current layout assembled in the Timeline window. You can play through the entire program on the Timeline using all the same controls and keyboard commands that are used in the Clip window. You can also display overlaid safe margins on the Monitor window to avoid working too close to the edges of the frames.

1 Open a Project

Start Premiere and open a project with some clips on the **Timeline**. To restore the windows and palettes to the default layout, choose **Window**, **Workspace**, **A/B Editing**.

Click

2 View the Monitor Window

The **Monitor** window is labeled Program at the top right because it displays the entire program currently laid out on the **Timeline**. As in the **Clip** window, use the **VCR controls** to play through the **Timeline**, or use the cursor control keys or keyboard shortcuts (see Part 9, "Trimming and Reusing Clips").

3 Show the Safe Margins

Click the triangle in the upper-right corner to open the **Monitor window** menu and select **Safe Margins for Program Side**.

Click

④ View the Safe Margins

Premiere displays a *safe zone* overlay on the **Monitor** window. Television sets typically do not display the entire video image but instead tend to *overscan* the display to cut off the image at the edge of the screen. The outer rectangle marks the safe area for action in the scene, and the inner rectangle marks the safe area for displaying titles on overscanned displays.

⑤ Open the Monitor Window Options

Click the triangle button to open the Monitor window menu and select **Monitor Window Options**.

⑥ Set the Safe Margins

Premiere displays the Monitor Window Options dialog. Use the Safe Margins section to resize the safe margins overlay, reflecting the type of display on which you expect your production to be viewed. Click **OK** when finished.

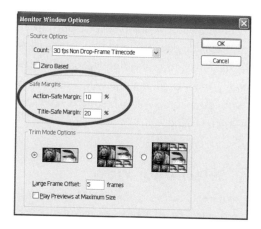

How-to Hint

Safe Margins

Use the safe margins as guidelines for editing your material, especially if you expect it to be viewed on overscanned television displays. To be sure that your viewers see what you intend, keep the important action in the scene within the outer rectangle, and keep text overlays within the inner region. If you are editing for viewing only on computers or on the Web, overscan is not an issue, and you can use the whole frame.

How to Set Up the Dual View Display

The Monitor window has a second part. In the dual view display, you can view and trim source clips in the Source view instead of needing to open separate Clip windows. And, to fit the Monitor window's editing style, you also can set the Premiere workspace for Single-Track Editing.

1 Select Dual View

Click the triangle button to open the **Monitor window** menu and select **Dual View**, or click the **Dual View** button at the top of the **Monitor** window.

Click

2 Adjust the Monitor Window

Premiere expands the **Monitor** window to dual view, with the Program area on the right and a Source area on the left for viewing and trimming source clips. (Move or close any palettes that are open over the expanded window.)

3 Load a Source Clip

Click a clip in the **Project** window and drag it to the Source section of the **Monitor** window.

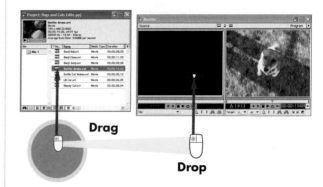

Drag

Drop

④ View the Source Clip

Premiere loads the clip into the Source view and displays its name in the **Select Source Clip** menu at the bottom left of the window. Use the VCR controls to play part way into the clip.

⑤ Select the Single-Track Editing Workspace

Choose **Window**, **Workspace**, **Single-Track Editing**.

Click

⑥ View the Single-Track Editing Workspace

Premiere adjusts the window layout to accommodate the dual-view **Monitor** window. It also collapses the **Timeline** window for single-track editing, showing a single row per track, without a separate transition track.

How-to Hint

Single-Track Editing

Single-track editing fits the style of professional video editors. It provides precise and efficient control by setting source and destination points and then clicking a single button (or using the keyboard equivalents).

Alternating Tracks in A/B Editing

In the A/B editing layout, you alternate clips between the Video 1A and 1B tracks and add transitions between them. As you edit, this alternating sequence may break down with two adjacent clips on the same track. You can switch to the single-track layout and drag a transition between the two clips. Premiere then rearranges the track layout, and you then can switch back to the A/B layout.

Even in single-track mode, click on the **Track Mode** icon to the right of the track name to expand the Video 1 track to see separate video and transition tracks as in the A/B editing layout.

How to Use the Monitor Source View

With the dual-view Monitor window, you can view and trim clips directly in the Source view and switch quickly between clips. You can prepare clips from bins in the Project window and edit clips already added to the Timeline window. Premiere also provides the option to still view individual clips at full size in a Clip window.

1 Open the General Preferences

Choose **Edit**, **Preferences**, **General and Still Image**.

2 Set the Open Movies Option

Premiere displays the General and Still Image section of the Preferences dialog. Uncheck **Open Movies in Clip Window** to have clips open in the Source view of the **Monitor** window, and not in an individual Clip window (as in the A/B Editing workspace). Click **OK** when finished.

3 Open a Project Clip

Double-click a new clip in the **Project** window.

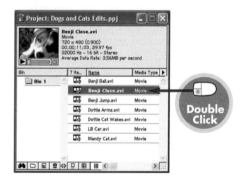

④ View the Source Clip

Premiere opens the clip in the **Source** view of the **Monitor** window, and not in a new clip window.

⑤ Open a Timeline Clip

Double-click a clip on the **Timeline** to open it, or (**Ctrl+click**) [**Right+click**] a clip and then choose **Open Clip** from the pop-up context menu.

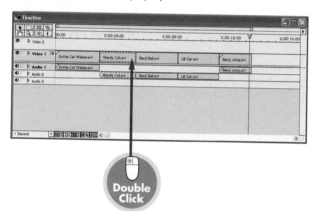

Double Click

⑥ View the Timeline Clip

Premiere loads the clip into the Source view of the **Monitor** window. Its timecode is displayed in the **Select Source Clip** menu at the bottom left of the Source view. Premiere also shows the extent of the clip within the entire program in the jog tread area at the bottom of the Program view.

How-to Hint

Viewing Source Clips

You can override the current **Open Movies in Clip Window** option by pressing (**Option**) [**Alt**] while you double-click. Also you can choose how to view a clip in the **Project** window; (**Ctrl+click**) [**Right+click**] the clip and then choose **Open in Source Monitor** or **Open in Clip Window** from the pop-up context menu.

Multiple Source Clips

You can add a group of clips to the **Select Source Clip** menu by selecting them in the **Project** window and double-clicking or dragging them into the **Source** view.

How to Trim in the Monitor Window

The Source view of the Monitor window has the same kinds of trim controls and menu options that you have seen in the Clip window. You can create instances of clips with different trim settings to add to the Timeline, and change the trim settings of clips already on the Timeline.

① View a Project Clip

Double-click a clip in the **Project** window to load it into the Source view of the **Monitor** window, or click the **Select Source Clip** menu at the bottom left of the **Source** view to switch between clips that you have loaded recently.

② Trim the Source Clip

Click the Source view **VCR controls** to play the clip. Use the trim controls to set the source trim points to a very short duration (that is, around **1:00**). You can **Set**, **Go to**, and **Clear** markers in the Source view by using the **Marker**, **Mark In**, and **Mark Out** button controls, respectively, or by using the **Clip Marker** commands in the pop-up context menus or **Clip** menu.

③ Add the Clip to the Timeline

Drag the trimmed clip from the **Source** window to the **Timeline** and add it to the current program.

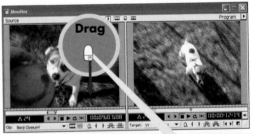

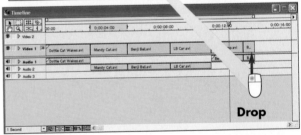

④ View the Clip from the Timeline

Double-click the clip in the **Timeline** to view it in the Source view. Premiere displays just the trimmed section of the clip in the Source view. The clip name is displayed in the **Select Source Clip** menu with the associated starting timecode in the **Timeline**.

⑤ Trim the Clip on the Timeline

Use the trim controls in the Source view to set new In and Out points.

⑥ Apply the Trim

Click the **Apply** button at the top of the **Source** view of the **Monitor** window to apply the new trim points to the clip on the **Timeline**.

Click

How-to Hint

Master Clip

Premiere keeps track of multiple instances of the same master clip as you trim and edit a clip, and reuse the same clip with different settings. As a result, instances of the same clip name can occur several times in the **Select Source Clip** menu.

To view the original master clip, choose **Open Master Clip** from the pop-up context menu (or the Clip menu).

How to Edit with the Monitor Window

The full power of the dual-view Monitor window comes from the capability to precisely control how clips are inserted and deleted in the Timeline. By selecting source and destination trim and edit points, you can use the Premiere edit controls to insert and delete, not just individual clips but also within clips and across multiple clips on the Timeline.

1 Trim the Source Clip

Start a new project with clips on the **Timeline**, and then load a clip into the Source view of the **Monitor** window. Trim the clip to a short duration (that is, around 1:00). You can disable individual tracks by clicking the **Take Video** or **Take Audio** buttons at the bottom of the Source view (as marked by a red diagonal line).

2 Set the Insertion Point

Position the edit line in the **Timeline** window to specify the insertion point for the clip. If needed, use the controls in the Program view of the **Monitor** window to move to an exact timecode. The insertion point can be at any place in the **Timeline**, including the middle of another clip.

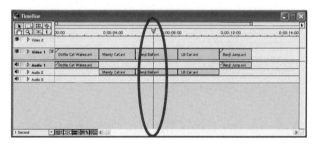

3 Set the Destination Tracks

Click the Video 1 and Audio 2 video and audio track names in the Timeline to select the destination tracks. Premiere highlights the selected tracks with the names in bold and the header region grayed.

④ Set the Destination Targets

Alternatively, you can open the **Select Video Target** and **Select Audio Target** menus in the **Monitor** window to specify the destination tracks. Choose **None** to disable the corresponding tracks. Premiere also highlights the selected tracks in the Timeline.

⑤ Insert at the Edit Line

Click the **Insert** button under the **Source** view to insert the clip at the current edit line position. (You also can type a comma (,) as a keyboard shortcut, or choose **Insert at Edit Line** from the pop-up context menu or **Clip** menu.)

⑥ View the Insertion

Premiere inserts the specified tracks of the source clip into the destination tracks and shifts over the existing contents of the **Timeline**. If the insertion point is in the middle of a clip, that clip is cut into two pieces.

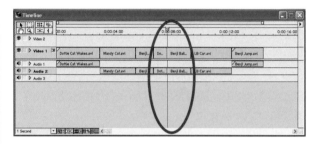

⑦ Overlay at the Edit Line

Undo the insert operation and then click the **Overlay** button under the **Source** view to overlay the clip at the current edit line position. (You also can type a period [.] as a keyboard shortcut, or choose **Overlay at Edit Line** from the pop-up context menu or **Clip** menu.)

8 View the Overlay

Premiere overlays the specified source tracks onto the destination tracks, on top of the existing contents of the **Timeline**. If the insert point is in the middle of a clip, portions of that clip will be replaced.

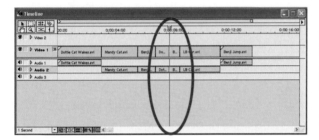

9 Set an Insertion Marker

Undo the overlay operation and then set an In point marker in the **Timeline** window to select the destination. You can **Set**, **Go to**, and **Clear** markers in the **Timeline** by using the **Marker**, **In**, and **Out** buttons under the Program view of the **Monitor** window (or by pressing the **I** and **O** keys).

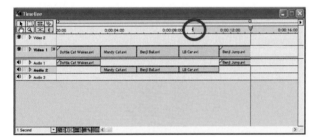

10 Insert at the Marker

Premiere displays the current In point under the Program view of the **Monitor** window. Click the **Insert** (or Overlay) button under the **Source** view. Premiere inserts (or overlays) the source clip in the **Timeline**, aligned to the specified In (or Out) point in the **Timeline**.

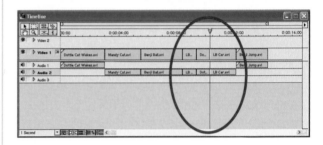

11 Set the Delete Region

Undo the insert operation and then set both an In and an Out point in the **Timeline**.

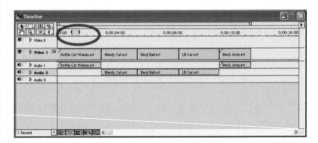

⑫ Lift Delete

Premiere displays the current trim region under the Program view of the **Monitor** window. Click the **Lift** button under the **Program** view.

⑬ View the Deletion

Premiere deletes the specified frames from the **Timeline** between the In and Out point and leaves the rest of the program unchanged with a gap in it.

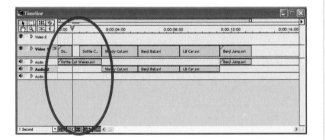

⑭ Extract Delete

Undo the delete operation and then click the **Extract** button (to the right of Lift) under the Program view of the **Monitor** window. Premiere ripple deletes the specified frames from the **Timeline** between the In and Out point, and shifts over the rest of the program to fill the gap.

How-to Hint

Timeline Markers

You can use markers in the **Timeline** window for more than setting In and Out points for insertions and deletions. You can mark important edit points and add comments to them.

You even can create Web Links that can be embedded in some exported movie formats and can cause an automatic jump to a Web address when the movies are played in a Web page.

How-to Hint

Three- and Four-Point Edits

By setting In and Out points in the **Source** and **Program** views, you can use the **Monitor** window controls to precisely determine where and how frames are inserted into the **Timeline**. In a three-point edit, you set any three markers; Premiere determines the fourth to match the duration. In a four-point edit, you set all four markers; Premiere displays a warning if the durations do not match.

Track Settings

The effect of these **Monitor** window editing operations on the destination tracks and the entire program are controlled by a number of settings. The On Insert section in the Timeline Window Options dialog specifies whether an insertion affects the target tracks, or all the tracks in the **Timeline**.

Task

12

Adding Titles

Premiere 6.5 includes the new Adobe Title Designer to design complex broadcast-quality titles for video productions. The Title Designer is a specialized text and graphics editor for creating and laying out titles. It can be used to create both main title screens and titles overlaid with transparency on video clips.

With the Title Designer, you can create text and graphic objects with sophisticated control over attributes and styles, including text along a curved path. You also can create titles with text in motion, for rolling or crawling credits.

Adobe provides more than 100 predefined templates, or you can customize your own styles and designs. You can save and use titles like any other clip in your projects.

Even with all this great flexibility, try to keep your titles relatively simple so that they are easy to read. Use fewer and larger words, with simple bold fonts, colored and shadowed to stand out well from the background.

How to Create Titles

The Premiere Title Designer window includes a main Drawing Area and a Toolbox with text and graphic drawing tools, and a Properties area with object attributes. You also can overlay the title design over a clip in your production to use in positioning the design.

1 Open a Title Window

Open the **File** menu and choose **New**, **Title**.

Click

2 Select the Type Tool

Premiere opens an empty **Title Designer** window Click to select the **Type** tool (with a "T" icon) at the top left of the Toolbox.

Click

3 Type a Title

Click inside the window and type a few lines of text Click the **Selection tool** (arrow) when finished to leave the new text object selected.

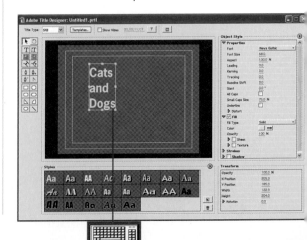

④ Change the Text Style

Click a text box in the **Styles** area to apply different predefined styles to the text. The **Object Style** and **Transform** areas on the right display the properties for the selected object. Use the **Styles** pop-up menu to manage your own style libraries.

Click

⑤ Change the Video Background

Make sure the **Show Video** box is checked to show the title design against the current video frame in the Timeline. Click and drag the timecode hot text control to show a different frame. Click the **Sync to Timeline** button to show the frame currently at the edit line.

Drag

⑥ Save and View the Title

Choose **File**, **Save** to save the current title design. Premiere adds it to the current project as a still image with alpha channel. Drag the title to the Video 2 track in the **Timeline** to view it overlaying your video.

Drag

Premiere 6.0 Titles

Premiere 6.5 still includes the **Premiere 6.0 Title** window to open old title files. You then can copy them into the new **Title Designer**.

Sharing Titles

You can open multiple copies of the **Title Designer** and access them through the **Window** menu. Titles are independent files that you can save and then import into your projects like any other clip. Titles are created at the resolution of the current project settings.

How to Use Templates

The Adobe Title Designer includes more than 100 templates to help you design titles. These are organized into various themes with appropriate design styles and background art, and include variations in positioning and layout (such as framed, or lower and upper third).

1 Display the Template Dialog

Click the **Templates** button (or choose **Title**, **Templates**) to display the Templates dialog.

2 Choose a Title Template

Click the triangle icons to explore the nested menus of predefined template categories. Click a template name to view a preview thumbnail image. Choose a "title" template for a full-screen title.

3 Choose a Frame Template

Choose a "frame" template to use as an overlay, with the center of your video showing through a frame.

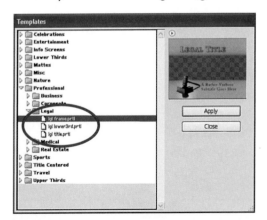

4 Choose an Overlay Template

Choose a "lower," "upper," or "centered" template to use as an overlay, with text positioned over the full video frame. Choose a "list" template for a title with additional lines of text.

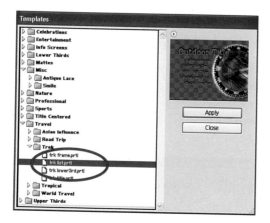

5 Create Custom Templates

Click to open the **Title Designer** window menu. Use Save and Import to create your own templates from titles. You also can set the **Restore Default Template, Rename Template,** and **Delete Template**.

6 Apply a Template

Finally, click **Apply** to apply the selected template to the current title. You then can add your own customizations by editing the sample text.

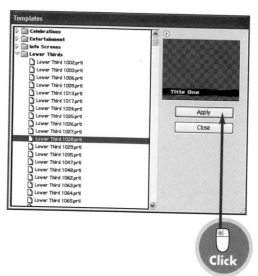

How-to Hint

Apply Templates First

When creating a new title, first apply a template and then add any additional text and graphics. Applying a template deletes any existing objects in the title.

Matte Templates

Use the **Matte Letterbox** and **Matte Pillbox** templates to frame the video in a widescreen (horizontal) or pillbox (vertical) black matte.

Safe Area

When displaying your projects on overscanned television displays, part of the edges may not be visible. Therefore, you should keep your text within the **Safe Title** and **Safe Action Margins** shown as rectangles near the edges of the Drawing area. Use **Title**, **View** to display these aids.

How to Add Text and Graphics

The Adobe Type Designer provides tools for creating text and a variety of graphics objects in the Drawing area. Text can have horizontal or vertical orientation, and an object's shape can be adjusted after it is created.

① Add Vertical Text

Click to select the **Vertical Type tool** (with the vertical arrow), click in the Drawing area, and type some text. Click the **Selection** tool when finished.

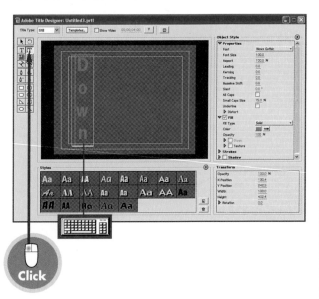

② Add a Text Paragraph

Click to select the **Horizontal** or **Vertical Paragraph tool** (in the next row). Click and drag in the Drawing area to create a rectangular text box, and then type some text. The text wraps within the enclosing box.

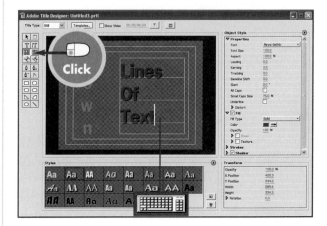

③ Create Rectangle Shapes

Use any of the Rectangle tools to draw filled objects: **Rectangle**, **Round Rectangle**, **Round-Corner Rectangle**, and **Clipped-Corner Rectangle**. Press **Shift** as you draw to constrain the aspect ratio, or press (**Option**) [**Alt**] to draw from the center.

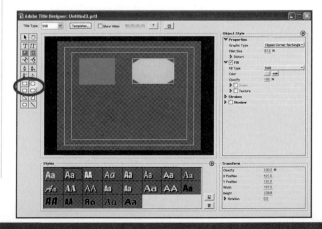

④ Create Circular Shapes

Use the **Wedge tool** and **Arc tool** to draw slices of objects. Use the **Ellipse tool** and **Line tool** to draw basic shapes. Drag across the edges, or drag diagonally across the corner points to flip the shape as you draw.

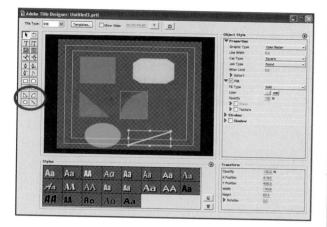

⑤ Change a Shape

To change an object's shape, (**Control+click**) [**Right+click**] and choose a shape option under **Graphic Type** in the pop-up context menu.

Click

⑥ View the New Shape

The selected object is changed to the specified shape. You then can adjust the new shape.

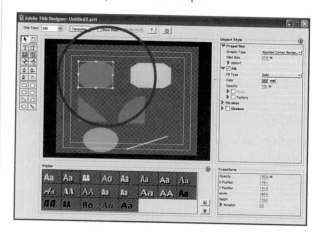

How-to Hint

Changing Text Orientation

To change text orientation, choose **Title**, **Orientation**, and select **Horizontal** or **Vertical**.

Flipping Objects

To flip an object, click it with the **Selection tool** and then drag a side or corner across the object.

How to Edit and Lay Out Objects

With the Adobe Type Designer, you can change a text or graphics object's position, size, and orientation. You also can use tools to adjust the layout of a group of objects.

1 Select Multiple Objects

To select multiple objects, use the **Selection tool** to click and drag a selection rectangle over a group of objects. Press **Shift** and click to add or remove individual objects from the current selection. The Type Designer displays a rectangular selection frame around the extent of all currently selected objects.

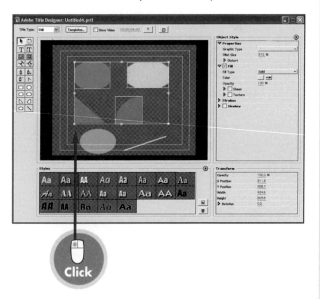

2 Move or Delete a Object

To move an object, choose the **Selection tool**, and then click in the interior of the object and drag it to a new location. Press **(Delete) [Backspace]** to delete the selected object (or objects).

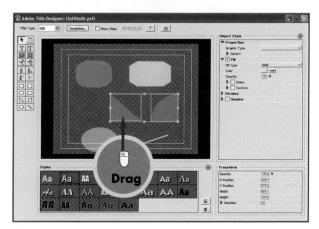

3 Resize an Object

To resize an object, hold the cursor over a box at the corner or side, and when the cursor becomes a scale icon (straight arrows), click and drag to resize the object.

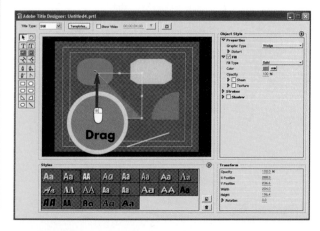

4 Rotate an Object

To rotate a text object, hold the cursor just outside a corner box, and when the cursor becomes a rotate icon (curved arrows), click and drag to rotate the object.

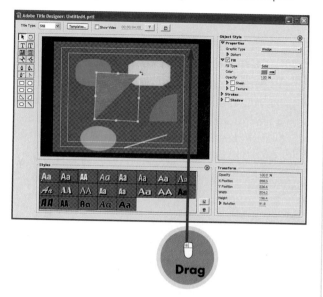

5 Layer Objects

Choose **Arrange** and select from the pop-up context menu to work with layered objects placed on top of each other.

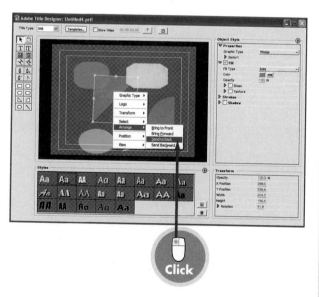

6 Align and Distribute Objects

Choose **Position** to position the selected object relative to the Drawing area. Choose **Align** or **Distribute Objects** to line up or evenly space the selected objects within the Drawing area, according to a horizontal or vertical layout.

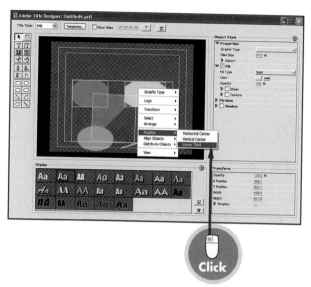

Rotate Tool

You can also use the **Rotate tool** (next to the Selection tool) to rotate the currently selected object or group of objects.

Precise Control

Use the **Transform** properties to view and set object position, size, and rotation values (or use the menu options under **Title, Transform**). Click and drag an underlined hot text value to change it (or click and type a new value). Or select **Transform** from the **Title** or pop-up context menus.

How to Format Text

Premiere provides extensive text formatting and typographic controls in the Title Designer, including text fonts and attributes, kerning and baseline, fills and blends, and even sheen and textures. Use a shadow to have the text stand out from the background.

1 Select Some Text

Use the **Selection tool** to select an entire text object, or use a **Text tool** to select only a group of adjacent characters.

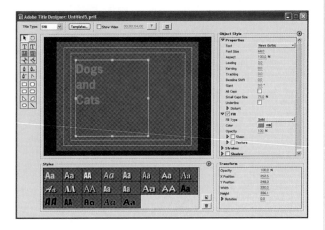

2 Choose the Font

In the **Properties** section at the top of the of the Object Style area, click the **Font** menu to select a different font (or use the pop-up context menu). Click and drag the underlined **Font Size** hot text value to change it (or click and type a new value).

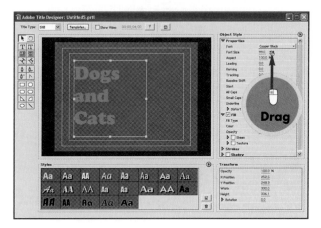

3 Change the Font Style

Use the Properties values to change the font style to **Small Caps** or **All Caps**, or to **Slant** or **Underline** the text. Use **Aspect** to make the text narrow or widen the text.

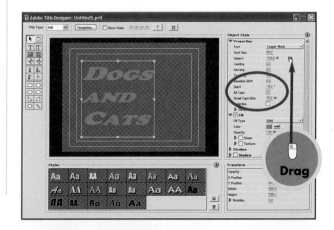

④ Distort the Text

Click to open the **Distort** options. Adjust the **X** and **Y** hot text values to manipulate the letter shapes.

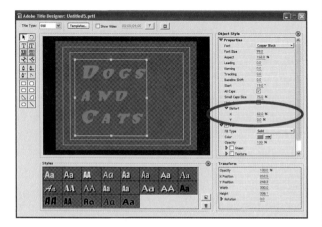

⑤ Adjust the Text Layout

Use **Tracking** to change the spacing between characters, and Kerning to adjust specific character pairs. Use **Leading** to change the spacing between lines, and **Baseline Shift** to raise or lower the characters. Also use the pop-up context menu to choose a **Type Alignment** and **Word Wrap**.

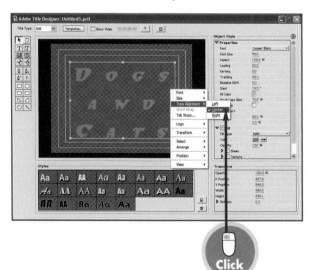

⑥ Add a Shadow

Click the **Shadow** check box to enable it. Click the **color chip** to set the shadow color from the Color Picker dialog. Set the shadow's **Opacity** against the background, the **Angle** and **Distance** offset from the text, and the **Size** and **Spread**.

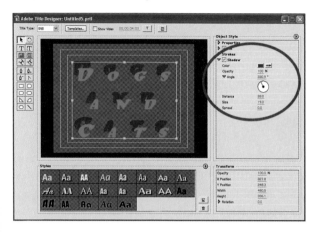

How to Set Color and Texture

The Adobe Type Designer provides extensive control over the fill color, transparency, and design of both text and graphic objects, as well as individual characters. Objects also can be textured with a still image.

1 Set the Fill Color

Select an entire object, or a group of characters, and enable and open the **Fill** properties. Click the **color chip** to set the fill color from the Color Picker dialog. Click and drag to adjust the **Opacity** value to make the object translucent.

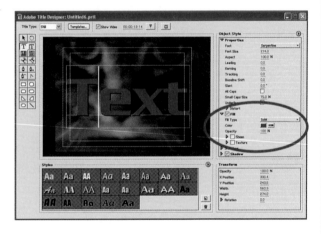

2 Select the Fill Style

Click the **Fill Type** menu to select a fill type and display its associated options. Use **Eliminate** to specify no fill or shadow. Choose **Ghost** to specify that only the shadow be drawn, but not the fill.

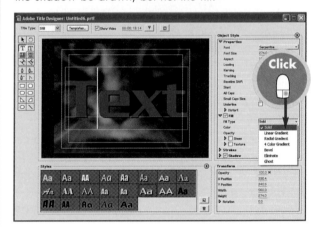

3 Set a Color Gradient

Use a **Linear Gradient** fill for a smooth transition between two colors. Use **Radial Gradient** for a circular gradient, or **4-Color Gradient** to fill from four corners. Click a **color chip** to set the Stop Color and Opacity. Set the gradient Angle and have the pattern Repeat.

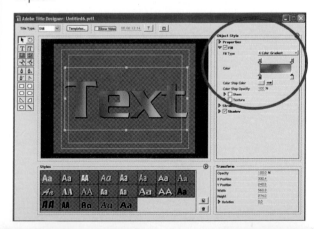

④ Add a Beveled Edge

Use a **Bevel** fill to add a beveled edge around the background of the object. Adjust the **Color**, **Opacity**, **Balance**, and **Size** of the Highlight and Shadow areas. Click **Lit** to add a Light effect, and adjust the **Light Angle** and **Light Magnitude**.

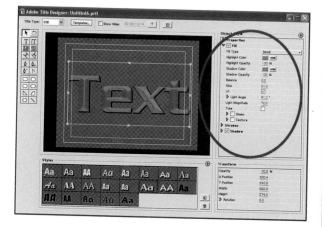

⑥ Add Outline Strokes

Click **Strokes** to add outline strokes around the inner or outer edge. The strokes then can be filled in different styles, even with a sheen and texture. Use the **Object Style** pop-up menu to add, delete, and reorder the strokes.

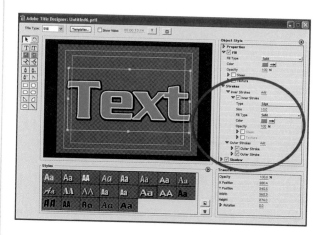

⑤ Add a Sheen

Click **Sheen** to add a streak of colored light across the object. Adjust the **Color**, **Opacity**, **Size**, **Angle**, and **Offset** from the center.

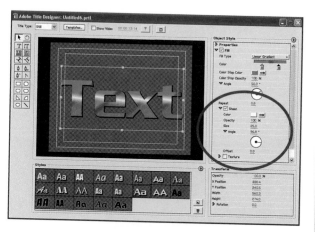

⑦ Fill with a Texture

Click **Texture** to map an image onto the object. Click the texture chip to select a bitmap or vector image file from the Load Texture dialog. Flip and rotate the texture with the object. Use **Scaling**, **Alignment**, and **Blending** to fit the texture to the object shape.

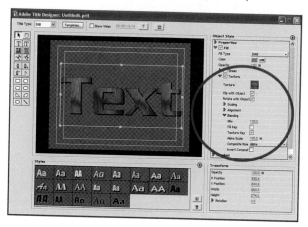

How to Use the Pen Tool

The Title Designer includes pen tools like Adobe Illustrator and Photoshop. Create objects from a set of anchor points, including straight lines and smooth curves. You also can create text that flows along a curved path.

❶ Create a Shape

Click to select the **Pen** tool, and then click to create a series of anchor point boxes that define a shape from connected lines. Finish by clicking on the **Selection tool** (to leave the shape open), or click the initial point to close the shape.

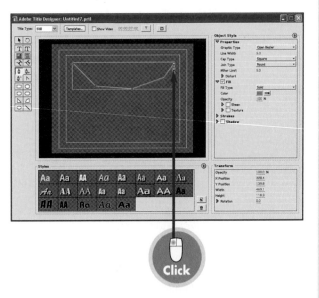

❷ Create a Curved Shape

To create a curved shape, click and drag at each anchor point to create direction lines that determine the shape and size of the curved segments at that point.

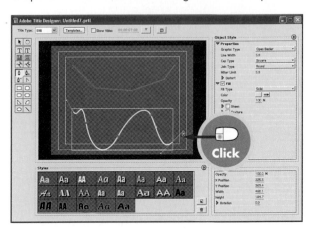

❸ Add or Remove Anchor Points

Select the **Add Anchor** tool (with the "+"), and then click to create a new anchor point between two existing points. Select the **Delete Anchor tool** (with the "-"), and then click to delete an anchor point. (Or just double-click with the **Pen tool**.)

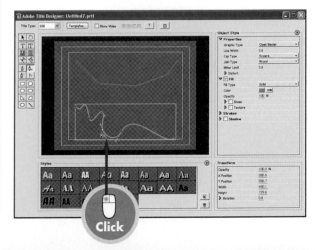

④ Adjust the Shape

To adjust the shape of an object, select the **Pen tool**, and then click to select an anchor point and drag it to a new position.

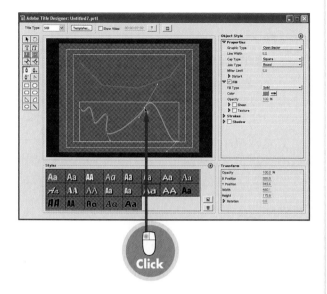

⑥ Change Anchor Point Type

Select the **Convert Anchor Point tool** and click and drag an anchor point to create new symmetric direction lines. Drag one end of a line to independently change both the angle and length. Click once to convert a curved line to straight.

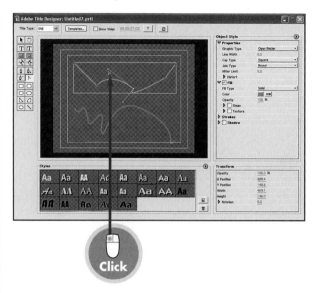

⑤ Adjust the Curves

Select the **Pen tool**, click to select an anchor point, and then drag an endpoint of the direction line to change the angle and size of the curve. The length of each end of the line can be set independently.

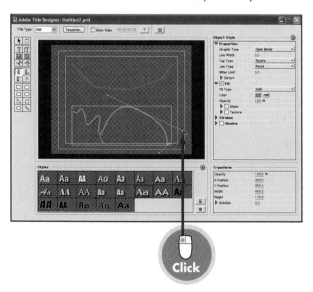

⑦ Draw Text on a Path

Click the **Text Path** tools to create a path with a pen tool and then type text along the path. The text is positioned along the top or right edge of the path, typically for a horizontal or vertical layout.

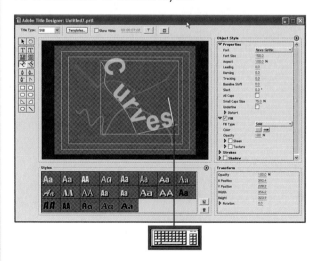

How to Create Rolling and Crawling Titles

The Title Designer can create titles that move across the screen, either rolling (moving vertically up or down) or crawling (moving horizontally left or right). When the Title clip is placed in a Timeline window, Premiere uses the duration of the clip to determine the speed that it moves.

1 Create a Crawling Title

Start a new title, and select **Crawl** from the **Title Type** menu in the top left of the window.

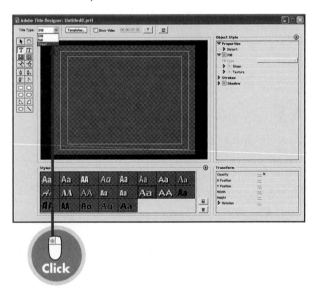

2 Enter Crawling Text

Select the **Type tool** and enter a long line of text to create a crawling title that scrolls left or right across the screen. The Drawing area window expands with a horizontal scrollbar to the horizontal crawling text.

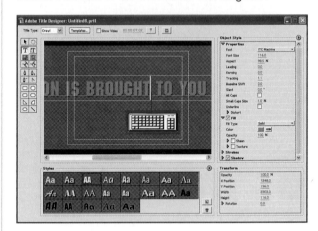

3 Enter Rolling Text

Select **Roll** from the **Title Type** menu, and enter multiple lines of text to create a rolling title that scrolls up or down the screen. The Drawing area window expands with a vertical scrollbar to view all the lines.

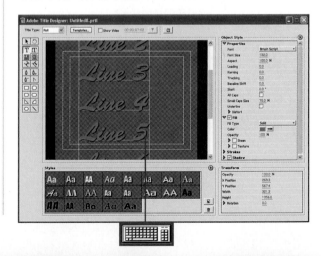

④ Align Lines with Tabs

Use **Tab** characters to consistently align the text in multiple lines. Choose **Title**, **Tab Stops** to set the position and justification of tab stops in your text. Choose **Title**, **View**, **Tab Markers** to view tab marker symbols in your text.

⑤ Set the Title Options

Choose **Title**, **Roll/Crawl Options**. Use the dialog to select whether the scrolling will **Start Off-Screen** and **End Off-Screen**. Enter the **Pre-Roll** number of frames to wait before starting the move, **Ease-In** and **Ease-Out** to accelerate into and decelerate down, and **Post-Roll** to stay motionless after ending. Then click **OK** to close the dialog.

⑥ Save and Preview the Title

Choose **File**, **Save** to save the title. Premiere automatically adds it in the open **Project** window. Drag the title to the Video 2 superimpose track to overlay the video in the Timeline. Then preview it in the **Monitor** window.

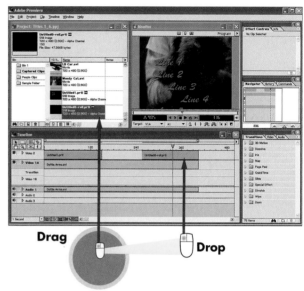

Drag   **Drop**

Editing Titles

To change a title, just double-click it in a **Bin** or the **Timeline**. Premiere opens the **Title Designer** window so that you can edit the title and then save the changes. Premiere updates the title file and your project.

Title Speed and Duration

The title rolls or crawls for the duration of the clip in the Timeline. If you reduce the duration, the title scrolls faster to complete the movement within the available time.

Task

13

Superimposing Images and Video Clips

In Part 4, "Adding Transitions Between Clips," you saw how to use the Transitions palette to create a variety of transition effects between consecutive clips, including dissolves, wipes, and zooms. You also can use transitions to show two clips at the same time with a split screen or inset.

After you have laid out your main program in the Video 1 track in the Timeline window, Premiere provides up to 97 additional *superimpose* tracks, starting in Video 2. These tracks can be layered on one another, each with transparency settings to show through to the underlying tracks. This is particularly useful for overlaying a title, graphical logo, or translucent watermark on top of a clip.

When superimposing tracks, you can use the Opacity rubberband line to to fade the entire clip in and out over time. You also can use the Transparency Settings dialog to define a *matte* shape as a transparent region in a clip, or to *key* the transparency on a color to *composite* overlaid areas of one clip on another. In this way, you can shoot a person talking or moving against a color screen, and then key away the background and to composite them into a totally different video clip.

With these tools, you also can display multiple clips with split-screen and picture-in-picture layouts.

How to Fade Overlay Tracks

When you add a clip to the Video 2 or other higher *superimpose track*, Premiere displays it on top of the program in the Video 1 tracks. You then must change the transparency of the superimpose track to see through to the underlying program tracks.

1 Add a Superimposed Image

Open a project and add a video clip to the **Timeline** in the Video 1A track. Then drag an image clip to the Video 2 clip to superimpose over the Video 1 track (for example, use the Veloman clip from the Sample Folder provided with Premiere).

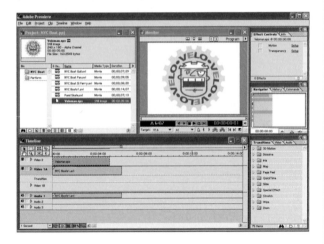

2 View the Opacity Rubberband

Click the triangle to the left of the Video 2 track name to expand the superimposed track. Then click the red **Display Opacity Rubberbands** icon under the track name to display the red Opacity rubberband line.

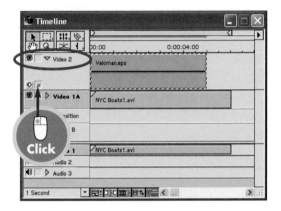

3 Adjust the Opacity

The red Opacity rubberband line at the top of the panel indicates that the superimposed image is fully opaque. Click the **Selection tool** (arrow icon) and click on the Opacity rubberband to create a handle (small red square). Drag the handle down to make the clip more translucent, or to the bottom of the panel to make it fully transparent.

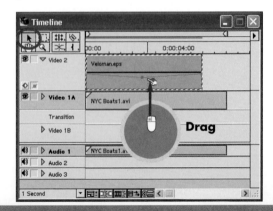

④ View the Info Palette

As you drag, Premiere updates the **Info** palette so that you can adjust the percentage opacity.

⑤ Create a Fade Effect

Add additional handles to the Opacity rubberband, for example, to fade the superimposed image in and out. Premiere adjusts the fade percentage over the duration of each line. Shorter and steeper lines cause faster fade effects.

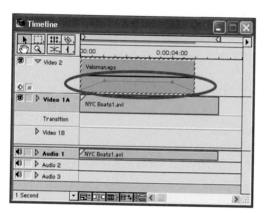

⑥ Preview the Result

Render-scrub through the **Timeline** to preview the effect: Press the (**Option**) [**Alt**] key, and then click and drag the edit line in the time ruler.

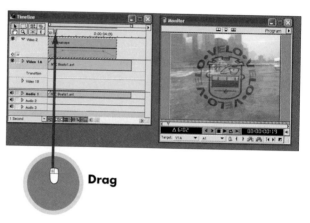

Drag

How-to Hint

Precise Percentages

To adjust the opacity percentage in exact 1% increments, hold down the **Shift** key as you drag the Opacity rubberband.

Delete Opacity Handles

To delete an Opacity handle, simply drag it outside the track.

Opacity Adjustments

Premiere provides additional Timeline tools for adjusting the Opacity rubberband. Use the **Fade Scissors tool** (scissors icon, with the Razor tools) to click and add two adjacent handles to create a sharp transition. Use the **Fade Adjustment tool** (up and down arrow icon, next to the **Zoom tool**) to drag an entire segment of the line up or down.

How to Use Transparency Keys

Even better than changing the transparency of an entire clip in a superimposed track, you also can *key* on a range of colors in a clip to cut out an object, title, or logo and lay it on top of the clip.

❶ Set the Transparency

Repeat the setup from Task 1, placing a simple image clip in the Video 2 superimpose track. Select the image clip and click **Setup** next to Transparency in the **Effect Controls** palette, or choose **Clip**, **Video Options**, **Transparency**.

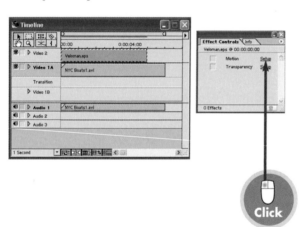

② Select the Key Type

Premiere displays the Transparency Settings dialog. Click the **Key type** drop-down menu and choose **Chroma** to key on a color value.

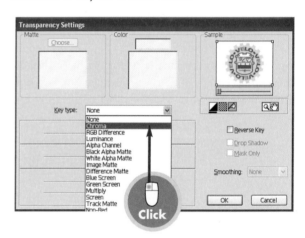

❸ Choose the Key Color

Click on the color swatch in the **Color** area to choose a key color, or click with the **eyedropper cursor** in the sample image.

④ Adjust the Keying Effect

Premiere previews the keying effect in the **Sample** area. Drag the sliders to adjust the effect: **Similarity** adjusts the range of matching colors, **Blend** controls the blending with the underlying clip, **Threshold** controls the amount of shadow in the color matching, and **Cutoff** darkens shadows up to the Threshold setting. Click the **Smoothing** drop-down menu to choose the sharpness or smoothing of edges.

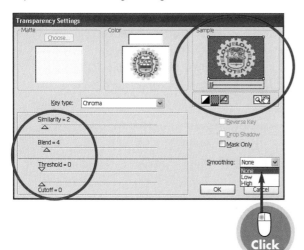

⑤ Preview the Keying Effect

Click the background icons under the **Sample** area to better view the keying effect. Click **Black/White** for a simple black or white background, **Checkerboard** for a checked pattern, and **Image** to display the underlying image.

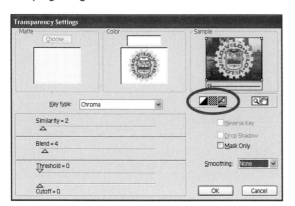

⑥ Examine the Transparency Effect

Drag the slider under the image to view the transparency effect across the duration of the clip. Click the **Zoom** icon and click in the sample image to zoom in for a more detailed view of the sample image, or hold down the (**Option**) [**Alt**] key and click to zoom out. Click the **Hand** icon to click and drag in the sample image. Click **OK** to close the dialog.

How-to Hint

Logos, Watermarks, and Titles

Use the Opacity rubberband to fade a watermark or title in and out, and the **Transparency** effects to overlay a logo with transparent regions.

Key Options

Some *key* types support the additional key options under the **Sample** area.

Use **Reverse Key** to reverse the opaque and transparent regions, and use **Drop Shadow** to add a gray shadow to help a superimposed title or graphic stand out better from the underlying clip.

How to Use Transparency Mattes

You can explicitly define a keying region using a matte image to define which portions of the clip are transparent. You can create an overlay image such as a logo with a matte stored with the image, or you can use a separate image as the matte for keying.

① Use an Alpha Channel Matte

Continuing from Task 2, display the Transparency Settings dialog. With the Chroma key set, all the white areas in the image are keyed out, including inside the logo. Click the **Key type** menu and choose **Alpha Channel**. Now only the area outside the logo is keyed out, because this image was prepared with an *alpha channel* using a tool like Adobe Photoshop or Illustrator.

② Use an Image Matte

Prepare a simple title image in an image editor such as Windows Paint, with plain, black text and graphics against a white background. Reopen the Transparency Settings dialog, click the **Key type** drop-down menu, and choose **Image Matte**. In the Matte section, click the **Choose** button and open the title file.

③ Preview the Image Matte

Premiere displays a thumbnail of the title in the **Matte** section and uses the non-white sections of the matte image to cut transparent areas in the superimposed track to see through to the underlying clip. Click **Reverse Key** to reverse the keying effect. Click **OK** to preview the matte effect in the Timeline.

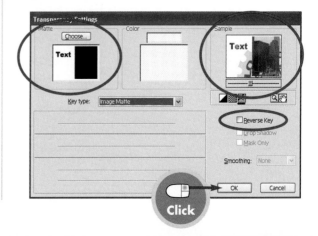

Click

④ Superimpose a Video Object

Delete the still image from the superimposed track, and drag a video clip to the Video 2 track, with a foreground object (or person) shot against a relatively solid background. Reopen the Transparency Settings dialog, click the **Key type** drop-down menu, and choose **Luminance** to key against the brightness of the background.

⑤ Key the Video Object

Adjust the **Threshold** and **Cutoff** sliders to mask out as much of the background as possible, without turning the entire foreground object transparent. Adjust the handles in the **Sample** area to create a garbage matte with only the center region of the image used with the foreground object.

⑥ Preview the Video Composite

Premiere displays the Transparency setting name on top of the clip in the superimposed track. Render-scrub through the **Timeline** to preview the effect. Depending on how accurately you were able to key, you should have created a ghostly person moving in the scene.

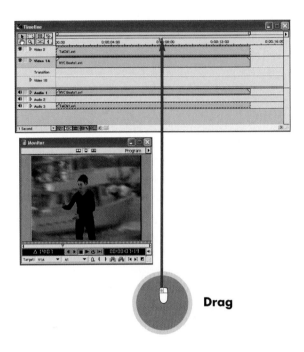

Drag

How-to Hint

Creating Mattes

You can create simple matte images with text and graphical shapes using the **Title** window. Or choose **File**, **New**, **Color Mattes** to create a solid color frame that can be used as a background image for titles.

Make a Split Screen

You can use the corner handles in the **Sample** area of the Transparency Settings dialog to create a split screen. Move the handles on one side of the thumbnail to the center of the screen, or use them to create a diagonal split instead.

Mixing Audio Tracks

Premiere can combine the visual effect of multiple video tracks with *transitions* (Part 4), *superimpositions* (Part 13), and *effects* (Part 15). You also can combine multiple audio tracks by *mixing* them together, for example, to add voice-over narration and background music. Premiere also provides audio effects to *sweeten*, or enhance and manipulate, the audio (Part 15).

Premiere helps you visualize audio clips with a *waveform* display in the Clip window or a Timeline window track, showing the relative strength of the sound over time. You then can adjust the volume of individual clips, cross-fade between clips, and pan or balance the sound between left and right stereo channels. You also can adjust the overall gain or volume of the entire production.

In addition, Premiere provides a separate Audio Mixer window to display and dynamically adjust the volume and pan settings for each channel from the Timeline. When Premiere processes your program for preview, play, or export, it applies the audio settings in a specific order.

First, it converts the audio based on the Audio Settings dialog (Task 1) and adjusts the stereo channels as set by the Audio Options menu (Task 5). Then it applies any audio effects (Part 15). Finally, it applies the volume and pan/balance settings for individual clips as set in the Timeline (Tasks 2 and 4), and then performs a gain adjustment for the overall program (Task 4).

How to Edit Audio Clips

Task 1

When you open an audio clip in a Clip window, Premiere provides an audio *waveform* display to help visualize the sound in the clip. Use the Audio Settings dialogs to convert audio clips between different formats, or to extract the audio channels from a video clip.

① Open a Project with Audio

Open a project with a variety of clips, including clips captured from DV and audio-only clips. Click an audio-only clip (such as the Music clip from the Sample Folder) in the **Project** window to select it, and then choose **Clip**, **Open Clip**, or (**Control+click**) [**Right+click**] and choose **Open in Clip Window**.

② Play and Edit the Audio Clip

Premiere opens a **Clip** window with the audio waveform. Use the **Zoom** button at the bottom left of the window to zoom the display. Use the VCR controls to play the clip and the In and Out marker controls to trim it (the In and Out points are shown with green I and a red O marks). Choose **Clip**, **Properties** (or choose it from the pop-up context menu).

③ View the Audio Properties

Premiere displays a **Properties** window for the clip. Click to select a stereo clip captured in DV format (see Part 8, "Capturing and Using DV"), and also display its properties. The audio-only Music clip is recorded in mono with 8-bit samples. This DV clip is recorded in stereo with 16-bit samples.

④ Export an Audio Clip

Close the **Properties** windows, click to select the DV clip from the **Project** window, and open it in a **Clip** window. Then choose **File**, **Export Clip**, **Audio** to export only the audio portion of the clip (see Part 6, "Exporting to Video and Audio Formats").

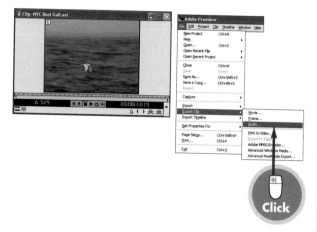

⑤ Set the Audio Export Settings

Premiere displays the Export Audio dialog. Navigate to the output folder and enter the output file name. Check the current audio export settings listed at the bottom left of the dialog. Click **Settings** to set the output audio file format.

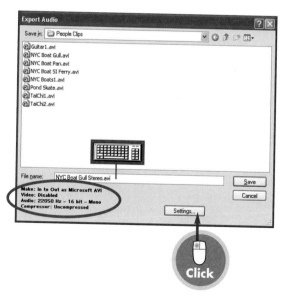

⑥ Save As Stereo or Mono

Choose the **File Type** (such as **Windows Waveform**) from the Export Audio Settings dialog, and then click the **Next** button to change the Audio settings. Use the **Format** list to save the audio in a **Stereo** (or **Mono**) format, and select the **Compressor** (such as **Microsoft ADPCM**). Click **OK** to close the dialog, and then click **Save** to save the audio-only file.

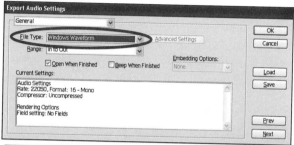

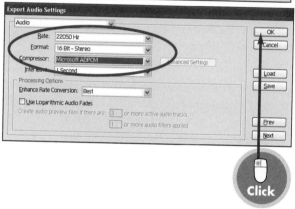

How-to Hint

Rate Conversion

Converting between different audio formats often requires a *rate conversion* or *resampling* between the different sample rates.

See the **Enhance Rate Conversion** list in the Audio Settings dialog.

Logarithmic Audio Fades

Use the **Use Logarithmic Audio Fades** option in the Project and Export Audio Settings dialogs to use more processing to replace simple linear volume changes with more natural nonlinear processing.

How to Adjust Audio Volume

In Premiere, rubberband lines are used for audio clips in the Timeline window to control their volume and pan/balance, similar to the Opacity rubberband line used for fading video clips (see Part 13). Use the red Volume rubberband line to adjust the volume within an individual clip, and to cross-fade between two overlapping clips in different tracks.

① Add an Audio Track

Open a project and add an audio clip to the **Timeline** window in the Audio 1 track (for example, you can use the Music clip from the Sample Folder provided with Premiere).

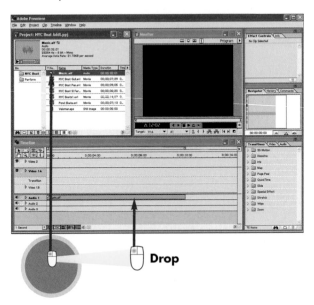

Drag

Drop

② Display the Audio Waveform

Click the triangle to the left of the Audio 1 track name to display the expanded audio track. Click the first **Show Audio Waveform** icon, if needed, to display the audio waveform in the **Timeline**. (This might require changing the **Draw audio when view is n Seconds or closer** option in the Timeline Window Options dialog.)

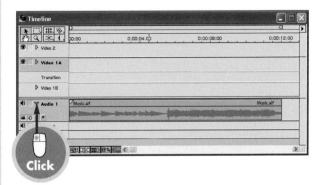

Click

③ Display the Volume Rubberband

Click the red **Display Volume Rubberbands** icon under the track name to display the red Volume rubberband line. The Volume rubberband runs through the center of the waveform, indicating that the volume is at 100% of the original setting for the clip.

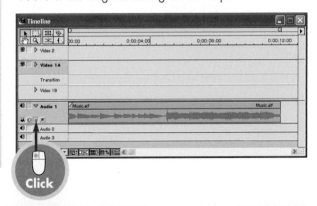

Click

④ Adjust the Volume

Click the **Selection tool** (arrow icon) and move the cursor over the Volume rubberband; it changes to a pointing finger with red plus and minus signs. Click on the line to create a handle (small red square), and drag the handle down (to 0%) to lower the volume at that point, or up (to 200%) to raise it. As you drag, the Info palette shows the **Fade Level** as a percentage.

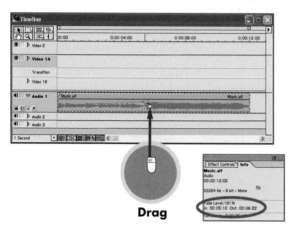

Drag

⑤ Fade In and Out

Add additional handles to the Volume rubberband, for example, to fade the volume up and then down over several segments. Premiere adjusts the fade percentage over the duration of each line. Shorter and steeper lines cause faster volume changes.

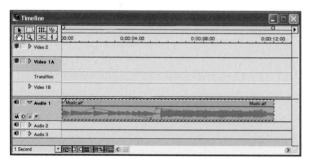

⑥ Adjust the Fade Effect

Premiere provides additional Timeline tools for adjusting the Volume rubberband. Use the **Fade Scissors tool** (scissors icon, with the Razor tools) to click and add two adjacent handles to create a sharp transition. Use the **Fade Adjustment tool** (up-and-down arrow icon) to drag an entire segment of the line up or down.

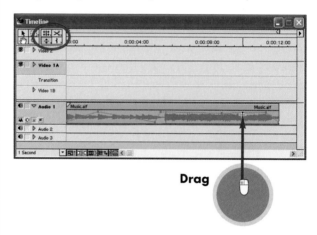

Drag

How-to Hint

Precise Percentages

To adjust the volume percentage in exact 1% increments, hold down the **Shift** key as you drag the Volume rubberband.

Delete Volume Handles

To delete a Volume handle, simply drag it outside the track.

Audio Edits

Use the **Fade Scissors tool** and **Fade Adjustment tool** for simple audio edits—for example, to cut out a small section of a clip.

How to Cross-Fade Audio Clips

Premiere's Cross-Fade tool enables you to automatically cross-fade between two overlapping audio clips, fading out the first while fading in the second. You also can cross-fade the audio between two adjacent video clips, even if they do not overlap, by performing a split edit.

1 Overlap Two Audio Clips

Clear the **Timeline** window and add two overlapping audio clips on different tracks, with one extending beyond the other. Click the triangle icon to to display the audio waveforms and click the red **Display Volume Rubberbands** icon to make it active (see Task 2).

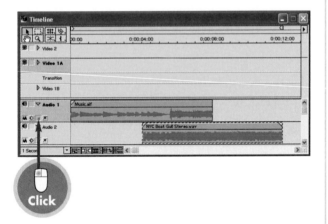

2 Select the Cross-Fade

Select the **Cross-Fade tool** (next to the **Zoom tool**). Click one of the clips to select it. Move the cursor over the second clip, and it changes to the cross-fade icon. Then click to select the second clip to be faded.

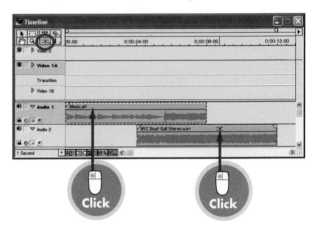

3 View the Cross-Fade

Premiere automatically adds volume handles to both clips, adjusted to fade out the volume of the first clip while fading in the second.

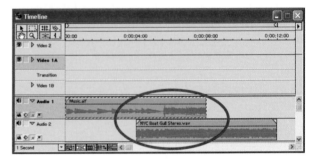

4 Overlap Video and Audio Clips

Clear the **Timeline** and add two adjacent video clips with audio. You can use a split edit to cross-fade the audio while cutting the video. First, click the **Toggle Sync Mode** button at the bottom of the **Timeline** window to unsync the video and audio tracks.

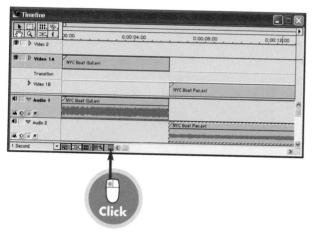

5 Perform a Split Edit

Click the **Selection tool** and extend the end of the first audio track to the right so that its Out point overlaps the second video clip. (Trim the clip's Out point, if needed, so that there is some extra material at the end.) This split edit is an L-cut, in which the audio Out point is extended beyond the video Out point so that the audio cuts after the video.

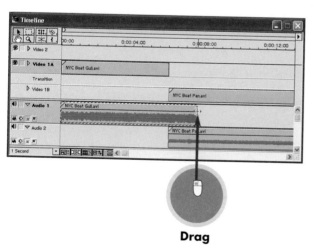

Drag

6 Perform the Cross-Fade

Next, click to select the **Cross-Fade tool** and then click the two audio clips. Premiere adjusts the volume handles of both clips to create the cross-fade effect where they overlap.

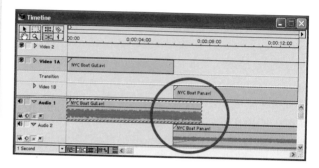

How-to Hint

J-Cuts

Another split edit is the *J-cut*, or *audio lead*. In a J-cut, the In point of the second clip overlaps the first so that the audio starts playing before the video as a lead-in to the visual cut.

Trimming for Cross-Fades

Split edits and cross-fades require trimming the In or Out points of the clips to provide some extra material at the ends to overlap with the neighboring clip.

Automate to Timeline

The Premiere Automate to Timeline function (see Part 4) also can automatically insert audio cross-fades.

How to Pan/Balance and Set Gain

The Pan controls (in blue) are for panning or balancing the audio. You pan the single channel of sound of a monophonic clip by setting its relative position from left to right, typically to match the position of the audio source in the video. You balance the two channels of a stereo clip between the left and right channels.

1 Add an Audio Clip

Clear the **Timeline** window and add an audio clip in the Audio 1 track. Click the triangle icon to expand the tracks to display the audio waveforms (see Task 2). Click the blue **Display Pan Rubberbands** button under the track name.

2 Display the Pan Rubberband

Premiere displays a blue Pan rubberband line through the audio waveform. Click the **Selection tool** and move the cursor over the blue Pan rubberband line; it changes to a pointing finger with left/right arrows.

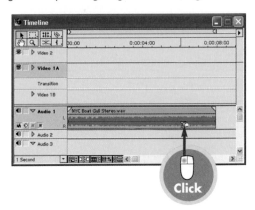

3 Adjust the Pan Rubberband

Click to add a handle to adjust the Pan rubberband line, and drag the handle up or down to pan or balance to the left or the right. Set a straight ramp from left to right (top to bottom) and then back again; then listen while you play the clip to confirm that your audio hardware is set up properly. As you drag the Pan rubberband line, Premiere displays the pan/balance percentage in the Info palette.

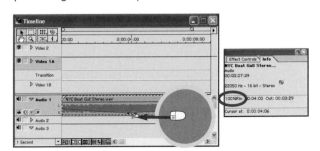

Drag

4️⃣ Adjust Overall Audio Gain

Choose **Clip**, **Audio Options**, **Audio Gain** (or (**Control+click**) [**Right+click**] and select **Audio Gain**).

5️⃣ Set the Audio Gain

Premiere displays the Audio Gain dialog. In the **Gain Value** field, type a percentage value for the overall gain. Enter a value greater than 100% to amplify the overall volume of the clip, or less than 100% to attenuate the clip, or make it quieter.

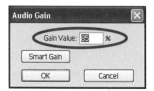

6️⃣ Automatically Adjust Audio Gain

Click **Smart Gain** to have Premiere automatically set the gain value, to boost the overall gain of the clip up to 200% so that the loudest part is at full volume. Click **OK** to close the dialog.

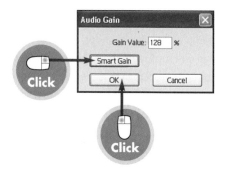

How-to Hint

Adjusting the Pan Rubberband Line

As with the Volume rubberband, specify precise percentages in 1% increments by pressing **Shift** as you drag the Pan rubberband line.

To remove a handle, drag it outside the track.

Mono and Stereo Projects

You must be editing a stereo project to edit across two channels. Use a **DV** preset, or change **Project Settings** under the **Audio** panel.

How to Use the Audio Mixer

The Audio Mixer window is used to automate the viewing and setting of volume and pan controls in real time as the program is playing. The Audio Mixer has VU volume meters, Pan/Balance control knobs, and Volume fader sliders for each audio track, and a master control for the overall program.

1 Open the Audio Mixer

Open a new Project and add a video clip with audio to the **Timeline** window, and a background audio clip to the Audio 2 track. Adjust both the volume and Pan rubberband lines for the two audio clips. Open the **Window** menu and choose **Workspace**, **Audio**.

2 Use the Audio Workspace

Premiere rearranges the workspace with the **Audio Mixer** window. (To just open the window, choose **Window**, **Audio Mixer**.)

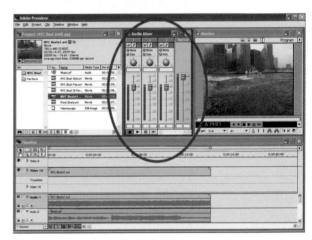

3 Play the Mixed Audio

Click the **VCR controls** at the bottom of the **Audio Mixer** to play through the **Timeline**. The Audio Mixer displays the audio level with a VU meter, and the master audio level in the rightmost column. The indicator above the VU meters turns red if the level is too high and would result in clipping, or distortion.

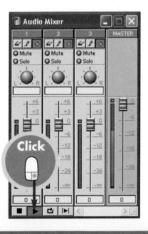

④ Play Individual Tracks

Click the **Mute** button for a track to silence it. Click the **Solo** button to listen to that track and mute all others that do not have Solo selected. You can watch the video in the **Monitor** window to synchronize the audio with the video.

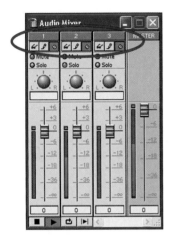

⑤ Adjust Stereo Channels

Choose **Clip**, **Audio Options** to adjust the channels of a stereo clip. Choose **Mute Left** or **Mute Right** to mute an individual channel, or **Swap Channels** to exchange the two channels. Choose **Duplicate Left** or **Duplicate Right** to use one channel for the entire clip. Choose **Normal** to restore the original audio settings.

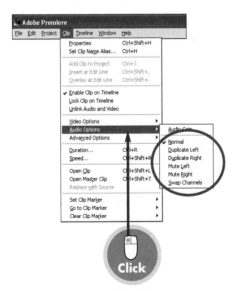

⑥ Read the Volume and Pan

Click the **Automation Read** button (eyeglasses icon) above the tracks in the **Audio Mixer** window, and then click the **Play** button. The Pan/Balance knob and Volume slider dynamically adjust to show the current settings at the edit line in the Timeline. (**Control+click**) [**Right+click**] in the title bar and choose **Audio Mixer Window Options**.

⑦ Record Volume and Pan Changes

In the Audio Mixer Window Options dialog, use the **Display Options** to customize the **Audio Fader** window to display the **Audio Tracks** or **Master Fader** controls.

Use the Automation Write Options to record your Audio Mixer adjustments to the Volume and/or Pan rubberband lines. (**Control+click**) [**Right+click**] the **Volume fader slider** in the **Audio Mixer** to **Gang** together multiple tracks to adjust simultaneously.

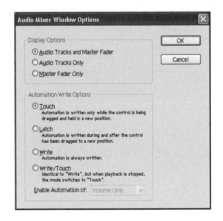

Task

Applying Audio and Video Effects

Premiere provides almost 80 built-in video effects and more than 20 audio effects for enhancing, improving, and distorting the clips in your productions with special effects. The available effects are listed in the Video Effects and Audio Effects palettes, organized into folders by category.

More than 30 of the video effects included with Premiere are Adobe After Effects plug-ins. If you also own After Effects, Adobe's professional animation, compositing, and effects program, it provides additional plug-ins that also can be used in Premiere.

As you edit in the Timeline window, Premiere displays the list of effects applied to each clip in the Effect Controls palette. You then can adjust the effect settings and view the results in the Monitor window. As with other controls in Premiere, you also can add multiple keyframes to each clip to modify the effect settings and have Premiere interpolate the settings from keyframe to keyframe along the clip.

How to Use the Effects Palettes

Premiere organizes the available video and audio effects into different categories in the Video Effects and Audio Effects palettes. Much like the Transitions palette (see Part 4, "Adding Transitions Between Clips"), you can customize these palettes by reorganizing the effects into folders. This makes it more convenient to find and apply your favorite effects to your productions.

1 Display the Effects Palette

Open a project with a variety of clips, and copy a video and an audio clip to the **Timeline** window. Choose **Window**, **Workspace**, **Effects**.

2 Review the Effects Workspace

Premiere reorganizes the palette windows to make more room for the **Effect Controls** palette at the top right of the window.

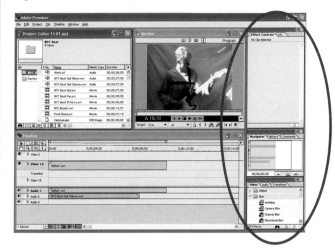

3 Expand Audio Effects Palette

Click the **Audio** tab to display the **Audio Effects** palette, with a collection of more than 20 predefined effects organized into categories as folders in the palette. Resize the window and click on the triangles to the left of the folders to expand them to show the included effects.

④ Review the Video Effects Palette

Click the **Video** tab in the Palette window (or choose **Window, Show Video Effects**). Premiere displays the **Video Effects** palette, with a collection of more than 70 predefined effects organized into categories.

⑤ Expand the Video Effects Palette

Click on the triangles to the left of the folders to expand them to show the included effects. Premiere includes both built-in video effects (with a filmstrip icon and the letter "V") and many Adobe After Effects effects (with the After Effects icon).

Click

⑥ Scroll Through the Effects

Click to open the **Effects** palette menu to choose **Expand all Folders** or **Collapse all Folders**. These options will help you scroll through the effects in the palette.

Click

How-to Hint

Customizing the Effects Palettes

Use the pop-up palette menu (or palette buttons) to customize the effects with **Create Folder**, **Rename Folder**, and **Delete Folder**. Choose **Hide Selected** and **Show Hidden** to hide and reveal effects to simplify the list. Then reorganize the effects as you like, and even drag your favorites into a new folder at the front of the list.

Finding Effects

You also can search for effects by name by choosing **Find** from the palette menu, or by clicking the **Find** button (binoculars icon) at the bottom of the window.

How to Apply Effects to Clips

Apply effects to clips in the Timeline window by simply dragging them from the Effects palettes. Use the Effect Controls palette to view and tweak the settings for each effect. You then can preview the results of the effects in the Monitor window.

❶ Add an Effect to a Clip

In the **Video Effects** palette, click on the triangle to expand the **Adjust** effects folder. Then click the **Posterize** effect, and drag it on top of the clip in the video track of the **Timeline** window.

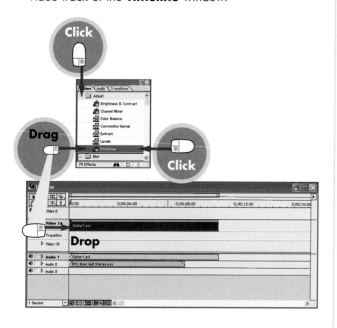

❷ Adjust the Effect Controls

Premiere displays the **Effect Controls** palette, with the **Posterize** effect and its controls. Drag the **Level** slider to a low number to strengthen the effect. Premiere provides a preview of the result of the effect in the **Monitor** window.

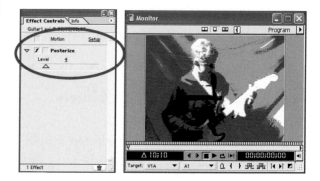

❸ Add Another Effect

Click to select the **Color Balance** effect in the **Adjust** folder of the **Audio Effects** palette, and drag it into the open **Effects Control** palette (or drag it onto the same clip in the Timeline). Premiere adds the **Color Balance** effect to the **Effect Controls** palette as a second effect to apply to the clip.

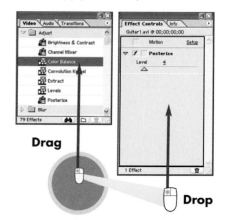

④ Set Up the Effect

You can click the **Effect Enabled** button ("f") to the left of an effect name to temporarily disable that effect for the clip. **Color Balance** is a Premiere effect, and not an After Effects effect, so click **Setup** to the right of the effect name to set its controls.

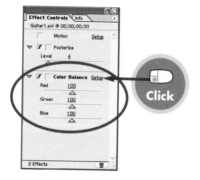

⑤ Adjust the Effect Settings

Premiere displays the Color Balance Settings dialog, with the available controls for the effect and a preview image. Drag the sliders to adjust the colors and then click **OK**.

⑥ Preview the Combined Effects

Premiere displays the result of applying both effects in the **Monitor** window. You can change the order of the effects in the list in the **Effect Controls** palette by clicking the triangle buttons to the left of each effect to collapse the list, and then dragging the effect to a new position in the list.

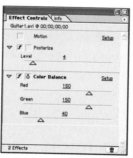

⑦ Edit and Preview the Effects

Click the arrow button to open the **Effect Controls** palette menu. Use **Remove Selected Effect** and **Remove All Effects From Clip** to delete effects from the clip. Use **Preview During Adjust** to update the **Monitor** window continuously while adjusting the effects controls. Use **Best Quality** to improve the visual quality of the effect preview.

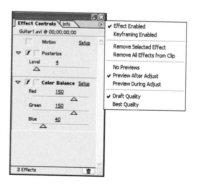

How to Use Keyframes

Premiere also can change the settings for each effect over time by interpolating the values from one time point to another. You can add multiple keyframes to the Timeline window to define points where the settings change, and Premiere will adjust the settings from one point to the next.

1 Expand the Video Tracks

Continuing from Task 2, click the triangle to the left of the Video 1A track to expand it. The Video 1A track is marked with the effect name and a blue line for setting keyframes.

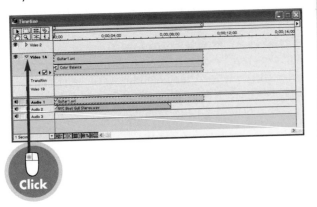

2 Add a New Keyframe

The clip has two keyframes, indicated by white boxes at each end, with the same settings over the entire clip. Click and drag the edit line in the clip, and then click the **Add/Delete Keyframe** box to the left of the track.

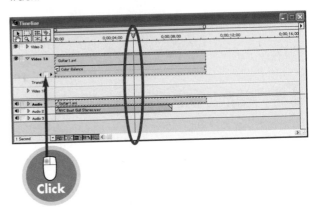

3 View the New Keyframe

Premiere adds a new keyframe at the edit line, indicated by a white diamond. The beginning and end keyframes can now be set independently. The **Add/Delete Keyframe** box is checked to indicate that the edit line is positioned on a keyframe. Use the Keyframe Navigator arrows to jump to the previous and next keyframe.

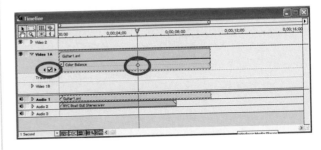

④ Change the Effect Settings

Premiere updates the first line of the **Effect Controls** palette to display the timecode for the current keyframe. It also displays a stopwatch icon in the **Enable Keyframing** box to the left of the effect name. You can then change the effect settings at the current keyframe, and view the result in the **Monitor** window.

⑤ Preview the Effect

Render-scrub through the **Timeline** to preview the effect. Watch as Premiere interpolates the effect values simultaneously for all the effects, in the **Effect Controls** palette and the **Monitor** window.

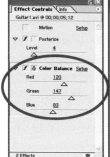

⑥ Select Other Effects for Keyframes

Click the effect pop-up menu to the left of the effect name on the keyframe line to select from multiple effects applied to the selected clip. Then add keyframes for the other effects, as desired.

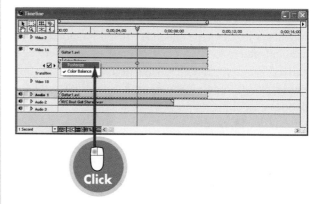

Click

Copying Effects

Use **Paste Attributes** in the **Edit** menu to copy effects from one clip to another. This copies the effects and settings, although the keyframe positions may need adjusting when copying to a clip with a different duration.

Moving Keyframes

Click and drag the diamond icon to move a keyframe to a different point in the clip. Drag the beginning and end keyframes into the clip to change the starting and ending time for the effect.

Removing Keyframes

Uncheck the **Add/Delete Keyframe** box to remove a single keyframe. Or drag the diamond icon off the keyframe line.

To remove all keyframes from a clip, select the clip, and then click the **stopwatch** icon in the **Effect Controls** palette.

How to Choose Audio Effects

Premiere provides more than 20 audio effects, including filters to clean or enhance the audio signal, and special effects to add more interest or detail to the sound. The available effects are organized into seven categories as folders in the Audio Effects palette. Here's a brief tour of the different audio effects.

1 Use Bandpass Effects

Use the effects in the **Bandpass** folder to remove specific frequencies from an audio clip. **Highpass** removes low frequencies such as hisses, and **Lowpass** removes high frequencies such as high-pitched whines. **Notch/Hum Filter** removes a specific frequency range, such as the hum from a power line.

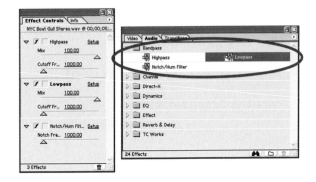

2 Use Stereo Channel Effects

Use the **Channel** effects to adjust the two channels of a stereo clip. **Fill Left** and **Fill Right** place the entire clip in the corresponding channel, and **Swap Left & Right** exchanges the two channels. Pan sets the pan/balance between the two channels, and **Auto Pan** pans between the two channels.

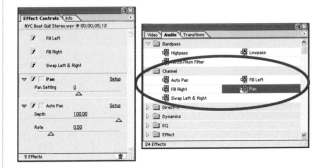

3 Use Dynamics Effects

Use the Dynamics effects to adjust the dynamic range (the difference between the loudest and softest sounds). **Boost** raises the apparent volume. **Compressor/Expander** provides more precise control over the dynamic range. Compress to raise soft sounds, or expand to increase the difference between volume levels. **Noise Gate** silences quiet passages by removing background noise.

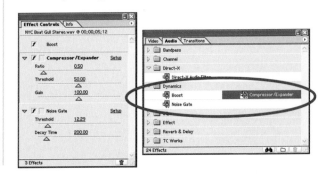

④ Use Equalization Effects

Use the **EQ** effects to adjust the tone and equalization of the audio. **Bass & Treble** boosts or weakens the low or high frequencies. **Equalize** adjusts specific frequency bands like a graphic equalizer. **Parametric Equalization** provides more precise control of equalization over frequency ranges.

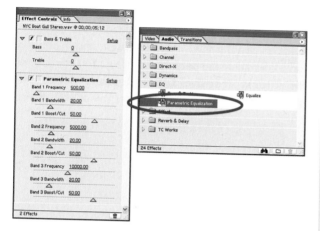

⑤ Use Audio Effect Effects

Use the **Effect** effects to add extra interest to the audio. **Chorus** adds a second copy of the sound at a slight offset to add depth. **Flanger** inverts the phase of the audio at its center frequency. **Multi-Effect** provides more precise control of echo and chorus effects by adjusting the delay and modulation.

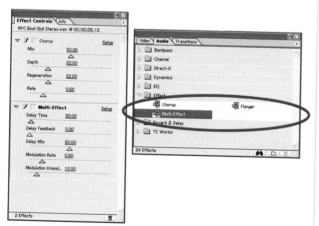

⑥ Use Reverb and Delay Effects

Use the **Reverb & Delay** effects to create a richer sound simulating a physical environment. **Echo** provides an echo after a delay. **Reverb** simulates the ambience of a room of a specific size and with sound-absorbent properties. **Multitap Delay** provides more precise control for delay effects.

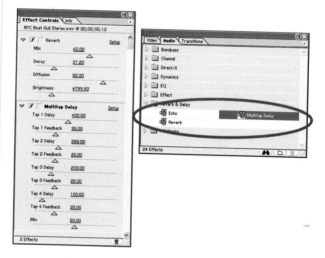

How-to Hint

Musical Time Calculator

The **Multitap Delay** effect dialog includes a **Musical Time Calculator** that you can use to calculate a delay time based on the Time Signature, Tempo, and Note value of the musical rhythm.

Direct-X Audio Filter

The **Direct-X** audio filter provides access to Windows Direct-X audio filters installed on your system.

How to Use TC Works Effects and SmartSound QuickTracks

Besides the Audio effects, Premiere includes powerful Windows and Macintosh sound engineering tools from TC Works.

Premiere also includes 27 SmartSound QuickTracks from Sonic Desktop to use to automatically create music and audio effects in a desired style, and to fit a custom duration in the Timeline.

❶ Use the TC Works Effects

On Windows, Premiere provides three DirectX audio plug-ins to sweeten audio. These provide control-panel interfaces to adjust the audio as it is playing. Click the **Preview** button to listen to the track play as you adjust it. Click the black bar at the bottom of the window to choose a built-in preset.

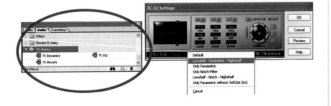

❷ Use the TC Dynamics Effect

Use the **TC Dynamics** effect to boost the sound quality of an audio track with compression and expansion tools to even out the peaks and valleys. You can control the **Attack**, **Threshold**, and **Release** of the compressor, and the amount of compression as a **Ratio**.

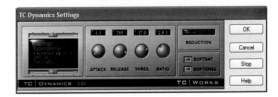

❸ Use the TC EQ Effect

Use the **TC EQ** effect to equalize an audio track by manipulating specific frequencies to highlight particular sounds or to minimize noise. It provides a three-band **EQ**, with **Notch** or **Parametric** controls to manipulate the frequency, bandwidth, or gain.

4 Use the TC Reverb Effect

Use the **TC Reverb** effect to add ambience by simulating the acoustics of sound in different environments. Select the room size and reflections, from a **Small Room** to a **Large Cathedral**, with **Bright** or **Dark** sound. Adjust the **Decay** time and the **Mix** ratio between the original and processed sound.

5 Use TC Works SparkLE

On the Macintosh, use the **TC Works SparkLE** stand-alone utility to play and edit high-resolution sound files in a variety of popular formats and without any additional audio hardware. You can assemble multiple tracks from the **File list** to the **Play list** window, navigate with the **Transport** window, edit in the **Wave Editor** window, and complete your recording using the controls in the **Master** window.

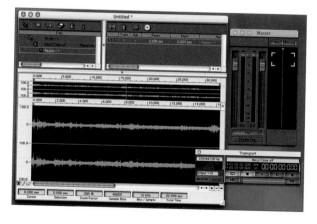

6 Use SmartSound QuickTracks

Choose **File**, **New**, **SmartSound**. Use the SmartSound Maestro Wizard to step through the process of creating a custom soundtrack. First, select the intended use of the soundtrack, and then click **Next** to specify the musical style.

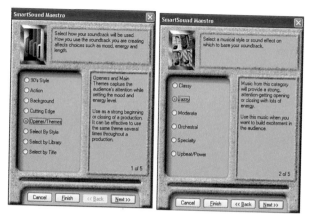

7 Select Soundtrack Duration

Finally, select the desired duration for the soundtrack and whether the track is loopable. Click **Finish** to have the SmartSound Maestro create your custom track as an audio file and add it to the Timeline. You also can double-click the track later to adjust the duration and create a new track.

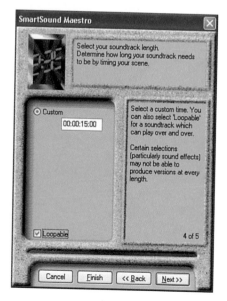

How to Choose Video Effects

Premiere provides almost 80 video effects, including color adjustments, and distortions and transformations. In addition to these effects, you also can use the Motions Settings dialog to animate clips and logos (see Part 16). The available effects are organized into folders in the Video Effects palette, with both Adobe After Effects and Premiere effects (with a "V" filmstrip icon).

① Use Adjust Effects

Use the effects in the **Adjust** folder to adjust the brightness and color of the image. Adjust **Brightness & Contrast**, **Color Balance** or the **Channel Mixer**, and **Extract** a range of colors. Perform sophisticated adjustments with a **Convolution Kernel**, and manipulate **Levels**. Reduce the color range for a **Posterize** effect.

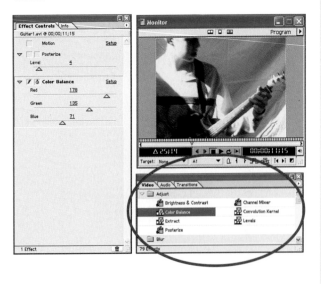

② Use Blur Effects

Simulate a **Camera Blur**, or a rotating **Radial Blur**. Smooth sharp edges with **Antialias**, or remove noise with **Gaussian Blur** or a simpler **Fast Blur**. Simulate glows with a **Channel Blur**. Simulate motion with a **Directional Blur** or **Ghosting**.

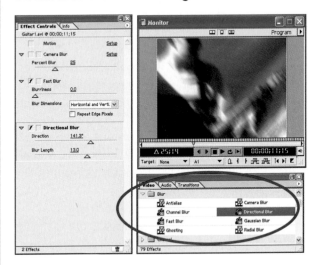

③ Use Channel Effects

Use the **Invert** effect in the **Channel** folder to invert the colors in the image and optionally blend the result with the original. Use the **Blend** effect to create transitions between clips with cross-fades and transparency.

4 Use Distort Effects

Use the **Distort** effects to **Bend** and **Pinch**, **Mirror** and **Shear**, **Ripple** and **Twirl**, **Wave**, **Zig-Zag**, and mangle the image. Distort with **Polar Coordinates**, simulate the effect of **Lens Distortion**, or **Spherize** to wrap the image around a 3D globe.

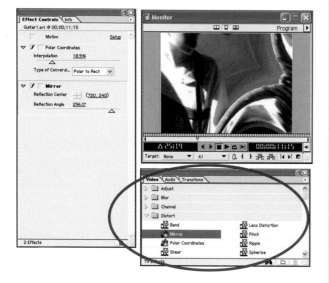

5 Use the Transform Effect

The **Transform** effect in the **Distort** folder provides precise control over animating a clip with zooming, rotation, and distortions along a motion path. The Motion Settings dialog (see Part 16) also provides similar effects.

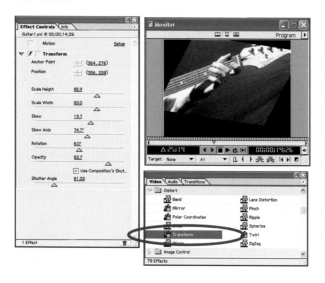

6 Use Image Control Effects

Use the **Image Control** effects to apply color filters. Convert to **Black & White**, **Tint** with color, or apply **Color Pass** to retain a color range. Change the **Color Balance**, **Color Replace** a color range, or shift a **Color Offset**. Apply a **Median** filter to remove noise or create a painterly effect, or use **Gamma Correction** to brighten or darken the image.

7 Use Perspective Effects

Use the **Perspective** effects to create 3D effects. Add a **Drop Shadow**, or use **Bevel Alpha** and **Bevel Edges** to create chiseled, three-dimensional edges. Rotate the clip in two dimensions with Transform, or in 3D space with **Basic 3D**.

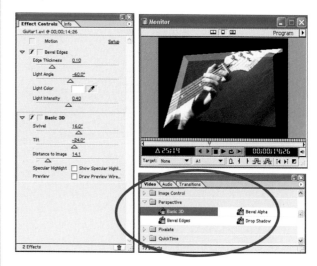

⑧ Use Pixelate Effects

Use the **Pixelate** effects to break up the image by merging adjacent pixels into larger clumps. **Crystallize** pixels into polygonal cells, or group similar colors into **Facets**, or **Pointillize** into dots.

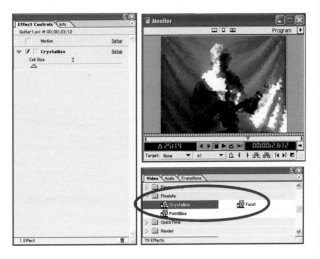

⑨ Use QuickTime Effects

Use the **QuickTime Effects** to display the QuickTime Select Effect dialog box to access the additional video effects built in to the QuickTime format.

⑩ Use Render Effects

Use the **Render** effects to add dramatic elements to your clips. Use **Lens Flare** to simulate the flare from a bright light shining into the camera lens. Use **Ramp** to smoothly blend color gradients with the original footage. Create **Lightning** bolts or other electrical effects.

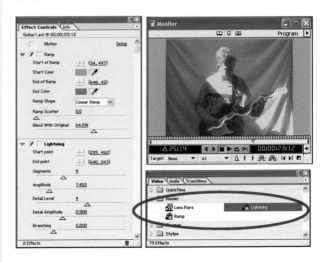

⑪ Use Sharpen Effects

Use the **Sharpen** effects to **Sharpen** the image, or to **Gaussian Sharpen** it more, or to **Sharpen Edges** when there are large color changes in the image.

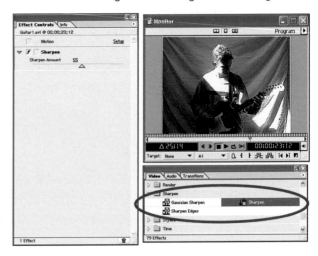

12 Use Stylize Effects

Use the **Stylize** effects to enhance the edges of the clip with **Find Edges**, **Emboss**, or **Color Emboss**. Distort with **Noise** or **Wind**, or brighten with **Solarize** or periodic **Strobe Light** flashes. Break up the image with a **Mosaic** or into **Tiles**, or **Replicate** in tiles. Use other images to **Texturize**, or apply an **Alpha Glow** around a masked alpha channel.

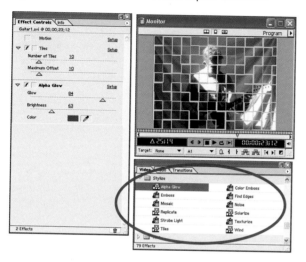

14 Use Transform Effects

Use the **Transform** effects to **Clip**, **Crop**, or **Resize** the image, or reverse it with **Horizontal Flip** or **Vertical Flip**. Adjust like a television screen with **Horizontal Hold** or **Vertical Hold**, or **Roll** on a cylinder. Simulate panning over the image with **Image Pan**, or viewing from different angles with **Camera View**. Use **Edge Feather** for a beveled look.

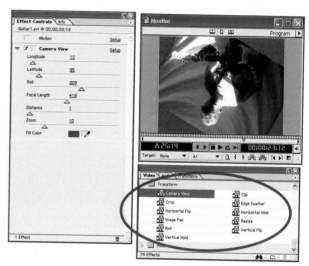

13 Use Time Effects

Use the **Time** effects to affect multiple frames over time. Combine and **Echo** multiple frames for a ghosting or streaking multi-image effect, or **Posterize Time** to strobe playback at a different frame rate.

15 Use Video Effects

Use the **Video** effects to apply video corrections. Limit the clip to legal **Broadcast Colors**, or use **Field Interpolate** or **Reduce Interlace Flicker** to correct video footage with television interlaced lines.

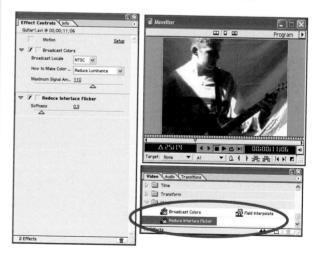

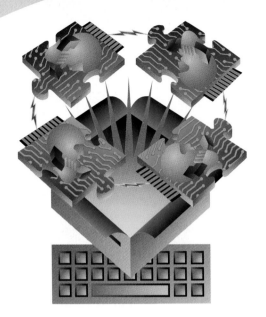

Animating Clips in Motion

In this book, you have seen how to edit video and audio clips; organize them on the Timeline; and then add interest with transitions, titles, superimpositions, and effects. But Premiere also can combine these effects by animating clips, putting video and overlays in motion across the screen.

With the Motion Settings dialog, you can define a path for the clip to follow across the frame; coordinate the timing and speed of the motion; and cause the overlay to zoom in and out, rotate, and even distort its shape. This motion is controlled by keyframes, as other effects in Premiere are. Therefore, not only the motion, but also the zooming, rotation, and distortion can be smoothly interpolated from keyframe to keyframe across the screen.

You also can use the Transform effect in the Effects palette for even more precise control in animating clips (see Part 15, "Applying Audio and Video Effects"), but the Motion Settings dialog provides a convenient interface for performing a wide range of useful animations.

This part uses the Sample Folder of clips installed with Premiere (see Part 1). It includes a movie file (zfinal) that was edited together from the sample clips. The movie includes multiple video clips with a transition, an audio music track, and a superimposed animated logo. The folder also includes a Premiere project file that you can open to see how the movie and the motion effect were created.

16

How to View the ztour Project

To understand how the zfinal movie in the Sample Folder was created, you can explore the ztour.ppj Premiere project file. The Timeline window shows you the layout of the clips, transitions between clips, and where different kinds of effects have been applied to clips.

❶ Open the Sample Project

Choose **File**, **Open** to display the Open dialog. Navigate to the Sample Folder and select the ztour project file. Then click **Open** to open the ztour project.

❷ Display the A/B Editing Workspace

Choose **Window**, **Workspace**, **Single-Track Editing** to use a single-track layout with the dual-view **Monitor** window. Then choose **Window**, **Workspace**, **A/B Editing** to reposition the windows in the layout you have been using with separate Video 1A and Video 1B tracks, and the Transition track in between them.

❸ Preview the Project

The **Timeline** window has four video clips, a still image logo, and an audio soundtrack. The Transition track has a cross-dissolve between the first two video clips. Render-scrub through the **Timeline** to preview all the effects. The project plays through the video clips and, near the end, the logo image zooms into the frame and then spins away.

4 View the Video Effect

The Finale video clip has a blue line above it to indicate that it has an effect applied to it. Click the triangle to the left of the Video 1A track name to expand the track. Premiere displays the name of the Camera Blur effect applied to the Finale clip as the logo spins over it.

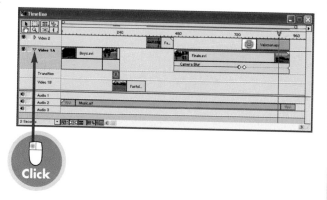

5 View the Effect Keyframes

Click the white diamond keyframes to see the settings applied to the effect in the **Effect Controls** palette (see Part 15). The **Camera Blur** effect starts at 0% in the middle of the clip, ramps quickly up to 80% as the Veloman logo appears, and ramps down again as the logo spins away.

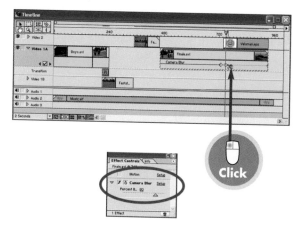

6 View the Logo Transparency

Click the **Veloman** still image clip in the Video 2 superimposed track to display its settings in the **Effect Controls** palette. Both a **Motion** and a **Transparency** effect are enabled. You can click on **Setup** to the right of the **Transparency** item to display the **Transparency Settings** and see that the logo is superimposed using a White Alpha Matte (see Part 13, "Superimposing Images and Video Clips").

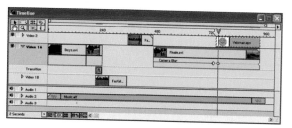

How-to Hint

Time Display

The **Duration** field at the bottom right of the Project window displays video frames or audio samples, not the timecode that you saw in earlier parts. To change the time display for the project, choose **Project**, **Project Settings**, **General**. In the Project Settings dialog, change the **Time Display** from **Frames/Samples** to **30 fps Drop-Frame Timecode**.

How to Define a Motion Path

The Motion Settings dialog provides a visual summary of the animation, with the motion path across the screen, keyframes and timing, and settings applied at each keyframe. The motion path can extend beyond the edges of the frame so that the object can enter and exit across the edges of the screen.

1 Open the Motion Settings

Continuing from Task 1, click to select the Veloman still image clip in the Video 2 superimposed track. Click **Setup** to the right of the **Motion** item in the **Effect Controls** palette to display the Motion Settings dialog (or choose **Clip**, **Video Options**, **Motion**).

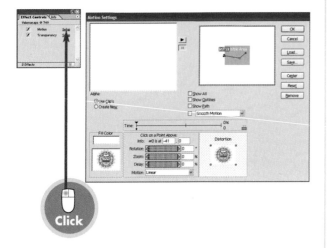

2 Preview the Motion Effect

The **Motion Path** window at the top right shows the path of the motion through the frame (the lines) and the keyframe points along the path (the squares). Click the **Play** and **Pause** buttons to preview the motion in the left **Sample** window.

3 View Motion in the Program

Premiere also displays the keyframes as hash marks along the Motion Path Timeline in the **Time** area. Click and drag the arrow to play through the motion. Check **Show All** to display the motion on top of the other tracks.

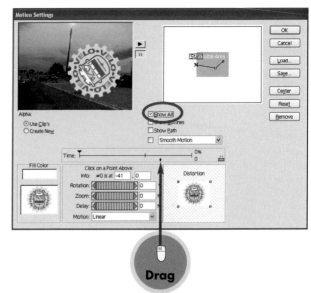

4 Change the Motion Path

Move the cursor over the first **Start** keyframe box in the **Motion Path** window, and it changes to a pointing finger icon. Click the **Start** box and drag it off the side of the visible area of the frame.

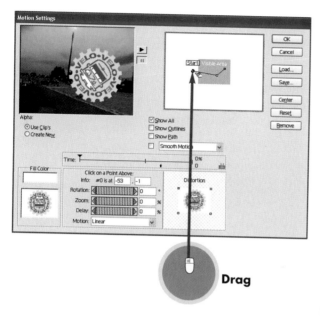

Drag

6 Add a New Keyframe

Move the cursor over the first line segment in the motion path and click to create a new keyframe point. Drag the keyframe box close to the bottom of the visible area to have the logo sweep down and then up into the frame.

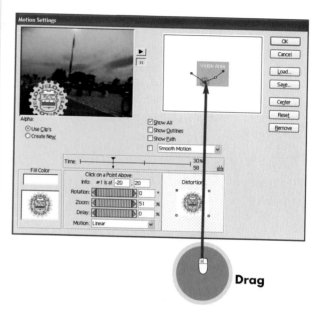

Drag

5 Preview the New Motion

Click **Play** or drag the upward-facing arrow in the Motion Path Timeline to preview the motion, as the logo now appears to fly in from offscreen.

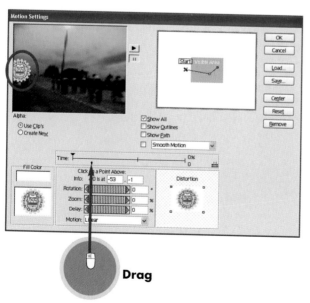

Drag

How-to Hint

Adjusting Positions

To adjust a keyframe position one pixel at a time, select it and use the cursor control arrow keys. Or hold down **Shift** and press the **arrow** keys to move in 5-pixel increments. Click the **Center** button to move the keyframe to the center of the frame.

Entering Positions

The keyframe information in the **Info** area is shown in pixels from the center of the image. You can type coordinates directly into these fields and use fractional values for more precision.

Delete a Keyframe

To delete a keyframe, click to select it and then press the **Delete** key.

How to Change Speeds, Rotate, and Zoom

After you define the motion path and keyframes in the Motion Path window, you can adjust the timing of the motion between each keyframe. You can also animate the motion by adjusting the Zoom and Rotation settings.

① View Keyframe Timing

Continuing from Task 2, click the second keyframe (#1) to select it. The Motion Path Timeline shows the current position with a black downward triangle above the Timeline. Click the two red arrows to the right to switch between displaying the Time for the clip and for the entire program.

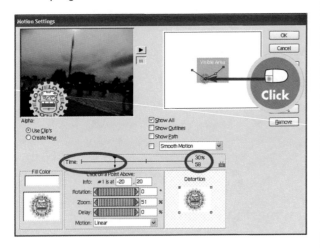

② Change Motion Speed

Click and drag the triangle to the left on the Timeline so that this keyframe is reached 10% of the way through the effect. Click **Show Path** to view a dotted motion path between each keyframe.

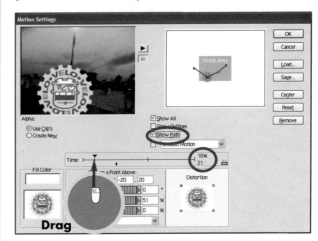

③ View Zoom Settings

Click the third keyframe (#2) to select it. Notice the **Zoom** value for the keyframes increases from 0% to 51% to 100%, causing the logo to grow in size as it moves onscreen.

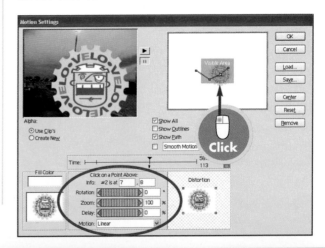

④ Change the Zoom

Drag the **Zoom** slider, or type a value between 0% and 500%, to decrease or increase the size of the logo at that keyframe. Click **Show Outlines** to view an outline of the clip's size and rotation at each keyframe.

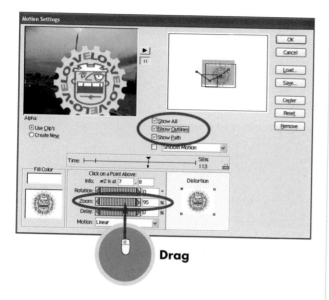

Drag

⑤ View Rotation Settings

Click the End keyframe (#3) to select it. Notice the **Rotation** value for the keyframes changes from 0 to 720 degrees, causing the logo to spin through two full 360-degree rotations as it moves and shrinks offscreen.

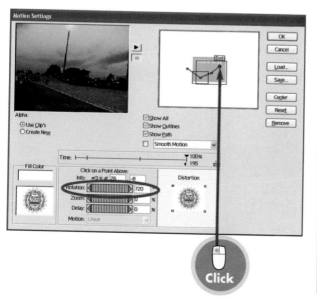

Click

⑥ Change the Rotation

Click to add another keyframe before the end, and drag the **Rotation** slider or type a value between –1440 degrees (counterclockwise movement) and 1440 degrees (clockwise), to spin the logo even faster, up to eight times between two keyframes.

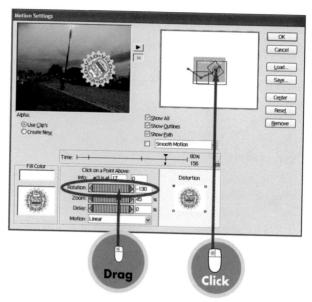

Drag   **Click**

How-to Hint

Undo Changes

When you complete a series of changes in the Motion Settings dialog, click OK to close it, and then reopen it to experiment with further changes. This way, you can click **Cancel** to reject the new changes, or use **Undo** to step back through several sets of changes. Click **Reset** to remove all the settings for a specific keyframe.

Remove or Disable Motion Settings

Click **Remove** in the Motion Settings dialog to remove all the motion effect settings applied to a clip. Or disable any effect by clicking the **Enable Effect** button to the left of the Motion entry in the **Effect Controls** palette.

How to Delay and Distort Clips

Finally, Premiere provides several more controls to animate the motion more precisely. Use the Delay setting to pause the motion along the path; the Motion setting to add acceleration; and Distort to perform arbitrary distortions, resizing, and rotations.

❶ Add a Delay

Click to select the middle keyframe (#2). Drag the **Delay** slider or type a value to have the motion settings pause at the keyframe for the specified time (up to the duration to the next keyframe). Premiere displays a blue bar on the Motion Path Timeline to show the delay period.

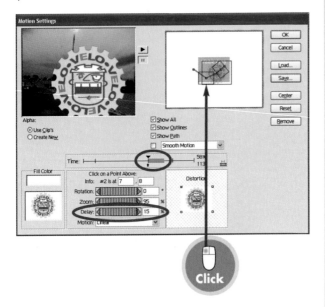

❷ Accelerate or Decelerate

Click the **Motion** drop-down list to choose the type of motion to use up to the next keyframe. The motion can be **Linear** (constant), or can **Accelerate** or **Decelerate** to make the motion seem more natural.

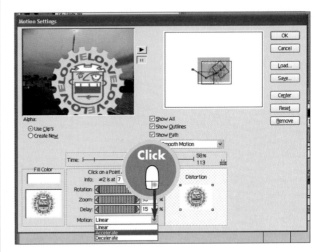

❸ Distort a Corner

Click and drag a corner of the sample image in the **Distortion** area to resize the image and stretch and distort its shape.

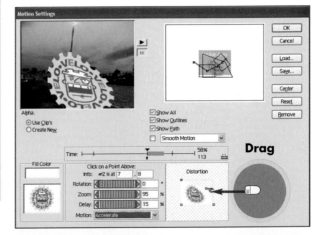

④ Distort and Rotate

Hold down the **(Option) [Alt]** key and drag a corner to rotate the clip around its center to provide arbitrary rotation from keyframe to keyframe.

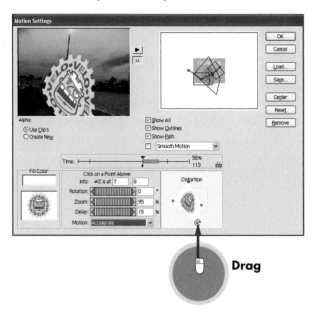

Drag

⑤ Distort and Move

Drag in the center to move all four corner points together to reposition the distortion.

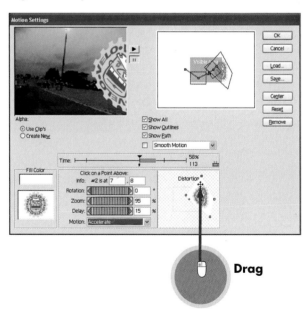

Drag

⑥ Smooth Motion

Click **Smooth Motion** and choose a smoothing option from the list to smooth out abrupt changes in direction, rotation, and distortion. Choose the amount of smoothing to be applied, from **Smooth Motion** (the least) to **Averaging-High** (the most).

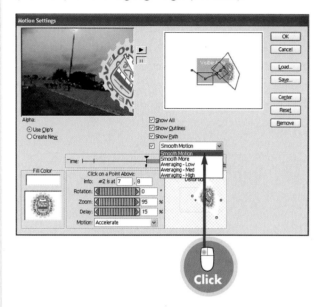

Click

How-to Hint

Moving Between Keyframes

After clicking on a keyframe in the **Motion Path** window, press **Tab** to move to the next keyframe, or hold down **Shift** and press **Tab** to move to the previous keyframe.

Selecting the Alpha Channel

Use the **Alpha** settings to control how the clip is superimposed, using the clip's own alpha channel, or **Create New** for clips without an alpha channel (see Part 13).

Background Fill Color

Use the **Fill Color** area at the bottom left of the dialog to specify a fill color to be used behind the clip for previews, or if the clip is in the Video 1 track.

How to Create Image Pans and Flying Video

The Motion Settings dialog provides a convenient interface for creating quick effects such as panning and zooming over a still image and adding multiple layers of flying video windows. For more control, try the Video Effects palette to layer effects including Camera View, Image Pan, and Transform.

1 Import an Image to Pan

Import a large still image and add it to the **Timeline** in the Video 1A track. Click the image to select it, open the **Effects** palette, and then click **Setup** to define the Motion effect.

2 Set the Start Position

In the Motion Settings dialog, click the **Start** keyframe to select it, and then click **Center** to start the motion with the image filling the screen.

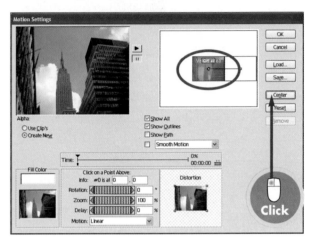

3 Define the Pan and Zoom

Click the **End** keyframe to select it. Set the **Zoom** slider to 150% and then drag the keyframe to have the motion zoom in on a point of interest. Preview the image pan and zoom to check the motion. Or add more keyframes for more interesting motions.

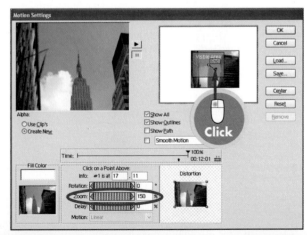

④ Create a Video Window

Start a new project with a still image in the Video 1A track of the **Timeline**. Add a video clip to the Video 2 overlay track. Click the overlay clip to select it, open the **Effects** palette, and then click **Setup** to define the Motion effect.

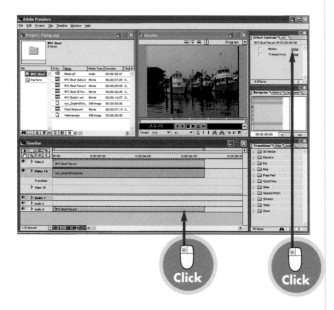

Click   **Click**

⑤ Set the Start Position

In the the Motion Settings dialog, click the **Start** keyframe to select it. Set the **Zoom** slider to 33% to shrink the overlayed clip, and then drag the keyframe to start at the left side of the frame.

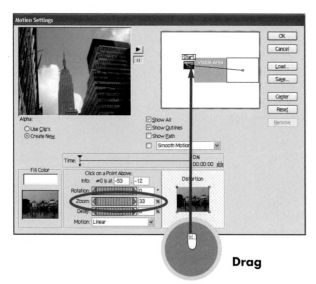

Drag

⑥ Define the Flying Video

Click the **End** keyframe to select it. Set the **Zoom** slider to the same 33% size, and then drag the keyframe to the right edge of the frame. Click **OK** to save the motion settings.

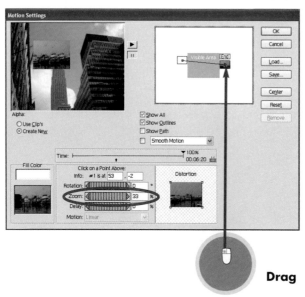

Drag

⑦ Add a Picture in Picture Clip

Drop a second video clip onto the top of the **Timeline** to create a new Video 3 overlay track. Use the Motion Settings dialog to have it fly across the bottom of the screen. In this way, you can layer multiple overlaid video clips. Preview the result in the **Monitor** window.

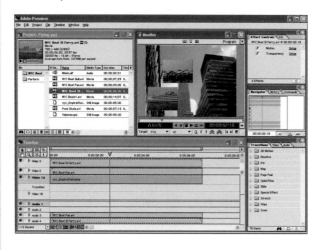

Glossary

NUMBERS

1394 See *FireWire*.

A

A/B editing   A style of editing in which you edit together clips in pairs—A and B—typically with a transition from one to the next. In Premiere, the A/B Editing workspace configures the Monitor window in Program view and the Timeline with separate expanded tracks for Video 1A, Video 1B, and Transitions. This style is useful for assembling a program with simple drag-and-drop convenience. See also *single-track editing*.

AIFF   Acronym for Audio Interchange File Format; Macintosh audio file format. Can be used for uncompressed and compressed data. See also *WAV*.

alpha channel   Extra information stored with an image to define transparent areas used for keying and superimpositions. Also called an *alpha mask*. Sometimes present in files prepared using a tool such as Adobe Photoshop or Illustrator. See *key*.

amplify   Increase the audio volume.

analog media   Audio sources, such as audio cassettes and microphones, and video sources, such as VHS and 8mm VCRs and camcorders, that must be digitized and converted into digital format for processing by a computer. Newer digital formats such as DV and DVD have higher resolution and quality than older consumer formats such as VHS and also do not degrade in quality when they are copied from one generation to the next. See also *component video, composite video, digital media*.

animate   To move and manipulate an object over time, such as a title, a superimposed logo, or a transition between frames.

antialias   To smooth out a jagged or stair-step appearance or motion between adjacent points so that it appears continuous.

aspect ratio   The shape of an image or frame, expressed as the width-to-height ratio. Widescreen film uses a 16:9 aspect ratio (1.78:1), whereas standard television uses 4:3 aspect ratio (1.33:1).

attenuate   To reduce audio strength or volume.

Audio Effects palette   A small floating window along the right side of the Premiere workspace that lists the available audio effects, grouped by type. Used to access effects to be applied to an audio clip. You can also reorganize and customize the list.

audio lead   See *J-cut*.

Audio Mixer window   The Premiere window used to dynamically monitor and control the volume level and pan/balance of multiple audio tracks on the Timeline to combine them into a final program.

audio waveform   A graphical representation of an audio clip, helping to visualize the sound in the clip by showing the signal levels. Premiere can show a waveform in audio tracks in the Timeline and in a separate Clip window when you open an audio clip.

AVI   Acronym for Audio Video Interleave. The old multimedia file format used under Windows for interleaved video and audio streams. See also *Video for Windows, Windows Media*.

B

balance   To distribute two channels of a stereo clip between the left and right channels. See also *pan*.

bandpass effects   Audio effects designed to remove specific frequencies from an audio clip (manifested as hisses, whines, and hums).

bandwidth   The amount and rate of data that can be processed or transmitted by a given device. An analog modem has very little bandwidth compared to a high-speed cable modem, for instance, so the former cannot download video from the Internet nearly as quickly as the latter. See *data rate*.

baseband video   See *composite video*.

batch capture   The automated process of capturing an entire group of clips (such as from a DV camcorder) as defined by a batch list.

batch list   A list of clips with the timecode values for each In and Out point (also called a *timecode log*) to be used in a batch capture process. See also *batch capture*, *log*, *timecode*.

Bin window   The area of the Premiere Project window used to import and organize folders of source clips.

bit   A binary digit. The fundamental element of computer logic and numbers. Represents one of two values: zero or one, off or on, false or true. See also *byte*.

bit rate   See *data rate*.

bitstream   A collection of data, as in video or audio data compressed to a file or transmitted between devices.

blue screen   A specially colored backdrop (typically blue or green) that can be matched with a color key and made transparent so that it can be replaced with another video layer. For example, you can cut out a subject from the blue screen background and composite it into another scene. See also *matte*, *key*.

BMP   The standard Windows bitmap still image file format. Bitmap files are not compressed and are therefore significantly larger than the same image stored in formats such as GIF and JPEG.

byte   A data element containing eight bits, or 256 distinct values. Commonly used to store a single text character. Computer data transfer rates are traditionally measured in bits, as in Mb for Megabits (millions of bits, with a lowercase "b"); whereas computer data storage is traditionally measured in bytes, as in MB, for megabytes (millions of bytes, with an uppercase "B"). See also *bit, GB, KB, MB*.

C

caption   Title text that labels a scene or identifies a location or person onscreen.

capture   To digitize, or import and convert, video and/or audio into digital format on your computer from an external device, such as a camcorder or VCR. You typically use a special video capture card to input analog video into your computer, and then convert and save it into digital files on your disk. With DV camcorders, you transfer digital data directly into your computer over a FireWire/1394 interface. See *import*.

CD   See *compact disc*.

CD-Audio   A consumer electronics format for prerecorded music on compact disc. CD-Audio discs include only the audio data for each track. Other ancillary information, such as song titles or album and artist information can be accessed from online databases.

channel   The subcomponents of a clip. For images, an alpha channel can contain a matte or mask image to key certain regions of the image to be transparent. For audio, the separate left and right channels of a stereo clip.

chrominance   The color of a video signal. Video signals are split into separate luma and chroma (color) components for higher-quality and more efficient transmission and encoding. The chroma signal is typically split into two components or color difference signals, such as YUV format. See also *luminance*.

clip   A short piece of video and/or audio, often containing an individual *scene*. When creating a video project, you import clip files into bins in your Premiere project and often trim longer clips into individual scenes. You then edit the clips together on the Timeline to play in sequential order to tell the "story" of your production, with transitions between clips and other added effects.

Clip window   The Premiere window used to view and trim individual clips. See also *Monitor window, Source view*.

codec　A video or audio compression component that can both compress and decompress (encode and decode) files. Media formats and players, such as Windows Media, RealMedia, and QuickTime have a selection of codecs built in and can add additional codecs to support new file formats. See also *compression*.

Commands palette　A small floating window along the right side of the Premiere workspace that contains a list of preset commands. You can customize the palette to define buttons and function keys for fast access to often-used commands.

compact disc (CD)　An optical digital disc format used both for prerecorded content, especially music (CD-Audio), and as recordable media for consumer devices and computers (CD-R and CD-RW). The full-size 120mm (12cm) diameter disc originally stored 650MB, or 60 minutes of audio, and is now also available in 700MB/80-minute capacity. Also available in smaller sizes and specialty shapes (business cards, for example). See also *DVD*.

composite　See *superimpose*.

composite video　A video signal that combines the brightness (luminance or luma) and the color (chrominance or chroma) video information into one signal. Because the signal is not modulated, composite video provides higher quality than RF video. Requires a separate audio signal and connector. Also called *baseband video*. See also *component video, DV, RF video, S-Video*.

component video　A video signal that separates the video signal into three separate signals (and three separate wires) to avoid any quality loss from mixing signals. The components can be RGB (red, green, and blue); luma (Y) and two chroma signals, such as Y, Y-R, Y-B; or other formats including YUV, YCbCr, or Y Pr Pb. Requires a separate audio signal and connector. See also *composite video, DV, RF video, S-Video*.

compress　To reduce the size of audio or video data through the use of a compression scheme. Also called *encode*. See also *decompress, lossy,* and *lossless*.

compressor　Program by which files are *compressed*. A compressor that also *decompresses* files (returns them to their original state) is called a *codec*. See also *compress*.

crawl　To scroll a line of title text sideways, left or right across the screen. See also *roll*.

credit　Title text that identifies the people who contributed to a production. Usually scrolled at the end of a show.

crop　To make an image physically smaller by trimming away one or more edges. This reduces the dimensions of the image and reduces the size of the computer file.

cross-fade　See *fade*.

cut　To switch instantly from one clip to another. A video cut appears suddenly onscreen without any other kind of transition effect. The cut is the most basic kind of transition for changing scenes and dropping titles onto the screen. See also *fade, transition*.

D

data rate　The speed at which data is transferred, as in bytes per second. Also called *bit rate*. For example, the speed to download or stream a video file over the Internet, or the speed at which the file must play from a hard disk. When you create a video or audio file, you can specify the target bit rate at which the file will be played. See also *bandwidth*.

decode　See *decompress*.

decompress　To process a compressed bitstream and recover the original data (if lossless compression), or an approximation of the original (if lossy compression). Also called *decode*. See also *compress*.

deinterlace　To process *interlaced* television video, in which each frame contains alternating pairs of lines from two separate fields captured at slightly different times. The motion between fields can cause visible tearing when displayed on a computer monitor. Deinterlacing uses every other line from one field and interpolates new in-between lines without tearing. See also *interlace, NTSC*.

delay　An audio effect that provides an echo of a sound after a specified time period.

digital media　Audio and video sources such as audio CD, DV, miniDV, Digital8 camcorders, and DVD that store the audio and video in digital format. As a result, the data can be imported and processed directly by a computer, and copied without any loss from one generation to the next. See also *analog media, DV*.

disc   Term commonly used to refer to optical storage devices such as DVD and CD. See also *disk*.

disk   Term commonly used to refer to magnetic storage devices such as hard disks. See also *disc*.

dissolve   A video transition in which one video clip fades into the next. See also *fade, transition*.

downmix   To convert from a multichannel audio program to fewer channels. For viewers who do not have a surround-sound audio system, DVD players can downmix the DVD soundtrack to two-channel analog stereo so that the DVD can be played on a television or stereo system.

dub   To duplicate or make a copy of a production, traditionally from one tape (usually a master tape) to another tape.

duration   A length of time. For a clip, the length of time that it will play, determined by its overall length. Or if the clip has been trimmed, the difference in time between its In point and Out point. See also *timecode*.

DV   A Digital Video tape and compression format for consumer and professional video equipment. The DV compression format is used for DV and Digital-8 camcorders. DV format video and audio can be captured using a FireWire/IEEE 1394 interface and then saved and edited in Premiere. The consumer tape format is more accurately called mini-DV. See also *analog media*.

DVD   Originally an acronym for Digital Versatile Disc (or Digital Video Disc). A family of optical disc formats used both for prerecorded content, especially movies, and as recordable media for consumer devices and computers (that is, DVD-ROM, DVD-R, DVD-RW, DVD-RAM). A family of data format standards for video, audio, and data storage (that is, DVD-Video and DVD-Audio) for consumer electronics products and computers. DVD discs are the same diameter as CD discs, and most formats hold 4.7GB (actually billion bytes) of data on a side. See also *compact disc (CD)*.

DVD authoring   The process of creating a DVD production. This involves designing the overall navigational structure; preparing the multimedia assets (video, audio, images); designing the graphical look; laying out the assets into tracks, streams, and chapters; designing interactive menus; linking the elements into the navigational structure; and building the final production.

dynamic range   The difference between the softest and loudest sounds. Decrease to compress the range and reduce noise, or expand to emphasize volume differences.

E

edit line   The current editing point in the Timeline, as displayed in the Monitor window and used for inserts and deletes. In Premiere, shown by a triangle control in the time ruler with a vertical line down through the Timeline tracks.

effect   The result of processing audio and video clips to enhance, improve, or distort them. See also *filter*.

Effect Controls palette   A small floating window along the right side of the Premiere workspace that lists the current effects applied to an audio or video clip. Used to adjust the order of effects and change effect settings.

encode   See *compress*.

equalize   To adjust the tonal quality of an audio clip. As with graphic equalizers found in home or auto audio equipment, Premiere's equalize effect permits you to boost or cut the original signal at different frequency bands.

export   To save your production to a file or to an external video device. Premiere can export both individual clips and entire productions on the Timeline to a variety of disk and Web media file formats. See also *import*.

F

fade   A gradual transition from one clip to another. With video, the clip changes from transparent to fully opaque (or vice versa) to fade in or out. With audio, the gain changes between silence and full volume.

field   For interlaced video sources, a full frame is constructed from alternating odd and even lines from two video fields captured at slightly different times. See also *interlaced video*.

filter   A transformation applied to a video or audio clip to enhance it or create a visual or auditory effect. See also *effect*.

FireWire A digital data interface standard that provides a high-speed Plug-and-Play interface for personal computers. Used for connecting DV camcorders to computers, as well as to hard disk drives and DVD drives. Supports up to 480Mbps data rate. Also known as *IEEE 1394* and *Sony iLink*. See also *USB*.

FireWire connector A roughly rectangular, hot-pluggable connector used for FireWire/IEEE 1394 digital connections, especially digital video signals such as from DV camcorders. The connectors can vary in size: full-size (6-pin) for connecting to a computer or hub, and smaller (4-pin) for connecting to equipment such as DV camcorders.

four-point edit A method of setting In and Out points to precisely control where and how frames are inserted into a Timeline. In a four-point edit, you set all four In and Out markers, and Premiere displays a warning dialog if the durations do not match. See also *three-point edit*.

fps Frames per second. See also *frame rate*.

frames The individual video images that make up a moving sequence. Video formats and individual clips are typically described in terms of the resolution of the individual frames and the frame rate at which they are played. See also *frame rate, field*.

frame rate Playback speed as determined in frames per second.

freeze frame A technique in which a particular frame of video is held onscreen. Sometimes the audio portion of the scene continues playing.

G

gain Overall audio output volume. Increase gain to *amplify* a clip, or decrease gain to *attenuate* a clip, making it quieter.

gamma A display setting related to the brightness of the middle tones of an image. You can adjust the gamma of an image to lighten or darken the midtones (the middle-gray levels), without significantly changing the dark and light areas (the shadows and highlights).

gang To adjust multiple tracks at the same time, as in the Premiere Audio Mixer window.

garbage matte A mask used in a keying operation to remove a region of a frame that contains unwanted objects.

GB Gigabytes (billions of bytes). In computer use, a gigabyte actually represents the closest binary power of 2 to a billion, or 1024 cubed. In general use in advertising DVD disc capacity, however, the number of "GB" is actually used to specify a different value, a billion decimal. See also *byte, KB, MB*.

GIF Acronym for Graphics Interchange Format. A still image file format commonly used on Web pages for simple illustrations and animations. Use the JPEG format for photographic images.

gradient Gradual change from one color (or intensity level) to another. Gradient colors can also become opaque or transparent, varying in translucency from one side to the other.

H

History palette A small floating window along the right side of the Premiere workspace that displays a list of your recent actions during the current working session. Used to undo recent operations and return to a previous state of the project.

Hz Hertz. A measurement used for audio sampling rate, as in the number of audio samples per second. See also *sample rate*.

I

IEEE 1394 See *FireWire*.

iLink See *FireWire*.

import To bring media elements into your current working space. Premiere can import video and audio clips, still images, and animated sequences in a variety of formats. You can import both individual clips and folders of clips, and add them to bins in an open Project. See also *capture, export*.

In point A placeholder used to mark a specific timecode as the starting point of a segment in a longer sequence. You can use In and Out points to mark a clip to be captured from a source tape, to mark part of a clip to be trimmed, or to mark a portion of the Timeline to be played. See also *marker, Out point*.

Info palette A small floating window along the right side of the Premiere workspace that displays information about a selected clip or transition.

interlaced video   A technique used for television video formats, such as NTSC and PAL, in which each full frame of video actually consists of alternating lines taken from two separate fields captured at slightly different times. The two fields are then interlaced or interleaved into the alternating odd and even lines of the full video frame. When displayed on television equipment, the alternating fields are displayed in sequence, depending on the *field dominance* of the source material. See also *progressive video*.

interpolate   To automatically create graduated steps between two or more keyframes to create smooth transitions for video, audio, and motion effects.

J

J-cut   A split edit in which the In point of a clip is adjusted to overlap the preceding clip so that the audio portion of the later clip starts playing before its video as a lead-in to the visual cut. Also called an *audio lead*. See also *L-cut*.

jog   To move slowly through a program, as with frame advance or frame reverse VCR controls. Use the Premiere jog tread to step frame by frame through a clip or program to position to a specific frame. See also *shuttle*.

JPEG   A still image file format developed by the Joint Photographic Experts Group that can compress photographic images into much smaller file sizes while sacrificing only a little image quality. Commonly used for photographs on Web pages and in email. See also *GIF*.

K

kerning   The spacing between adjacent characters in a text string, as in a title.

key   To specify a region of an image or video clip to be used as a mask for transparency. Used to make part of the scene transparent or semitransparent, and then composite it with other superimposed images or video tracks. The region can be specified using features such as color (a color key) or intensity, or with a separate alpha mask or image matte. See also *blue screen*, *matte*.

keyframe   A point along a timeline or path that defines where and how the settings for an effect will change. Premiere can interpolate one or more settings from keyframe to keyframe to create the appearance of a smoothly changing effect over a series of frames or along a motion path. See also *interpolate*.

L

L-cut   A split edit in which the audio Out point of a clip is extended beyond the video Out point, so that the audio cuts after the video and continues playing over the beginning of the next clip. See also *J-cut*.

leader   The beginning of the physical tape on a videocassette or extra material before the beginning of a clip. A tape leader is a strip of nonrecording material that connects the actual recording tape to the spindle on the cassette. Most cassette tapes have about five seconds of leader before the actual recording media portion of the tape begins.

log   A list of clips in a longer sequence, identified by starting and ending timecodes. Use the Premiere batch log to build a list of clips to be batch captured from a tape.

lossless   Any compression scheme, especially for audio and video data, that uses a nondestructive method that retains all the original information, and therefore does not degrade sound or video quality.

lossy   Any compression scheme, especially for audio and video data, that removes some of the original information to significantly reduce the size of the compressed data. Lossy image and audio compression schemes such as JPEG and MP3 try to eliminate information in subtle ways so that the change is barely perceptible, and sound or video quality is not seriously degraded.

luminance   The intensity or brightness of a video signal, usually represented by the letter Y. Video signals are split into separate luma and chroma (color) components for higher-quality and more efficient transmission and encoding. In YUV color format, for example, the color information stored in U and V (the color difference signals).

M

magnetic disk Term used for storage media such as hard disks and floppy discs that record data using magnetic fields. See also *optical disc.*

marker A placeholder used to mark a specific time-code in a sequence. Used to keep track of changes, events, or synchronization points in a longer sequence. You can use the In and Out point markers to mark a clip to be captured from a source tape, to mark part of a clip to be trimmed, or to mark a portion of the Timeline to be played. See also *In Point, Out Point.*

mask An image that defines areas in a frame to be used as a transparency key or matte. Each pixel in the mask image indicates the degree of transparency to be used for the corresponding pixel position in each frame. See also *key, matte.*

master For video, the original video or audio source, or final video production with analog media, the first tape you create from your PC video file, also known as the first-generation tape. The master tape is a high-quality source to which you should return whenever you want to make more copies. Although you could use the file on your hard drive as a master, you won't want to keep that file forever because it takes up so much storage space. If you're using analog video, however, the PC file is your master source and first generation; the first physical tape you record is considered to be a second-generation tape. See also *analog media, DV, digital media.*

matte An image mask used to define the transparent areas of each frame to be used in superimposing multiple clips. See also *key.*

MB Megabytes—millions of bytes. In computer use, a megabyte actually represents the closest binary power of 2 to a million, or 1024 squared. See also *byte, GB, KB.*

Monitor window The Premiere window used to preview and edit the Source view of individual video clips and the Program view of the material being assembled on the Timeline. See also *Clip window.*

mono Monophonic audio—a single channel of audio. See also *stereo.*

motion blur The effect of tracking a speeding object and thus blurring the background because of the motion.

MOV QuickTime Movie format. See also *QuickTime.*

Movie Capture window The Premiere window used to preview and record from DV and analog video and audio devices. Also used for batch capture of a group of clips.

MP3 An audio file format, especially popular for downloading songs from the Web and for storing music in portable music players. Named for Moving Picture Experts Group (MPEG) 1, Layer 3. Uses lossy compression to significantly reduce file size but often with little perceptible loss in sound quality. Used to store large song collections on hard disk, download audio to portable audio players, and save multiple hours of music to CD. See also *WAV, Windows Media Audio.*

MPEG A family of popular multimedia file formats and associated compression schemes defined by the Moving Pictures Expert Group. MPEG-1 video was designed for use on CD-ROMs and provides picture quality somewhat comparable to VHS. MPEG-2 video was designed for consumer video and is used on DVD, and can provide high-quality full-screen, full-rate video with smaller file sizes. MPEG-4 video is designed for a broad range of multimedia applications and is used for Web and wireless streaming video. MP3 is a commonly used audio compression format, especially for Web downloads and portable music players.

MPEG-1 An older digital video compression format developed in the early 1990s by the Moving Picture Experts Group. MPEG-1 video was designed for lower-resolution video played from CD-ROM and provides picture quality somewhat comparable to VHS (typically 352×240 resolution).

MPEG-2 A TV-quality digital video compression format developed in the mid-1990s by the Moving Picture Experts Group. MPEG-2 video provides high-quality full-screen, full-rate video (720×480 resolutiosn for NTSC) with smaller file sizes than MPEG-1. Used for DVD discs.

multichannel audio Audio stored in more than one component, typically representing different spatial positions, to be played on different speakers. Includes stereo (two-channel) and surround-sound audio.

N

narration   A voice that explains what is happening on a video. Voiceover narration can add tremendous value to a video by explaining the situation being shown to viewers.

Navigator palette   A small floating window along the right side of the Premiere workspace that displays a miniature view of the current Timeline work area within the overall program. Used to scroll and zoom the program in the Timeline view.

NTSC   A television video format used in the United States and elsewhere. Displayed 525 lines of resolution at 60 fields per second, 30 frames per second (actually a fractional value near 29.97). Named for the National Television Standards Committee. See also *PAL*.

NTSC safe colors   Colors inside the safe region for NTSC television video. Title colors outside this range can display badly and bleed on NTSC televisions. See also *safe area*.

O

opaque   Regions of a superimposed image that are solid (not transparent) and therefore cover the underlying image. See also *transparent*.

optical disc   Removable storage medium, such as DVD and CD, that is read (and written) with laser light. See also *magnetic disk*.

Out point   A placeholder used to mark a specific timecode as the end point of a segment in a longer sequence. You can use In and Out points to mark a clip to be captured from a source tape, to mark part of a clip to be trimmed, or to mark a portion of the Timeline to be played. See also *marker, In point*.

overscan   The outer edges of a video image that are typically cut off by consumer television sets to ensure that the image fills the entire display. See also *safe area*.

P

PAL   Acronym for Phase Alternation Line. A television video format used in Europe and elsewhere. Displayed with 625 lines of resolution at 50 fields per second, 25 frames per second. See also *NTSC*.

palette windows   Small floating Premiere windows that provide convenient access to information, options, and commands used in video editing. Palettes can be adjusted, hidden, and docked as desired to accommodate your editing style.

pan   To move the apparent location of a mono audio track to position it between the left and right stereo channels. With stereo clips, you adjust the balance between the two channels. See also *balance*.

PCM   Acronym for Pulse Code Modulation. An uncompressed (lossless) digital audio format.

perceptual compression   A compression technique that takes advantage of knowledge of how humans perceive; that is, by eliminating visual detail that the eye cannot easily see or audio frequencies that the ear cannot easily hear.

PICT   The standard Apple Macintosh still image Picture file format.

pixel   The individual *picture elements*, or "dots" of color, that are arranged in a two-dimensional array to define a digital image or video frame. The dimensions or resolution of an image are described in terms of the horizontal and vertical pixel count.

preroll   To start a tape spinning up to speed before beginning playback or capture to ensure that the operation is synchronized properly.

preview   To play a program on the Timeline and view the appearance of the final production, including transitions and effects. See also *scrub*.

preview file   Temporary file created by Premiere to save the results of rendering a portion of the Timeline. With these files, Premiere can preview the results of your editing on the Timeline at full playback rate, including transitions and effects. See also *scratch disk*.

Program view   The Monitor window view that displays the production being assembled on the Timeline. Depending on the current settings, this can be a simple preview of the cuts between adjacent clips, or a fully rendered preview with transitions and effects. See also *Source view*.

progressive download   A technique for downloading Internet video and/or audio clips so that they can be viewed at the same time that they are being transferred to your computer. This provides some of the benefits of streaming media without requiring a special streaming server. See also *streaming media*.

progressive scan Video display in which the entire screen is refreshed (redrawn) at once. Typically used for computer monitors and high-end video systems. See also *interlaced video*.

progressive video Video consisting of complete frames, not interlaced fields. Each individual frame is a coherent image captured by the camera at a single moment in time. See also *interlaced video*.

Project window The main Premiere window, used to import and save clips used in the program you are editing and organize them into bins. You save each editing activity in a separate Project file, including the imported material and editing context.

Q

QuickTime Multiplatform, multimedia Movie file format from Apple Computer (.MOV).

R

real-time preview To play back a program in the Timeline at full rate, while showing edits such as transitions, effects, overlays, and titles. Allows viewing the effects of edits immediately, without the need to wait and render the program each time. Premiere simulates the frame rate and appearance of the final program as close as possible depending on the complexity of the program and the system performance.

RealMedia Multiplatform, multimedia Web streaming file format from Real Networks (.RM, .RAM).

render To generate a video production in its final form, including transitions, effects, and superimposed tracks. You can render portions of a Timeline to preview your edits at that point, or render the entire production before exporting it in its final form to a disk file or out to tape.

render-scrub To preview a program in the Premiere Timeline and display the visual effects of transitions or other effects but not at full playback speed. Used to preview a portion of the Timeline before rendering it. See also *scrub*, *real-time preview*.

resolution The dimensions of an image, in pixels, typically expressed as the number of horizontal pixels across and the number of vertical pixels down. See also *aspect ratio*.

reverb An audio effect that simulates the ambience of a room of a specific size and with different sound-absorbent properties.

RGB Acronym for Red, Green, Blue. Full-color video signal format, consisting of three elements. See also *YUV*.

ripple edit A method of editing in the Timeline so that when new material is inserted, or existing material is deleted, other material is adjusted to fit. In a ripple edit, the change ripples through the rest of the material, as the existing clips slide apart to make room for the new material, or slide together to fill a gap. See also *rolling edit*, *slide edit*, *slip edit*.

roll To scroll lines of title text vertically up or down the screen. See also *crawl*.

rolling edit A method of editing in the Timeline by adjusting and trimming two adjacent clips. When you roll the cut point between the adjacent clips, the durations of the two clips are adjusted to keep the overall program duration unchanged. The Out point of the first clip is changed in tandem with the In point of the second clip so that, as one increases in duration, the other decreases to match it. See also *ripple edit*, *slide edit*, *slip edit*.

rough cut A quick assembly of raw clips to approximate the desired final program. As a first step in editing, arranging a collection of clips in the desired order as a storyboard of the production.

S

safe area Also known as the *safe zone*. Margins left around the edge of the image. Used when working with material intended for display on television. Safe margins keep titles from bleeding off the screen. See also *overscan*.

sample rate The rate at which samples of a continuous signal, such as music or a sound, are captured into a digital representation of the original signal. A higher audio sampling rate, with more samples per second, creates a more accurate representation of the original sound. See also *Hz*.

scale To reduce or enlarge an image or video sequence by squeezing or stretching the entire image to a smaller or larger image resolution.

scene A single video sequence, typically shot in one continuous take. For editing purposes, it is useful to capture or trim your video material so that each scene is stored as an individual clip that can then be edited on the Timeline. See also *clip*.

scratch disk A dedicated work area on hard disk. Used by Premiere for temporary storage and for saving preview files.

scrub To play a program in the Premiere Timeline by dragging the edit line. You can also render-scrub to show the visual effects of transitions or other effects, but not at full playback speed. See also *real-time preview*.

shuttle To move rapidly through a program, as with scan forward or scan reverse VCR controls. Use the Premiere shuttle slider control to scan rapidly through a clip or program to move to a general area in the material. See also *jog*.

single-track editing A style of editing in which the Timeline is condensed to a single row per track. In Premiere, the Single-Track Editing workspace configures a dual-view Monitor window and a collapsed Timeline window showing a single row per track, without a separate transition track. This is the Premiere workspace used most often by video professionals. See also *A/B editing*.

slide edit A method of editing in the Timeline by moving a clip and trimming neighboring clips to adjust to the change. When you slide a clip earlier or later in the program, the neighboring clips are trimmed accordingly by changing their In and Out points so that the duration of the overall program remains unchanged. See also *ripple edit, rolling edit, slip edit*.

slip edit A method of editing in the Timeline by changing the trim points in a clip. When you slip the trim points earlier or later in a clip, the In and Out points are adjusted correspondingly so that the duration of the clip is unchanged. A slip edit also does not affect the rest of the program on the Timeline. See also *ripple edit, rolling edit, slip edit*.

Source view The Monitor window view that displays a source clip for viewing and editing on the Timeline. The source clip can be from a bin in the Project window, or from a track on the Timeline. See also *Program view*.

split edit To adjust the video and audio portions of a clip separately so that they start or end at different times. Used for audio cross-fading so that the audio can lead in or fade out independently from the cut in the video. See also *L-cut* and *J-cut*.

split-screen A divided display that shows two clips, or portions of clips, side by side.

stereo Two-channel audio, with left and right channels. See also *mono, surround sound*.

still frame A single image or single frame of a video clip. See also *freeze frame*.

storyboard In video production, a series of cartoonlike panels drawn to describe a movie, shot by shot. In video editing, an interface that allows you to organize the sequential flow of your production by arranging thumbnails of each video clip. See also *Timeline*.

Storyboard window The Premiere window used to organize a group of clips into a sequence. You can use this window to quickly lay out the scenes to include in your production into a rough cut and then move them into the Timeline for further editing. See also *Timeline window*.

streaming media Internet video and/or audio clips that can play directly over the Internet, without needing to be downloaded first onto a computer. Used to view and hear broadcasts, and to interactively play and seek in stored clips. See also *progressive download*.

stripe To prepare a new videotape for a recording by prerecording a consistent timecode over the full length of the tape.

subtitle A text overlay on video materials, typically used to display the audio dialog in various languages, or to transcribe hard-to-understand speech.

superimpose To layer multiple tracks onto the Timeline. To composite portions of multiple clips into the final production by overlaying clips with transparent regions to allow the underlying tracks to show through. See also *key*.

superimpose track In Premiere, the Video 2 track and above, which can include titles, logos, and other material to be overlaid on the bottom Video 1 track.

sweeten   To use audio effects to enhance and manipulate the audio sound.

synchronize   To keep two sequences playing at the same rate (in sync). A slide show or a series of video clips can be synced to the beat on an audio track. A talking-head video needs to maintain lip-sync, so that the audio matches the mouth movements of the speaker.

T

talking head   A clip that shows just the head and shoulders of a person who is talking. This tight focus is often used in interview situations where the background is not as important as the talking subject. It is also convenient in a movie destined for the Web because the small amount of movement in a talking-head shot compresses well for the Internet.

three-point edit   A method of setting In and Out points to precisely control where and how frames are inserted into a Timeline. In a three-point edit, you set any three such markers, and Premiere determines the fourth to match the specified duration. See also *four-point edit*.

TIFF   A lossless image file format designed for photographic images that compresses the image size while preserving all the image quality. The resulting files are therefore larger than those with JPEG compression, which sacrifices some detail to significantly reduce the image size.

timecode   An exact time used to identify a specific frame in a clip or production. Measured in hours, minutes, seconds, and frames. See also *duration*.

time ruler   The time display row along the top of the Timeline, showing the time code along the production. See also *edit line*.

timecode log   See *batch list*.

Timeline   In video editing, an interface that allows you to assemble a collection of clips into a production with multiple overlapping tracks. A Timeline provides a view of multiple sources being combined over time, with separate tracks for video, audio, and superimposed video, as well as transitions and effects. See also *storyboard*.

Timeline window   The Premiere window used to assemble, trim, arrange, and superimpose video, audio, and image clips into a program. See also *Storyboard window*.

title   Onscreen text (and associated graphics) that can be used to add information to your production. Used as a title screen at the beginning of your production, for subtitles superimposed under the video, and for rolling credits at the end.

Title window   The Premiere window used to lay out and design title text and graphics.

track   A sequence of video or audio clips in the Premiere Timeline that are to be combined and superimposed into a final production.

transcode   To convert from one compression format to another (that is, from DV video from a camcorder to MPEG-2 for DVD). Preferably done intelligently to minimize loss of quality from repeated compression, and not requiring fully decompressing the input and then recompressing to the output.

transition   A visual effect to segue from the end of one clip or scene to the start of the next. The most basic transition is a *cut*, in which the last frame of one clip is immediately followed by the first frame of the next clip. More interesting transition effects include *fades*, *dissolves*, and *wipes* between adjacent clips.

Transitions palette   A small floating window along the right side of the Premiere workspace that lists the available video transitions, grouped by type. Used to access transitions to be applied to the Timeline. You can also reorganize and customize the list.

transparent   Regions of a superimposed image that are invisible, and therefore show through to the underlying image, as used for logo overlays and blue-screen effects. May be defined using a key color or alpha mask. Technically, overlays also can be translucent and blend portions of the two images. See also *opaque*.

trim   To cut out a segment of a clip by removing frames from the beginning and/or end. To adjust the In or Out points of a clip to identify the portion to be used in the final production.

U

USB (Universal Serial Bus)   A digital data interface standard providing a Plug-and-Play interface for personal computers. Typically used for lower-speed peripherals such as mice, keyboards, printers, and scanners. Also used for interfacing to digital cameras. The existing USB 1 standard provides up to 12Mbps (million bits per second) data rate. The new USB 2 standard supports up to 480Mbps data rate. See also *FireWire*.

V

Video Effects palette   A small floating window along the right side of the Premiere workspace that lists the available video effects, grouped by type. Used to access effects to be applied to a video clip. You can also reorganize and customize the list.

VU meter   An audio mixer's display of audio levels for each track.

Video for Windows   The media file format used with Microsoft Windows (.AVI). Supports many different video and audio compression formats (*codecs*). See also *Windows Media*.

VTR   Video Tape Recorder. Also called *VCR* (Video Cassette Recorder).

W–Z

watermark   A small, semitransparent graphic that identifies a scene or speaker. Many TV broadcasts use a watermark to let you know what channel you're watching.

WAV   The uncompressed Wave audio file format used with Microsoft Windows. See also *AIFF, MP3, WAV, Windows Media Audio*.

Windows Media   The multimedia platform built into Microsoft Windows, and a series of formats for storing and transmitting video and audio. Uses ASF, WMA, and WMF file types. See also *Video for Windows, Windows Media Audio, Windows Media Video*.

Windows Media Audio (WMA)   The Microsoft Windows Media native audio file format. Used for compressing, storing, and organizing CDs and downloaded audio in albums on disk. Also used to download audio to portable audio players. Some consumer audio players and set-top DVD players can play WMA audio files stored on CD-R/RW discs. See also *MP3, WAV, Windows Media*.

Windows Media Video (WMV)   The Microsoft Windows Media format for compressed video and audio files on CD and DVD discs. See also *Windows Media Audio*.

wipe   A video transition in which the new video physically moves into the frame while displacing the old video.

YUV   Full-color video signal format, consisting of three elements: Y (luminance), and U and V (chrominance). See also *RGB*.

Index

How can we make this index more useful? Email us at indexes@quepublishing.com

D

How can we make this index more useful? Email us at indexes@quepublishing.com

How can we make this index more useful? Email us at indexes@quepublishing.com

How can we make this index more useful? Email us at indexes@quepublishing.com

S

How can we make this index more useful? Email us at indexes@quepublishing.com

How can we make this index more useful? Email us at indexes@quepublishing.com

W

How can we make this index more useful? Email us at indexes@quepublishing.com